CHARLES WILLIAMS
POET OF THEOLOGY

CHARLES WILLIAMS
POET OF THEOLOGY

Glen Cavaliero

William B. Eerdmans Publishing Company
Grand Rapids, Michigan

First published in the UK 1983 by
THE MACMILLAN PRESS LTD

*This American edition published 1983
through special arrangement with Macmillan by*
WILLIAM B. EERDMANS PUBLISHING CO.,
*255 Jefferson Avenue, S.E.,
Grand Rapids,
MI 49503*

ISBN 0-8028-3579-1

Printed in Hong Kong

Library of Congress Cataloging in Publication Data

Cavaliero, Glen, 1927–
    Charles Williams: poet of theology.

Bibliography: p. 190
    Includes index.
    1. Williams, Charles, 1886–1945 — Criticism and
interpretation.   2. Theology in literature.
3. Christianity in literature.   I. Title.
PR6045.I5Z6   1983   828'.91209   82-11420
ISBN 0-8028-3579-1

For Paris Leary

*and in memory of
Michal Williams*

I have learnt that the place wherein Thou art found unveiled is girt round with the coincidence of contradictories, and this is the wall of Paradise wherein Thou dost abide.

Nicholas of Cusa, *The Vision of God*

The moment of the rose and the moment of the yew-tree
Are of equal duration. A people without history
Is not redeemed from time, for history is a pattern
Of timeless moments.

T. S. Eliot, *Little Gidding*

The glory of God is in facts; and those devoted to the glory have to deal with facts.

Charles Williams, *Flecker of Dean Close*

Contents

Preface		viii
Acknowledgements		x
1	The Life	1
2	The Early Poetry	9
3	Criticism, Biographies and Plays	22
4	The Novels	54
5	The Arthurian Poems	97
6	Theology	126
	Conclusion	158
	Appendix	178
	Notes	180
	Bibliography	190
	Index	193

Preface

Charles Williams was a prolific writer. In addition to working in a publishing house as literary adviser, editor and anthologist, he produced seven books of verse, four of criticism, four of theology, seven biographies, seven novels and over a dozen plays, as well as many articles and book reviews. No account of so multi-faceted an author can, therefore, hope to be fully comprehensive. This book, while considering his achievement as a whole, concentrates less on any single aspect of his work than on the interaction within it of literature with theology. For what distinguishes Williams from other imaginative writers of his time is the essentially theological nature of his inspiration. Like Hilaire Belloc, G. K. Chesterton and C. S. Lewis, he was a Christian apologist; but unlike them he did not write polemically. His work as a theologian, while faithful to the mainstream of Catholic tradition and independent of shifting theological emphases, is unique in its engendering by his own imaginative vision. But he was no mere individualist. His writing is idiosyncratic in the mode of its expression, not in unorthodoxy of content. Williams leaves the reader free to respond in a way characteristic of poets rather than of evangelists. He is an artist in theology.

His work focuses on two complementary themes. The first of these is the interrelatedness of every aspect of human experience: it is summed up in the words 'co-inherence' and 'exchange'. 'Co-inherence' was first used by the Early Church Fathers to describe the relationship between the divine and human natures of Christ, and was subsequently adopted to describe the mutual indwelling of the three Persons of the Holy Trinity; it is also a reality of nature, a 'play of interaction among separate identities'.[1] 'Exchange' signifies the active acceptance of co-inherence, a reciprocal movement of love within it by those who acknowledge mutual derivation. The nature of what makes for community is the object of a lasting intellectual and imaginative quest on Williams's part.

The second theme is the absolute relativity of all human apprehensions of truth. Such a conclusion arose from Williams's literary studies, and it is summed up in another of his verbal coinages, 'the Affirmation of Images': its motto is 'This also is Thou: neither is this Thou.'[2] Williams was a phrase-maker, but not in any frivolous or merely decorative manner. For him, theological expression went beyond the rearrangement of already accepted verbal formulations, and was the result of a variety of literary undertakings and experiments.

A study of his literary gifts is therefore inseparable from a study of his theology, for it is in their interaction that the vitality of each is found. Accordingly, this book discusses his work in the context of its time, so as to demonstrate that interaction and to relate it not only to Williams's output as a whole, but also to the process by which that output was achieved. Because much of his work is currently not in print, a good deal of exposition has been necessary; but, with so essentially intellectual an artist, that in any case was unavoidable. Fortunately Williams is also a writer with style and a gift for the illuminating phrase, unusual in being both a visionary and a wit. Wide-ranging in knowledge and interests, he was a genuine original whose diverse talents remain significant for an age outside his own.

Among the many people who have helped me I am particularly grateful to Mary W. McDougall, who read this book in manuscript form and gave me valuable assistance; and also to Mrs Alice Mary Hadfield, Mr Kenneth Hopkins, the Revd Dr Brian Horne, Professor Clyde S. Kilby, Miss Lois Lang-Sims, Canon John Lee, Mrs Anne Ridler, Mrs Thelma Shuttleworth, Miss Margaret Sinclair, Mr Mark Tucker, Mr Edmund de Waal and the late James Webb.

Cambridge   G.C.

Acknowledgements

The author and publishers wish to thank David Higham Associates Ltd and the executors of the Estate of the late Charles Williams, for permission to quote from the works of Charles Williams. They would also like to thank the Aquarian Press Ltd, for permission to quote from the author's Introduction to *Witchcraft* by Charles Williams. A portion of Chapter 3 first appeared in no. 24 of the *Newsletter* of the Charles Williams Society, to whom acknowledgement is likewise due.

1 The Life

For most of his life Charles Williams was a Londoner. City life was the perennial inspiration of his work; a vision of diversity in unity, of the interconnection of innumerable parts within a living whole. Houses, streets, subways, shops, churches provide the background of his early poetry, while the way in which they functioned was to be the mainspring of his interpretation of literature, history and religion. At the root of everything he wrote is his feeling for community.

He was born in Holloway in 1886. Eight years later his parents moved to St Albans, where Charles attended the Abbey School, and thus grew up in the presence of two historically embodied ghosts, the Abbey Church (since 1877 a cathedral) and the extensive remains of the Roman city of Verulamium: images of organised power and authority, civic and ecclesiastical, earthly and spiritual, were part of his awareness for the rest of his life. But so were more mundane considerations. The move from London had followed the liquidation of the firm for which his father worked, and he was therefore from an early age made acquainted with the far-reaching consequences of other people's business and financial ventures. Indeed, shortage of money was to dog him all his life, though characteristically he was to make the philosophical understanding of money a theme in his mature poetry.

His boyhood was centred on family as much as on school; and it lacked the privileges and expectations of most other future men of letters of his time. He once referred to himself as 'a Cockney bourgeois'[1] and he remained unaffected by the ethos and moral fashions of the public schools. He was unconventional likewise in his relative indifference to rural life and to the end of his days was to remain sceptical about the curative powers of nature.

The *relevance* of Nature to man is the problem. A high artistic moment makes it plausible, but the multiplication of those moments does not, in fact, make it more than plausible.[2]

1

Such moments came to Williams through ideas rather than through objects, and from the start of his career he was to create a world out of material limitation.

Limitation – and possibly frustration: in 1902, having won a county scholarship, he enrolled at University College, London, only to withdraw two years later, for financial reasons and without taking a degree. (A similar misfortune had attended Samuel Johnson.) Instead, Williams took a job in the Methodist Bookroom in Holborn, and enrolled at the Working Men's College, where, later on, E. M. Forster was to teach; then, in 1908, he joined the staff of the Oxford University Press. He stayed with them for the rest of his life, his first task being to act as proof-reader for the Collected Works of Thackeray, a writer with whom his own work was to have nothing in common at all. It was an irony he may subsequently have appreciated.

In the same year he met Florence Conway, his future wife. Impulsive, perceptive, with a tart sense of humour and at times a childlike spontaneity, she was to remain a pervasive, though frequently secluded, influence on her husband. His own exuberance met its match in hers. One instance was to have a lasting effect. Williams delighted in chanting passages of verse while walking in the street, and 'Not for my meek passivity on these occasions did Charles re-name me Michal, after Saul's daughter.'³ To bestow a nickname from the Bible was characteristic of him. Evolving dramas and fantasies while young, he continued in his later years to make his life resound with heroic names and to transform the routine of everyday into a ritual. There was about him much of the boy – not only his slender, youthful figure, but also his ready interest and excitement, and his flair for dramatising. He bestowed pseudonyms freely on his friends. His imagination lived in a world of courts and ceremonies, though he was always quick to perceive an absurdity and to laugh at the incongruous.

Michal was to be the inspiration of his first book of poems, a sonnet sequence called *The Silver Stair*. The inspiration or the occasion? The poems are fervent but impersonal, full of ideas but devoid of intimacy or particularity of reference. Falling in love is the subject, not the loved woman in herself. Here Williams was following Dante: the sonnets derive their style and tone from Dante Gabriel Rossetti's translation of *La Vita Nuova*. They were published in 1912, with the financial help of Alice and Wilfrid Meynell, who presumably found the young poet's work sympathe-

tic, since its imagery recalled that of their protégé, Francis
Thompson. Not that Williams was so very young. He was twenty-
six, and already writing with assurance, like Yeats employing a
poetic mask, 'The Lover'; in his later verse the mask became that
of 'Taliessin', King Arthur's poet. Although the intermediate
collections contain work in a tentatively colloquial idiom, as a
poet he was instinctively impersonal and formal. His next five
books (three of poems and two of verse plays) were published by
the Oxford University Press, and sold badly: four of them were
available as late as 1947.

Williams's eyesight had made him unfit to serve in the First
World War, and he continued to work for the Press. His two
closest friends were killed in France, and the grief and deprival of
the time is met and to some extent resolved in his early poems. In
1917 he and Michal were married, and in 1922 their only child, a
son, was born. Throughout these years Williams went back and
forth between Hampstead and the Press, and scarcely ever took a
holiday; he was also a dedicated teacher at night schools, at the
City of London Literary Institute and elsewhere. His life was
regular and settled, but impecunious, and his literary ambitions
were unsatisfied. However, the outward drabness masked an
inward light: the poems of the 1920s reveal an awareness of a
spiritual dimension ready to break through, a sense of momen-
tousness in daily happenings, casual gestures, human organisa-
tions. In this it resembles the work of G. K. Chesterton, another
writer whose entire output of novels, criticism, poems and
journalism reflects a sacramental sense of physical reality.

This visionary quality in Williams's personal life was trans-
ferred to his work at the Press. More than one of his fellow
workers have described what it meant.

> C.W. could make each one seem important and interest-
> ing, a vital gift to most of us, but even more than that, he could
> make life important and interesting, not some life removed
> from us by money, opportunity or gifts, but the very life we had
> to lead and should probably go on leading for years.[4]

This from Alice Mary Hadfield, his first biographer; another
colleague, Gerard Hopkins, claimed that by 'sheer force of love
and enthusiasm he created about him an atmosphere that must
be unique in the history of business houses'.[5] One of his later

friends, C. S. Lewis, was to describe him as 'a masculine angel, a spirit burning with intelligence and charity'.[6] T. S. Eliot, who first met him through Lady Ottoline Morrell, also admired and liked him, and wrote an appreciative obituary notice;[7] while W. H. Auden was to go so far as to attribute his conversion to Christianity in part to Williams's influence.

> ... for the first time in my life [I] felt myself in the presence of personal sanctity. I had met many good people before who made me feel ashamed of my own shortcomings, but in the presence of this man ... I did not feel ashamed. I felt transformed into a person who was incapable of doing or thinking anything base or unloving.[8]

But Williams could have a very different effect on other people. Lois Lang-Sims gives a disturbing account of their relationship, emphasising his magnetism, but also what sounds like emotional deficiency where normal human contacts were concerned.

> I had submitted myself to Charles Williams as a disciple submits himself to a Master: it was this that he expected of me and I felt as if I had not been permitted a moment of choice ... He was totally identified with his own myth.[9]

Williams was enormously attractive to women, and inspired devotion. On the other hand, Richard Heron Ward, who acted in a number of his plays, viewed him with dislike.[10] Whatever else, it was impossible to regard him with indifference.

In 1917 Williams joined for a while the Hermetic Order of the Golden Dawn, which was devoted to a study of the principles of magic and the teachings of the Cabbala: this particular branch was founded by A. E. Waite, a dedicated Christian scholar of the occult, whose voluminous books provided much of the imagery for Williams's novels. Other members of the original order included, at one time or another, W. B. Yeats, Arthur Machen, Algernon Blackwood and the theologian Evelyn Underhill. Little is known about the Order for the very good reason that its members were sworn to secrecy. Williams's involvement with it demonstrates his gnostic tendencies at this time, but, although he was interested in magic, he was not an occultist; and the idea of a secret knowledge was to be put to better use when in his later years, long after he had left the Golden Dawn, he became the centre of a group of people whom he designated 'The Companions of the Co-inherence'. At their request he drew up a Constitution in which they were enjoined to orient their lives towards their function as members one of another; to draw together in prayer and recollection; and to live as members of the co-inherent Body of Christ. This sense of the mutual interdependence of human beings was basic to Williams's view of life, and constitutes his ultimate rejection of the exclusiveness of gnosticism and magic.

Williams's influence on the corporate life of the Press really began with its removal to Amen House, near St Paul's, in 1924 (the year of the publication of the most despondent of his books of verse, *Windows of Night*). It was now that he fell in love with the 'Phillida' of the masques written for private performance at this time,[11] the 'Celia' of the many unpublished poems he wrote to her. This was no ordinary personal crisis. Williams never left his wife; nor, apparently, was their relationship destroyed. But this second love, perhaps for the very reason that it was never fulfilled and was only for a while returned, seems to have caused a self-questioning that was to result in the release of his full creative powers. It forced upon him the tragic awareness of a division within the good. Williams's innate pessimism and his thwarted romanticism made him peculiarly susceptible to this contradictory situation, which was to be a leading theme in his writings of the 1930s. Its handling by the major English poets is examined in his two critical books *The English Poetic Mind* (1932) and *Reason and Beauty in the Poetic Mind* (1933), fruits of his lectures at the City of London Literary Institute; and it surfaces also in the five historical biographies he wrote between 1933 and 1937. Its most satisfactory dramatic embodiment is in his play *Thomas Cranmer of Canterbury* (1936); and he elaborated the conception theologically in those that followed it – all of them, like the biographies, commissioned work. Also in the early 1930s he was publishing thrillers with a theological message. In these the personal crisis is discussed more generally: in each one the supernatural threatens to overwhelm the natural order, and equilibrium is only restored by those who can accept both aspects of reality.

In addition to his reputation at the Press as editor and literary

adviser, Williams had, by the late 1930s, made another one as a
book-reviewer in Lady Rhondda's *Time and Tide,* the *Dublin
Review* and other literary and theological journals; he was also
associated with the socio-theological Christendom group. His
work in this field was unmistakably his own. At times it smacks of
the oracular, and his prose is often so concentrated as to be
crabbed, a limitation that may in part be owing to the fact that
he wrote on small pads of notepaper, short lines encouraging
short sentences: posture can have great influence on style. He
himself complained that he could never learn to expand what he
had written; but at its best his terse and vigorous precision is a
tonic. Much of his writing was done at home, and then read
aloud to his wife in the small hours; and he claimed that an
author was only worth his salt if he could go on composing when
in the London Underground. That remark is significant, for it
shows that he never took his writing too solemnly. He enjoyed it;
he constantly experimented with it; he did far too much of it; but
it was always subordinate to the ideas emerging through it. His
weakness as an artist was due most immediately and practically to
the fact that he wrote too plentifully and too often, for reasons
both of the pocket and the heart: he responded generously to
requests and scrupulously to commissions, his astringent yet
debonair intelligence implicit in everything he undertook.

In 1938 he published *He Came Down from Heaven,* a poet's
interpretation of Christianity; and he followed it with *The
Descent of the Dove* (1939), a history of the Church which effects
a rare combination of visionary insight with intellectual analysis.
Witchcraft (1941) complements it, the dark side of this particular
moon, while the remedial nature of love is explored both in *The
Forgiveness of Sins* (1942) and in a study of Dante, *The Figure of
Beatrice* (1943). These five books provide a unique case of
theology illumined by a specifically poetic and literary
intelligence.

Most of them appeared after Williams had moved with the
Press to Oxford at the outbreak of the Second World War.
Michal Williams stayed in London, and Charles was drawn into
the company of friends known to posterity as 'The Inklings', of
whom C. S. Lewis and J. R. R. Tolkien are the most celebrated.
Although Williams shared many of their beliefs and interests, he
appears to have been peripheral to the group, and the donnish
atmosphere was alien to him. However, Oxford did bring him a

belated recognition. His impassioned lectures drew large audiences; *The Figure of Beatrice* confirmed his reputation as a critic; and in 1943 he was awarded an Honorary Degree. Among friends made at this time were Lord David Cecil, Maurice Bowra and Dorothy L. Sayers.

Over a period of six years Williams concentrated on theology. He continued to write articles and to review books, but his original work came almost to a stop. He wrote no criticism, biography or fiction, and only one play of any length; but what the writing of theology appears to have done for him was to objectify the workings of his personal mythology. His final books represent an evolving fusion of the two areas of theological and literary concern.

Each aspect of Williams's work is represented in them. *The Figure of Beatrice* constitutes a definitive interplay of theology with his own particular brand of literary exposition: among those who otherwise find his work uncongenial it is, not surprisingly, the most generally admired of his books. The plays matured steadily into a perfect blend of natural with supernatural in *The House of the Octopus* (1945), while *All Hallows' Eve* (1945) offers a kind of spiritual gloss upon the previous novels. Even the short commissioned biography *Flecker of Dean Close* (1946, but written concurrently with the novel) affords, through its portrait of an Evangelical headmaster, one final glimpse of Williams's interpretation of human life as part of an overall supernatural design. Although his death may have been untimely, his literary achievement had found its proper balance and perspective. Whether its powers of expression would have increased it is, of course, impossible to say. What is certain is that he had plans for several other books, including studies of Wordsworth and of Dickens. The mental discipline of writing theology now bore imaginative fruit, his art becoming more confident and more impersonal.

One piece of work was continuous throughout these years. Since the 1920s Williams had been composing a sequence of poems which would make use of the Arthurian myth to express his own understanding of reality; those published during that period are wordy, contained rather than sustained by their metres. But in 1930 he edited the second edition of the poems of Gerard Manley Hopkins; and these appear to have exercised a beneficial influence. The Arthurian poems that he began to write round about 1934 and published in *Taliessin through Logres*

(1938) owe everything to the rhythmic energy of his plays and little or nothing to the early verse. A second collection followed in 1944. Neither of them caused the least stir (indeed the Press declined to publish *The Region of the Summer Stars*, which came out under the imprint of M. J. Tambimuttu's Poetry London). *All Hallows' Eve* appeared early in 1945; and in May of that year Charles Williams died. He was at the height of his imaginative and intellectual powers, and the fame that had eluded him was beginning to be his. His death was but one more example of the ironic ways of providence which it had been his lifetime's work to trace.

2 The Early Poetry

It is usual to dismiss Charles Williams's early poetry as a false start, interesting because several of his ideas are expressed in it, but unimportant in itself. However it is not merely a quarry for ideas. It constitutes a way of seeing and feeling which gives one the clue to much that he wrote later.

It is not easy to determine the perspective from which these poems should be read; but to approach them with the hindsight of the Arthurian poems is unhelpful. Nor is it particularly to the point to read them as Georgian poetry, at any rate of the kind generally meant when that term is used as a literary marker. Williams did not share the pastoral preoccupations of, say, Edmund Blunden or Wilfrid Gibson (both of them poets he admired). His early poems are almost exclusively theological: never was poet more concerned with doctrine as such. And the more doctrinal the content, the more clearly Williams's authentic voice is heard. Sometimes the bulky shade of Chesterton looms large, or one hears the more fastidious tones of Belloc; but the poems really derive from late Victorian rather than from Georgian verse.

Williams was drawing on two distinct traditions, one metaphysical, the other devotional. The metaphysical tradition had its immediate precursors in Coventry Patmore and Francis Thompson, and was bound up with the premises of orthodox Western Catholic theology. In that theology the Incarnation of Christ forms the central human reality, of which the motherhood of Mary is the vehicle, a vehicle in itself derivative from, and representative of, human love. The divine and the human, flesh and spirit, being seen as eternally commingled, the poetry of Catholicism celebrates sacramental realities in devotional or doctrinal terms, safe in the assurance of the propriety of interfusing these two realms of human discourse.

In the work of the late nineteenth-century Catholic poets the devotional and theological elements are inseparable. The workings of grace are objectified in accepted and venerated formulae, Patmore, for example, building 'The Child's Purchase' out of a series of definitions of the Blessed Virgin's role and function that suggests a Litany of the Saints.

> Sweet Girlhood without guile,
> The extreme of God's creative energy;
> Sunshiny Peak of human personality;
> The world's sad aspirations' one Success;
> Bright Blush, that sav'st our shame from shamelessness;
> Chief Stone of stumbling; Sign built in the way
> To set the foolish everywhere a-bray;
> Hem of God's robe, which all who touch are heal'd;

and so on. The phrases are dense with scriptural references and theological overtones. The fragmentation characteristic of T. S. Eliot or David Jones is here compacted, charged with rhythmic energy that dictates a speed in tension with the density of thought. Both this method and its impact were influential on Williams's later verse; but Patmore's effect on the early work comes, superficially, through the domesticated sublimities of *The Angel in the House*, for it was the regular metres of that quintessential Victorian poem which Williams was to use.

Another influence was Robert Stephen Hawker. The Cornish poet's 'The Quest of the Sangraal' was one Victorian treatment of that theme which Williams genuinely admired; and the swinging rhythms Hawker affected, and the robust medievalism that was integrated into his daily concerns, would seem to lie behind many of Williams's early poems. Hawker was also on occasion capable of the kind of theological compression found in Patmore: 'Aishah Schechinah' takes its place with the most exalted and exact Mariological poems.

> Round her, too pure to mingle with the day,
>   Light, that was life, abode;
> Folded within her fibres meekly lay
>   The link of boundless God.
>
> So linked, so blent, that when, with pulse fulfilled,

> Moved but that infant hand,
> Far, far away, His conscious Godhead thrilled,
> And stars might understand....
>
> The Zone, where two glad worlds for ever meet,
> Beneath that bosom ran: –
> Deep in that womb, the conquering Paraclete
> Smote Godhead on to man!

This union of the mythological and the dramatic is found in Williams's later poems: his earlier work, while it shares Hawker's vision, lacks his vigour. Indeed, its principal inspirer would seem to be neither Patmore nor Hawker, but Francis Thompson.

Thompson is now generally known only as the author of 'The Hound of Heaven'; but in Williams's young manhood he enjoyed a wider fame. The blend of pagan and Christian imagery, a staple of Williams's early verse, is found already in such poems as 'Laus Amara Doloris' or 'An Anthem of Earth', while the verse form of 'Carmen Genesis' is employed repeatedly in Williams's *Poems of Conformity* and *Divorce*.

> Sing how the uncreated Light
> Moved first upon the deep and night,
> And, at Its *fiat lux*,
> Created light unfurled, to be
> God's pinions – stirred perpetually
> In flux and in reflux.

In 'Any Saint' one finds not only echoes of Patmore's rhapsodic definitions but anticipations of Williams's own poetic cosmology.

> Primer where the angels all
> God's grammar spell in small,
> Nor spell
> The highest too well!
>
> Point for the great descants
> Of starry disputants;
> Equation
> Of creation!

Such close-packed definitions also appear in the poems of Gerard Manley Hopkins, such as 'The Blessed Virgin Compared to the Air We Breathe' or, more completely assimilated, in 'As kingfishers catch fire'; but in Hopkins's work the relation of theological definition to natural forces is one not of illustration but of perfect fusion, reflected in a style that is based on speech rhythms – in itself also a kind of fusion. But the theology of Duns Scotus which Hopkins espoused, a theology which asserts the priority as well as the centrality of the Incarnation, is appropriate to the method and message of all these poets. By juxtaposing similitudes and images in this compacted manner they posit a spatial rather than a temporal revelation: the spiritual dimension does not so much correct the material one as inhere in it. Williams's own poetic procedures were to work towards the enunciation of such a belief.

Being, like Hawker, an Anglican, Williams was not involved in the polemical fervour of his predecessors. As a result he casts his net widely: Islam, Buddhism, Greek mythology all come within his terms of reference. He was first and foremost a poet moved to verse by the stimulation of ideas; but in the early work the poems are containers, rather than generators, of their own thought-forms. He was hampered by the literary, as distinct from the metaphysical, tradition he inherited. In place of the rhythmic inequalities and controlled free verse of Patmore's odes, or even the staccato rhythms and explosive enjambments of Thompson, one finds the jogging measures of a hundred hymn writers. The rhythms inevitably control the sensibility; Williams was essaying 'the plain style', a versification based on a translucent vocabulary and a syntax which is only inappropriate for prose to the extent that the governing metre may determine an inversion. But the kind of complexity that filled his mind needed to be approached obliquely. Direct confrontation made for anything but lucidity; or say, rather, that to spell it out was to defuse the spell. This is why those of Williams's readers who come to his early poems for the first time have an experience resembling the recognition of a familiar figure peering from old-fashioned clothing in a faded photograph. To work one's way through the jaunty metres, the verbal abstractions, the poems about Proserpina, Hecuba and Troy, and the sonnets and ballades of an earlier age, is a frustrating business: one turns up familiar image and idea after familiar image and idea, all treated statically without the gift of life.

II

Although the sonnets of *The Silver Stair* are now irrecoverably embedded in their own mannerisms, they are the work of a distinctive mind. Images relating to the City predominate: 'the gated world', 'balconies of prayer', 'Love's palaces', 'the city of my soul'.

> What song hath any road except it be
> Of men and towns, of lights and fires that glow?[1]

The lovers meet against a social and hierarchical background in which even the abstractions Life and Love become personified. But the personifications lack vitality: the poet is explaining their meaning to himself.

An ambiguity towards the experience of love, a wavering between acceptance and rejection, informs the sequence as a whole. From the outset of his career Williams was aware of the relativity of human absolutes. While the poet hails his beloved as 'Regent from the immovable throne of God', the identity of their love with the Love that is God involves them in the fate of Love incarnate.

> It is the wont of lovers, who delight
>   In time of shadows and in secrecy,
> To linger under summer trees by night.
> But on our lips the words fail, and our eyes
> Look not to one another: a man dies
>   In dusk of noon upon a barren tree.[2]

The choice remains between acceptance of a proffered joy and its renunciation, 'The bondage of the gold or silver cord'. (That 'bondage' is an early example of what was to be a continuing irony.)

> Cold roads of winter and green roads of spring
> Are not more wide than twain loves' hand-locking,
>   Each doubled way meet for a doubled boon.
> For lonelier feet, more clear and sheer than this,
> One bright bridge spans the dark of Time's abyss,
>   One single silver gleam beneath the moon.[3]

The bridge appears twenty years later in Williams's novel *Shadows of Ecstasy*, where it denotes the virginity of the deductive intellect: here the image of chastity is enlarged by military and nuptial metaphors. Chastity is presented as an activity as well as an abstention, and it is in this idea, poetically affirmed and explored, that Williams's imaginative world is grounded. Order and discipline springing from an understood relationship between substance and function: the craft of verse, the art of living and the dogmas of religion all partake of a common law which relates them and interprets them to each other. Everything Williams wrote was working towards an apprehension of that fundamental unity.

In *The Silver Stair* unity is asserted more than realised. The human element which is the poems' occasion is overwhelmed by the weight of biblical and liturgical imagery, while the archaic diction and Pre-Raphaelite echoes induce a sense of stuffiness. But, for all this, it is an interesting collection, purposeful, thoughtful, and free from emotional self-indulgence. Emotional inhibition may lie behind it; but, if so, there is not a trace of bitterness or compensatory posturing. And, if in these early poems Williams can be seen to experience the romantic and religious states in a tension so great that religion, as formally expressed, smothers the romantic impulse, it is from the continuing struggle that he was to restate that same religion, no longer in spite of his literary art, but through it.

III

In considering the poems that followed, one needs to remember Williams's upbringing and background. His parents were neither prosperous nor particularly sophisticated; and they were devout churchpeople. Williams himself never seems to have wavered in his intellectual assent to Christian doctrine, even though he was alive to the case that could be made against it. He was a believer and, moreover, a believer attracted to the Church more by what it taught than by what it made him feel. (Indeed, he was to remark that 'Christianity, like all religions, is, frequently, almost unmitigated boredom or even a slow misery, in which the command to rejoice always is the most difficult of all)'[4] He was a religious, as distinct from merely a devotional, poet. But, though

his early verse is in spirit more like that of Patmore than that of
John Keble, it none the less lacks Patmore's passionate assertion of
belief, passionate because proclamatory against a background of
doubt. Williams's early verse is unquestioningly affirmative, and
when it darkens it is a matter of self-awareness and self-
knowledge, not of unbelief.

Their diction and metres make the poems foreign to us today:
it is hard to credit that *Poems of Conformity* came out in 1917,
the year of *Prufrock and Other Observations*. But this is to point
an extreme and unfair contrast: familiarity and the selective
reading encouraged by examination syllabuses make it easy to
forget how experimental Eliot's poems were. And, though
Williams may not have been an innovator, he was far removed in
thought and sensibility from the average religious poet of his day.

Poems of Conformity coincided also with the author's
marriage. The 'conformity' is that of human love to the divine, as
it is known by the eternally present life of Christ in Church and
sacrament. Known 'by' rather than 'in': Love and the lovers relate
as people do. To express his sense of this relationship Williams
deploys religious imagery such as the sacramental elements, the
offices of the Church and the festivals of the liturgical year,
putting them to a use more in conformity with the outlook of
George Herbert than with that of Patmore. The diction is
elaborate and ceremonial; metaphors of war and city life and a
use of Latinate words are frequent. But there are flashes of
originality. The belief that lovers may lawfully and justifiably
behold in their own 'amorous rites' a manifestation of the divine
into whose pale they have entered takes the insights of Patmore's
Unknown Eros to homely, not to say domestic, conclusions. 'More
wisdom on thy breast I learn / Than else upon my knees.'[5] Or,
again, 'If some agnostic mouth deride / These songs of private
Christendom',[6] the answer is to be found in the knowledge of
sexual love itself.

> Hands bound but to a simple pledge,
>   Discover new vocation;
> Instincts, our bodies' depths that dredge,
>   Grow teachers of salvation.[7]

In most love poetry it is the impact of love which is central, its
manifestation in sexual, emotional or even moral terms. But in

Williams's verse love is seen first of all as a way of life, one which lovers exist to practise, at once subordinate to them and yet spiritually their master. The relationship suggests the one between the Christ-child and his parents. As Williams portrays it, love, like the Christ-child, grows up to be betrayed and killed and to rise again – and to ascend into heaven: his full glory is withdrawn. Human love is unable to apprehend him fully.

> A cloud of days receives him in,
>   God unto God returns;
> To his profoundest origin
>   Love manifested yearns.
> But now he was! but now, my Fair,
> Flickered his presence in your hair.[8]

The absence of a capital 'H' shows Williams's reluctance to press the theological parallel too hard.

Three years later came *Divorce* (1920). The word reflects the change in mood. The theme and symbol of marriage which had dominated *Conformity* is now faced with its opposites: separation, division, schism. Something not unlike the antithesis between Blake's *Songs of Innocence* and his *Songs of Experience* is being attempted. The earlier poems welcome a vocation to love, and in the sequel the implications of that acceptance become evident. *Conformity* proclaims 'This also is Thou'; *Divorce*, 'neither is this Thou'. Stresses in marriage are apparent, and also anxiety and a bitter realisation of the poet's own frailty and half-hearted dedication.

The title poem is the key to the entire volume. It is a moving address to Williams's father, in which the sense seems to be trying to break loose from the resolute metrical pattern which contains it. Walter Williams's blindness has made him one of

> such souls as, torn with pain,
> Have proved all things and proved them vain
>   And have no joy thereof,
> Yet lifting their pale heads august
> Declare the frame of things is just,
>   Nor shall the balance move . . . .

It is affirmation in defeat, a condition anticipating the divorce of body from soul in death, and also one more bitter still,

> whose everlasting source
> Sprang up before the sun,
> Whose chill dividing waters roll
> 'Twixt flesh and spirit, mind and soul, –
> Than death more deeply run . . . .

There follows an analysis that anticipates Eliot's celebrated 'wounded surgeon' lyric in *East Coker*.

> Divorce, sole healer of divorce;
> For our deep sickness of remorse
> Sole draught medicinal . . . .

This human experience is an image of the operation of the Trinity.

> Divorce, itself for God and Lord
> By the profounder creeds adored:
> Who in eternity,
> A bright proceeding ardour, parts
> The filial and paternal hearts,
> And knits the riven three.

The thought here is characteristically compressed. The love which unites man and wife also detaches them from their parents: yet this is a distinction in love rather than a rupture of it. Divorce separates, but also defines, and can thus bring about reunion. *Divorce* and *Conformity* complement each other; and Williams achieves this insight through his father's loss of sight. In its theme, its structure and its derivation the poem anticipates his life-work of revivifying theological concepts.

The image of the City recurs repeatedly in this collection, mainly as a manifestation of the Celestial City, but known also in the assemblage of men and women who are met in the ideal of the Republic of free citizens, and in the refrain of the 'Ballade of Travellers', 'Through the whole world's towns is the Free Town one.' At other times the one world seems to slide into the other. 'Ghosts' anticipates a memorable passage in Williams's last novel.

> If that which earth from heaven divides
> Were softly all removed,
> And I at the next corner met

With you whom once I loved,

No friendship 'twixt your eyes and mine
  Should suddenly revive, –
Who, charged with heaven in all your veins,
  In a new London thrive.

Along this doubly-paved street
  Though you should walk with me,
No right communion should attend
  On that epiphany.

Wiser than such estranged sight
  To see your shadows loom
Along this shadowed road by night,
  Gloom visioned upon gloom:

While exhalations of the street
  And vapours of my mind
Mingle within the past, and drift
  Upon a ghostly wind.

It is possible that this poem made its way also into the second section of Eliot's *Little Gidding*.

In 1924 Williams published *Windows of Night*, his most varied collection to date. The note of disquiet heard in its predecessor is now intense, and several poems reveal a self-distrust that almost amounts to self-loathing – but never quite: the Christian allegiances hold firm. On the other hand, the love poems are tranquil and less exclamatory, celebrating 'the immortal friendliness of love', its 'clear contentment'. In a world of shadows and lurking dread, marriage becomes an assurance, the beloved more of a partner, less of a child. An exquisite 'Night Song' is written for Williams's infant son,[9] and there are several poems 'To Michal', highly intimate and full of warm affection.

Windows of Night is marked by a change of poetic style. Williams is starting to experiment, not always successfully. Long, unrhyming stanzas, a general toning down of language both in syntax and vocabulary, a cultivation of the prosaic, all lead occasionally to bathos. The poems are more interesting as a symptom than as an achievement: possibly Williams was anticipating Kenneth Mornington's injunction in *War in Heaven*, 'Better be modern than minor.' But the true Charles Williams was never modern. At its best his work has the contemporaneity of timelessness; and this uneasy attempt to forge a colloquial poetic style was regrettable in a minor poet of real distinction, and wisely he abandoned it.

This collection also reveals Williams's innate and unrelenting pessimism. He once wrote that 'our life is a continual losing of life, and death is only the end of the process',[10] and his later writings about joy were the result of bitter struggle. It is the most satisfying of his credentials: he knew, none better, the truth of what he was saying. Here the greater pessimism is evident in an altered awareness of co-inherence. The similitudes and analogies of *Conformity* have become a burden; the 'private Christendom' has been invaded from without and betrayed from within. Whereas in 'To Michal: On Bringing her Breakfast in Bed' 'from the buttery / In the land of the Trinity', the poet can envisage a mutuality of service leading to a single blessed end, as the past is gathered up into a joyous present, in 'The Window' he evokes the burden of heredity, the past becoming a suffocating threat: 'all that men were they are'. In the bitterly entitled 'Domesticity' every house is a house of the dead; domestic fires burn Ridley, bars of nursery windows suggest torture-chambers and prisons. It is the doctrine 'as in Adam all die' felt along the bone. The universal guilt makes a scapegoat of the criminal, whom society punishes for its own crimes. 'The Two Domes' (St Paul's and the Old Bailey), likened, grotesquely, in two of the worst lines Williams ever wrote, to 'the broken halves of the shell / Of the egg of life, whose overspilt yolk we are', none the less point forward to the realisation that justice and the ironical overthrow of justice, signified by law court and cathedral, encompass every human life, while somewhere between them is lost 'the unknown motive, the common truth of all lives'. The relation between them was to become one of Williams's theological preoccupations.

Another one is foreshadowed in the long poem 'To the Protector, or Angel, of Intellectual Doubt'. Williams's most arresting achievement to date, it offsets the negative awareness of co-inherence with the counter-knowledge of absolute relativity. He invokes the 'doubt of all things seen' as the twin of supernatural faith, the slayer of sloth and self-sufficiency, the secret of the joy of lovers, faith's guardian against hypocrisy and 'utter and intimate unbelief'. The quality of disbelief, as Williams came to call it, is not the same thing as *un*belief; the latter rejects belief as such, whereas disbelief tests and rejects all statements that are unworthy of the truth it seeks to know. Its saints are St Thomas Didymus (already saluted in a poem in *Divorce*) and the Blessed Virgin,

> Who, saying 'How shall this thing be?'
> In that one asking did retrieve
> The pale credulity of Eve . . . .

Similarly the Protector succours Christ in his crucifixion,

> When slipping, scourged, and nigh to fall,
> Was't not your whisper: *Is this all?*
> First lifted, stayed, and held him? . . .

> Did'st thou not then, ere Faith could turn
> Through tears her comfort to discern,
> In that great night, leap forth to clear
> A space to breathe about Him there?

That last phrase alerts one to the particular difficulty in reading Williams's early verse. As a body of work it is by no means undistinguished; many individual poems are witty or beautiful or thought-provoking or all three. But they are more interesting to students of Williams's thought than they are to critics of twentieth-century poetry. They have had their admirers, Robert Bridges among them; but, while revealing a mastery of the techniques of earlier ages (there are some beautiful exercises in pastiche), they show an almost total unawareness of the poetic currents of the time. There are few sensual or pictorial images, while the rigid adherence to theological language renders several of the poems dowdy. These 'songs of private Christendom' come from a world of the mind, and their effect is less the re-enactment of experience than the appraisal of it. However authentic Williams's own feelings, he is still expressing them through books (even if one of his models is a singularly good one – Cranmer's *Book of Common Prayer*). There is no vitalising relationship between form and content, one could almost say between word and Word. Williams's style and vocabulary are congealed in traditional religious attitudes and phrasing; his imagination does not yet exercise autonomy. In all this early work the artist is subordinate to the theologian, and thus both artist and theologian are deprived. Williams was not to find himself as a poet until his energies were released and his ideas expanded by his work in prose, especially in his novels and biographies. Those energies demanded a poetic symbolism and methodology which could adequately embody them; and he accordingly began to experiment in that direction in his plays. In the meantime, he was aware of the implications of the kind of work he had been producing, remarking that 'Sanctity too often amuses herself with her poor relations.'[11] It was an observation which he took to heart where more than poetry was concerned.

3 Criticism, Biographies and Plays

I

Second only in importance to his work at Oxford University Press were the lectures Williams delivered at evening classes during the 1920s and 1930s, for they made him a literary critic of an unusual kind. The general trend towards professionalism, whereby the critic is not only thorough and systematic in his method but also career-dominated in his aims, has tended to sway the market where published criticism is concerned; and the more personal, expository and receptive manner of reading is now accounted superficial and belletrist. Williams's approach had nothing trifling about it; but it was subjective in its concentration on selected texts, and alien to all but a few of his contemporaries in its belief that poetry (and it was poetry which primarily concerned him) could express a reality beyond itself. Such a view was easier for creative than for critical temperaments to understand: thus, while F. R. Leavis could dismiss Williams's Introduction to the World's Classics edition of Milton's English poems as 'the merest attitudinizing and gesturing of a man who had nothing critically relevant to say',[1] T. S. Eliot could endorse it as the work of 'a critic of the type to which I belong if I have any critical pretensions at all'.[2] But where Williams differed from both men was in his audience. Leavis's outlook was determined and coloured by the fact that it developed in the context of university teaching; while the cosmopolitan Eliot mainly appealed to a selectively educated cultural élite, and to those fellow writers who contributed regularly to the London literary journals. (The name of Eliot's own *Criterion* indicates an aristocratic selectivity which led him notoriously to undervalue the genius and social relevance of D. H. Lawrence, a writer whose work Williams, on the other hand, took as a text for an essay on the goodness of the human body.[3]) Williams's world was that of students who studied in their spare time, following a full day's work; for them there were no examinations and syllabuses to make a task or nuisance out of all but the most favoured writers. Those pupils who attended the classes were adults who did so for pure love of the written word.[4]

It was through these audiences that Williams came to enunciate his peculiarly theological understanding of poetry. By 'theological' is meant an approach which sees poetry as one expression of the word or activity of God, and which studies it as an articulation, both in its method and its resultant power, of that which conceives and sustains the world. Because Williams took his beliefs seriously, he took poetry seriously: and those beliefs were shaped by a reading of the great Romantics, Wordsworth most notably. To Williams, as to Blake and Keats, 'all great literature is canonical, and Shakespeare is as much a sacred text as Isaiah'.[5] Williams would probably in theory have conceded the uniquely covenanted nature of the Bible, but in practice he treated the poets as on an equality with the biblical writers. The *poets*: it is characteristic that his central text for expounding his doctrine of the sovereign reality of the imagination should be, not the *Biographia Literaria* nor *A Defence of Poetry*, but *The Prelude*.

Williams's particular attitude to criticism can be seen in a suggestion he made more than once, that criticism has not properly attempted to evaluate poetry by poetry – an enigmatic remark which, however, his own practice illuminates. When discussing themes and imaginative statements he ignores factors of historical relationship: for him the poets are communicating the laws of an eternal world. Nowhere in his criticism does he posit a Neo-Platonic view as such, and indeed his subsequent stress on the objective reality of poetic images gives the lie to it; but what he does postulate is a kind of communal poetic awareness in the minds of readers, a poetic realm created by poets which the reader can enter and in turn enlarge.

This is evident in his first published book of criticism. *Poetry at Present* (1930) is a collection of sixteen rather chatty appreciations of those contemporaries who had 'to however small an extent, enlarged the boundaries of English verse'. The approach is characteristic, and is furthered by the quaint little 'end-piece' poems, which attempt, with varying success, a kind of interpretative pastiche. The book belongs to the belletrist rather than to the academic tradition, and shows definitively that Williams was not a literary critic as the term is nowadays generally understood; but despite a good deal of tiresome archness (poetry, for example, being referred to throughout as 'she') it does throw retrospective light on poetic theories already tried and found wanting in the early verse.

In this book Williams's interests are theological rather than technical. In discussing the Elizabethans, in connection with the early work of Yeats, he comments that it is

> rather in ideas of the world than in the world that novelty and familiarity must lie, and it is by the recognition of the inner in the outer that most of us find satisfaction, by the accommodation of the phenomenal world to our beliefs and consistencies.[6]

The remark defines his own sensibility, for the phenomenal world as such seems to have interested him relatively little. But despite this assertion his own poetic concerns were less with philosophy than with the exploration in terms of myth of the interior world of consciousness. One can see the underlying metaphysical concept implicit in his description of Yeats's world of Faery as 'that world which is said to exist invisibly in this one',[7] a statement that in itself suggests that our own world may exist in a similar way inside another – certainly a concept which Williams himself would have found congenial, and one which he was to relate to the processes of poetic composition.

Further development of this theme comes in the essay on Walter de la Mare, a poet of whom Williams is more critical than most. De la Mare's avoidance of the intellectual arouses his mistrust.

> When doctrine, and with doctrine intellect, is subdued entirely to emotional desire; when the very desired end itself is called Nothing; when in some poems the communication is of a state in which our mere existence would destroy its calm – then it is almost inevitable that the music sometimes should seem to quiver with the void rather than with peace.[8]

'Doctrine' – the word is all-important for Williams; the mere experience of human states of feeling is never enough for him. They are to be analysed and understood.

The point is made still more forcefully in his account (a good one) of John Masefield. Here he defines the romantic mind as one which 'wholly abandons itself to some intense experience, and normally does not stabilize that by others'.[9] But 'experience can only be countercharged with experience, not by a gospel, a meditation, or a dream'.[10] This poetic doctrine was one that he was to follow when it came to writing theology; but it also provides evidence that he possessed what de la Mare himself, in an essay on Rupert Brooke, calls the 'intellectual' as distinct from the 'visionary' imagination. 'The one knows that beauty is truth, the other reveals that truth is beauty.'[11] The latter endeavour was at the heart of all Williams's writing; and it puts him with the Augustans rather than with the post-Romantics from Tennyson to Yeats. And, to the extent that the latter were the forerunners of the Modernists, it helps to explain his solitary position in the literary life of his time.

But, if *Poetry at Present* skates lightly over the question of the function of poetry, that question is implicit in everything that Williams subsequently wrote. It was a question of an attitude, a point of view; and he confronts the matter directly in his two books on the poetic mind. These are central to any understanding of his work. Not only do they express something of what he believed the poetic gift to be and to imply, but they also provided an objective framework within which he could elucidate the personal crisis which obsessed him. In so doing he began to work out a relationship between the nature of poetic and that of religious truth, and to examine the distinction drawn by de la Mare between the two attitudes to truth and beauty apparent in the work of the major English poets.

The personal crisis arose from Williams's own discovery of divided loyalties, even of divided truth, with regard to his love for 'Celia'. The experience haunts many poems in *Windows of Night*, but finds its most highly charged expression in an unperformed verse drama, *The Chaste Wanton*, published in *Three Plays* (1931). A somewhat leaden affair, on which the poetic hand of Lascelles Abercrombie weighs especially heavy, it presents the crisis in linear terms, bringing it to a mental resolution, the characters choosing the consciousness they will have of their predicament. The time is the Renaissance, the setting the elaborately ceremonial, insidiously materialistic court of Mantua: Williams's ornate diction is appropriate. The Duchess, on the

brink of a necessary state marriage, falls in love with a commoner
who liberates her from self-centredness into a love for duty
greater even than her love for himself. But having found love she
must serve it, and in doing so she brings anguish on them both,
since, love being a 'thing inseparate', they are 'impaled' upon
each other:

> . . . this is execution
> done on us fully by mere being; fly
> we cannot, nor would fly: is not your breath
> mine, whosoever meets it on your lips?[12]

They find their fulfilment in the exchange of his life for her
honour, her honour for his knowledge of death. 'Now we are
made each other's glory.'[13] That 'each other' is significant of
much to come in Williams's work.

However overwrought, the play has the ring of emotional
sincerity. It is a portrayal of the sublimation of forbidden sexual
impulses congenial to the time: instances can be found between
works as different as Housman's *A Shropshire Lad* (1896) and
David Lean's film *Brief Encounter* (1946), Charles Morgan's
novel *Portrait in a Mirror* (1929) being a particularly plangent
example. But the romantic nostalgia of these works is missing
here. Williams's imagination was rigorous, and he directed his
own sense of personal frustration not only into his play, but also
into an examination of the treatment of similar contradictions in
the work of the English poets, not so much in quest of fellow
feeling as in a search for the best way in which to contain and
control and understand the pain involved. He put his own
precepts about romanticism into practice. It was not a solitary
quest.

In 1943 he was to edit *The Letters of Evelyn Underhill*; and in
the Introduction he coins the phrase 'the Impossibility' for a
comparable crisis with his own. In Evelyn Underhill's case it involved the dilemma she faced when, already a Catholic postulant,
she was confronted in September 1907 by Pius X's encyclical
condemning theological Modernism: her proposed adherence to
Rome was barred by Rome's apparent attack on her own intellectual probity. Whether the situation was to her the agony that
Williams makes it out to be is open to question; but she continued
going to Mass while refraining from communion, thus living out a
contradiction in terms.

One is apparently left to live alone with an Impossibility. It is imperative, and in the end possible, to believe that the Impossibility does its own impossible work; to believe so, in whatever form the crisis takes, is of the substance of faith; especially if we add to it Kierkegaard's phrase that, in any resolution of the crisis, so far as the human spirit is concerned, 'before God man is always in the wrong'.[14]

Williams himself worked towards that conclusion in his critical books, biographies and plays.

II

The core of *The English Poetic Mind* and *Reason and Beauty in the Poetic Mind* is the treatment in English poetry of this theme of the divided consciousness. In seeking for his own solution to the crisis through the study of its handling by the greater poets, Williams was using a critical method that might fairly be called theological. It was certainly a method in accordance with his own beliefs. In his life of Francis Bacon, published in the same year (1933) as *Reason and Beauty*, he remarks that great verse 'contains not only experience but man's creation of that experience harmonized into a pattern which he knows to be his own pattern'.[15] Resting on that assumption, he could proceed to study the texts of the English poets very much as a theologian studies the text of the Bible.

In *The English Poetic Mind* Williams compares the treatment of the crisis by Shakespeare and Milton with that by Wordsworth and lesser poets. The crisis itself he defines as 'one common to all men; it is in a sense the only interior crisis worth talking about. It is that in which every nerve of the body, every consciousness of the mind, shrieks that something cannot be. Only it is.'[16] Shakespeare's Troilus endures the crisis when he discovers Cressida to be unchaste: she becomes a contradiction, the union of incompatible experiences of one woman in her inseparate personality. The situation implies the union of two natures in one person, even suggesting (albeit by poetic rather than by theological association) the image of the crucified Christ, who is at once Heavenly King and criminal outlaw. Williams's discussion of Milton's Satan takes the matter further. Satan is himself the personified awareness of contradiction: in him it is willed and chosen.[17]

In *Reason and Beauty* the crisis is related to the poetic under-standing of those two terms; and both in this book and in its predecessor Williams claims that Shakespeare and Milton are the two greatest English poets precisely because they alone fully confront contradiction and succeed in resolving it in their verse. Keats, in the 'Ode to a Nightingale' deliberately withdraws from 'the penetrating gaze of intellect':

> if the Beauty of the rainbow depends for its effectiveness on our *not* knowing its woof and texture, if to know the actual identity of any apparent loveliness is to destroy it, of what worth – even poetically – can that loveliness actually be? It depends on a point of view; it depends on keeping something out. And what use is any imagination in the end that depends on keeping something out?[18]

But Milton reconciles Beauty and Truth in his conception of a supreme controlling harmony, actualised in his blank verse; while Shakespeare's method is to explore the schism in reason itself, from the experience of states 'contemporaneous and hostile' to states 'contemporaneous, hostile and harmonious'. *The English Poetic Mind* is an exposition of that progress:[19] *Reason and Beauty* suggests how Shakespeare came to achieve it.

> It would almost be possible to imagine Shakespeare's genius proceeding by questions – not that it is likely to have done so but as a way of making its progress clear. (1) When does man act? (2) At his deepest crisis: what is that crisis? (3) This 'thing inseparate' dividing wider than the sky and earth: how does he receive it? (4) He madly avenges himself on the thing which typifies that division: but if he cannot? (5) He will break under it. *Lear* is the breaking, almost the dissolution, of man.[20]

Williams does not point out the theological implications of this development, though he enlarged on them in his later writings, most notably in his plays. His interpretation of Shakespeare clearly coloured his theology, especially his realisation of how, in *Antony and Cleopatra*, the style, with its coupling of opposing images in association, transfigures the whole tragedy, so that even death becomes a positive.

In these two books Williams, though at times laborious in his use of paraphrases, is selectively exegetical, employing the method of defining poetry by poetry. The same method underlies his anthology *The New Book of English Verse* (1935). The Introduction, highly mannered, compact but stimulating, is something of a personal statement. One notes an overriding concern with what he calls, with personal reference, 'the Celian moment' (the official occasion of the designation is Marvell's 'The Match') 'the moment which contains, almost equally, the actual and the potential'.[21] This constitutes the reverse side of the Impossibility; and under these two terms Williams is mythologising what are usually called ambiguity and irony. The complexity of verbal association examined and applauded by such influential critics as Sir William Empson and Cleanth Brooks is put by Charles Williams to existential use; while his very habit of transtemporal collocation is Jungian in its implications.[22] The enthusiasm, wide range of reading, familiarity with unfamiliar texts, and good-humoured tolerance of the second-rate might belong to any early twentieth-century man of letters of the more scholarly sort; they are given added seriousness by Williams's sense of underlying realities, his unswerving recollection that poets write of experiences that, however common, are momentous. If he is a Victorian in his ready movement from poet to poet (and irritatingly post-Victorian in his frequent whimsicality), he is modern in his insistence that it is syntax rather than vocabulary that generates poetic energy. Sinew, not ornament: the method had to be learned by himself. The early poems gestured towards the transcendent experiences they described; but in these critical books one can see Williams moving towards an equation between literary method and personal apprehension. The 'why' of poetry was implicit in its 'how': the discovery, which must have come naturally to one who was steeped in an incarnational theology, was to have a lasting impact on his development both as theologian and as artist.

Poetic art is a basic concern of Williams's thinking, especially with regard to his understanding of the nature of belief. In *Reason and Beauty* he draws a useful distinction between poetry and prose. Verse, as distinct from prose, presents a rhythmic pattern which proclaims it to be the deliberate creation of a human mind. This pattern or convention is not apparent in prose, though it may be present in it; and accordingly it is possible to forget that, whatever the proposition, that proposition is the work of human nature and not an absolute: 'prose persuades us that we can trust our natures to know things as they are; ostentatiously faithful to its own nature, poetry assures us that we cannot – we know only as we can'.[23] Williams's entire structure of thought rests on this awareness of the conditioned limitations of human knowledge. The function of poetry as the apprehension of the absolute through images he takes seriously enough to affirm those images as being images, no more but certainly no less.

It is perhaps for this reason that he prefers in his novels and verse to work through received mythologies, which he is able to enlarge and use as means of ordering his ideas. Surrender to the pattern of the mythology (occult, theological, Arthurian or whatever) frees his imagination. If the early plays and poems are unsuccessful it is partly because, in the one case, either he has to invent his own mythology, or else be constricted by the forms he employs and thus be prevented from expanding an existing one sufficiently; while in the other he imposes upon his emotional responses formulations that are insufficiently dynamic. It is precisely as he improves as an artist that he improves as a theologian.

To say that he is handling a myth in the theological books is, however, to beg certain questions. Certainly he believed in the reality of which the myth was speaking; but he is sufficiently a sceptic, or a realist, to avoid equating the symbol with that which it represented. Yet he also knows that to apprehend the reality it is necessary to explore the symbol. To use doctrine as myth, as Williams was to do in his theological writings, is to put it to its proper use; it relates it to the responsive imagination. Williams's 'disbelief' allows him to use the intellectual theological structure, to which he assented, as a provisional working model of reality; and since he is always concerned to relate it to inner awareness and spiritual need he is able to some extent to bridge the gap between metaphysics and psychology. He recognises that people have an emotional need for metaphysics; but he is insistent that metaphysics inevitably involves the use of imagery. Like poetry, it is a way of seeing, not itself sight or knowledge.

In the Introduction to *The New Book of English Verse* Williams provides further variations on the theme of absolute relativity. Discussing 'the Celian moment', he notes that 'it is perfect within its own limitations of subject or method, and its perfection relates it to greater things'. So 'This also is Thou; neither is this Thou.' Poetry is not in itself a vehicle for transcendent truth; but its technique and inmost quality are an image of that truth. The first contention Williams roundly condemns as 'cant'; and in his comments on that term he relates it specifically to idolatry.

> The language of poetry is bound to be ceremonial, however direct. It is when versifiers (that is, ceremonialists) use such a language without the intensity it should convey and concentrate that Cant begins to exist; it is when ceremony is willingly accepted as a substitute for intensity that it triumphs.[24]

Equally, the rejection of ceremony is a failure to appreciate the relative nature of all human absolutes; and to Williams the inevitable result is a simplistic attitude to metaphysics which results in idolatry and incoherence. Indeed, his account of the sin of Milton's Satan stands as his principal charge against the life of his own day. The *New Book of English Verse* Introduction is among other things a reasoned elegy for a ceremonial which had in earlier times rescued people from self-consciousness by giving them a role to perform. All Williams's criticism tends towards the study of those moments, both in literary expression and in literary technique, which signal the release from self-enclosure into the liberated dance of joy. Ceremony was the means. This explains not only his admiration for the poetry of Robert Bridges but also his choice of Arthurian mythology as a means of self-expression.

Williams's literary criticism is concerned not only with the perception of, to use Lawrence's term if not quite with Lawrence's intent, 'the living moment', but also with the exhibition of the place of poetic power in poetic language. His stress on the 'feeling intellect' rises from his own receptivity to verse – as his novel *Shadows of Ecstasy* makes abundantly clear. The words of G. Wilson Knight are apposite here: 'poetry gives us not the factual, which is dead, but the actual, which lives. It aims to reintegrate our abstractions into their only proper context in the whole of life.'[25] Indeed, language is not only the record of thought, it is the physical embodiment of thought; and myth is in this sense a pattern of images which must be shared if it is to be understood – or, better, known – unlike allegory, which leads to false abstraction and intellection. Poetic knowledge, the knowledge of the maker, is language which recognises co-inherence; and co-inherence only has meaning where individuation is accepted. It is the reverse of absorption.

For Williams, the language of poetry was its essence; and in this belief he could face in theory what he rebelled against in practice – the fact that the day of the great myths had passed. What he did analyse neatly was the modern attitude to the myths. 'The most important things now in our self-consciousness are the conscious knowledge of our consciousness and our revolt against our knowledge.'[26] All Williams's work, not only in literature but also in life, was directed towards resolving that particular contradiction.

III

Williams continued to explore 'the Impossibility' in his biographies. *Bacon* appeared in 1933, and was followed over the next four years by studies of King James I, the poet Rochester, the first Queen Elizabeth, and her grandfather Henry VII. (Williams also wrote a number of shorter lives of the famous, seven of which were published in 1937 as *Stories of Great Names*. At least one of them, 'Joan of Arc', is a small masterpiece).[27] The books were commissioned, and were in effect pot-boilers; but they were conscientiously carried out, and are examples not only of literary versatility but also of Williams's range of interests. The sixteenth and seventeenth centuries were especially congenial to him, and their literary achievements did in some measure provide the aspiration of his own: to that extent Williams was a modern, a sharer in Eliot's regret for 'the dissociated sensibility'.[28]

> Whatever divisions of controversy existed under Elizabeth and James, this at least was common to all disputants – a power of prose and verse that often arose from an almost conscious aspiration after unity of mind and body, so that they discovered in their speech an instrument of unity, and wildness and restraint lived together in their world.[29]

Williams's studies in this period provided him, as his theological books were to do, with an impersonal medium through which to test his own ideas.

The books belong to a genre of informed popularisation that had followed in the wake of Lytton Strachey's *Eminent Victorians* (1918). Colourful, dramatic historical biographies by men of letters who were not academical historians proliferated at this time: among them one may cite Hilaire Belloc's *Charles I* (1933), Roger Fulford's *George IV* (1934) and Milton Waldman's *Elizabeth and Leicester* (1944). Charles Williams's contribution takes an honourable place among these books, and exhibits, as much as any of his work, the distinction of his mind. His biographies stand out among their contemporaries by virtue of their greater reflectiveness; they digress constantly, but always to come homing back to the essential point. But they do not eschew romantic colour, for 'the picturesque is not necessarily opposed to learning, and where exaltation and learning are mingled the result is far more likely to correspond to truth than the more pedestrian journey along a flat road of unvaried statement'.[30] Although written for a widely read and knowledgeable public, they are not works of original research, and the treatment of their material is drastically selective, being more concerned with the portrayal of personality than with the chronicling of events. They tell us as much about their author as they do about his subjects.

In the Preface to *Henry VII* (the last and most perfunctory, as well as the most political, of the series) Williams, quoting Bacon's assessment of the king as a man whose fortune was indistinguishable from his nature, asserts the purpose of biography to be the making of a distinction between the two. The contradictory element in human experience continued to preoccupy him, and it is through that distinction that the Impossibility does its work,

> that strange and dreadful crisis in which a man becomes a mockery to himself, in which annihilation is his only desire and in which the whole power of the universe denies him annihilation and sustains and nourishes his imagination that it may be at the same time more terribly destroyed; the crisis of which the Athanasian phrase 'perish everlastingly' is the only satisfactory definition . . . .[31]

Williams demonstrates the existence of the Impossibility in the lives of James I and of Henry VII by relating it in the first instance to Prince Charles and the Duke of Buckingham, and in the second to Katherine of Aragon; showing how James, who throughout his life had allowed his sense of his own royalty to control his personal affections, was at the end of it to see that royalty despoiled by those affections. Similarly Henry VII, 'having built a great edifice of monarchy, and peering about it with a candle to provide against cracks, set light to a train of powder that shattered it'.[32] Williams portrays Rochester, a Romantic in the age of Hobbes and Charles II, as wrestling with the Impossibility all his life; and interprets Bacon's career as a search for a personal perfection which could only make itself known after it had seemingly been lost.

It is not so easy, between the clanging moral uproars of existence, to decide with what exchangers the divine talent makes profit. By the end of life all that we know is that it has gone. It is only then that the long error of our actions becomes clear, and had our actions been wholly other still their long error would have been clear. That extreme error is the only revelation vouchsafed to normal man, and that error (since man acts always here and now, and never there and then) is inevitable. Francis Bacon repented of the inevitable as we all do; that perhaps is man's greatest hope, for in that his submission and his defiance are curiously one.[33]

This statement, with its simultaneous inclusion of the concepts of predestination and free will, anticipates Williams's later treatment of the doctrine of the Atonement. His vision of life in these biographies is sombre, almost fatalistic; he writes of human wickedness in a cool, even offhand manner, seeing men and women as the victims of their own natures, only redeemed through the pitiless outraging of those natures by their fortunes, their remedial scourging by the Holy Ghost.

In the play *Thomas Cranmer of Canterbury* Williams embodies the idea of Fortune in a vivid piece of imagery, and develops it into a theological affirmation. In the biographies no deductions are drawn: a pattern only is presented. But it is presented insistently, and fivefold. Henry VII is shown as a man who conformed his fortune to his nature, and Elizabeth as a woman who adapted her nature to her fortune. Francis Bacon's nature is shown examining his fortune, James Stuart's as resisting his. In Rochester, nature and fortune draw even, an ironic stalemate. Nor is this a matter of the biographer's playing games:

the distinctions work towards a moral, not to say a philosophical end. Thus Williams comments on Henry's execution of the last claimant to his throne, 'He surrendered himself to some element in his heart. He became himself.'[34] Read in the context of Williams's novel *Descent into Hell* (written, but not published, a few years earlier), the words become a definition of damnation: certainly they are not intended to suggest the kind of affirmative fulfilment they would have in contemporary psychological discourse. From Williams's point of view, the execution of Warwick marked the moment when, after years in which the King's nature had responded mercurially to his fortune, his fortune became subdued to his nature. A more dramatic example of the crisis is provided by the execution of Mary Stuart, an 'impossible' event both for Elizabeth and for James. For Elizabeth especially, Mary's very existence was an impossibility; her royalty was sacred but at the same time a threat, so that the English people, for whom Elizabeth lived, demanded the disowning of that royal privilege which she herself relied on to maintain her. The position was to be both repeated and reversed when, again to preserve her own royal position, Elizabeth was forced to behead the beloved Essex.

The idea of royalty was sympathetic to Williams's imagination, which is why he was to prove so understanding a biographer of James I, warning against reading *The Trew Law of Free Monarchies* 'unsympathetically scornful of a political system alien from our own debased oligarchy'.[35] Williams brings this much derided monarch to life not simply as a 'character' but as a man of genuine intelligence and spiritual capacity.

It is not surprising that he was obstinate in his beliefs. Others had been put before him, but never very persuasively, never as a matter of amiable or academic discussion. ... For all his obstinacy James had a very real tolerance; he wanted to argue as much as to win. True, he wanted to win as much as to argue, but he had not been wisely trained to endure intellectual defeat and the beautiful grace of thinking one may be mistaken. He had spent all his life among those who were sure they were not. ... His conversion to something or other was always looming on the horizon of the garden where otherwise he could have happily sauntered or disputed. In public and in private he was prayed to and prayed for. Between sermons and Masses it is not surprising that the Will of God which they all invoked kept him where he was, only much more obstinate than before.[36]

Here is the voice of the mature Charles Williams, humane, ironic, analytically witty, mannered, dry. Brought to bear on theological matters it was to find itself, his own beliefs imparting a glow to what otherwise might have sounded excessively detached.

The portrait of Queen Elizabeth is equally effective. The shortest of the biographies, this book is a masterpiece of telescopic compression. (For once Williams's inability to expand stood him in good stead, for the book was written for a series of Griet Great Lives.)[37] It is notable that he cannot resist making a symbolic figure of the Queen, a living embodiment of the Impossibility. In an age of certainties Elizabeth, unlike James, was always uncertain and undogmatic: her temperament held a strong appeal for her biographer.

The study of Rochester is less successful. At once a brilliant and an infuriating piece of work, it cannot escape the charge of fancifulness and special pleading. Written in contorted and exceptionally mannered prose, it provides a series of spotlights rather than a continuous narrative; though full of memorable observations, it is inconclusive in its purpose. Williams's interest in Rochester includes a measure of self-identification, but is less a poet's interest than a theologian's. The book focuses on Rochester's mind as it contended with forces of faith and unbelief, supported by scepticism in the resultant tension. Williams regards his subjects as human beings, historically conditioned but contemporary in their spiritual problems. He treats their mental assumptions with seriousness, and in *Bacon* makes a withering aside about Lytton Strachey and his 'dainty jests at the Trinity and the Earl of Essex, at the death-agony of Philip of Spain and the life-agony of Elizabeth of England'.[38] Williams himself had no sense of 'period'.

His response to the concept of royalty may be over-romanticised; but, in addition to being sympathetic to the High Anglicanism of his personal religion, it also came as a reaction against the Whig tradition of history, 'and the doubtful thesis that the freedom and security of the upper and upper middle classes is the same thing as, or a better thing than, the freedom and security of the lower middle classes and of the poor'.[39] And

the life of Bacon makes it clear that he was no obscurantist where
the significance of science was concerned: to prefer the inductive
to the deductive method is but another way of loving necessity.
His account of Bacon's revolutionary change of scientific pro-
cedure looks ahead to the masterly discussions of Christian
doctrine in his later theological books.

Williams may have been critical of Strachey's ironic elegancies,
but Strachey's style is often echoed in his own. Which writer is
responsible for the following passage?

> Yet, perhaps, it is not fanciful to imagine that Shakespeare, in
> his tragedy of the Venetian outcast, glanced for a moment,
> under cover of a piece of amorous jesting, at that other tragedy
> of the royal physician. 'Ay,' says Portia to Bassanio,
>
> > but I fear you speak upon the rack,
> > Where men enforced do speak anything.
>
> The wisdom and the pity of the divine poet exquisitely reveal
> themselves in those light words.[40]

These light words are Strachey's; but the cadence (though not the
content and only some of the vocabulary) could belong to
Williams. At his worst Strachey is thin and pettifogging; at his,
Williams is pretentious and dubiously comprehensible. 'The great
affection and violent passion of love which was in him (so they
said – but he tasted it with his head rather than his heart; he took
delight in the apprehension of devotion) had had for long no
intense and permanent centre.'[41] Another irritating trick is a
private, short-circuiting use of words. Thus he remarks of
Elizabeth that 'The daughter of things, she was to be finally hurt
by things.'[42] Things, kings, what's the difference? one is tempted
to ask. But, if their style is often gnomic or pretentious, the biographies remain among Williams's most readable books, full of a
sparkle that betokens confidence. 'Incapacity is the mother of
pride, and often of morality also, in the many marriages she
makes with men.'[43] 'It is as pleasant as unusual to see thoroughly
good people getting their deserts.'[44] The barb in that last word is
most adroitly launched. At times his manner becomes Gibbonian.
'Three and a half centuries afterwards, it is not possible to feel
quite certain such a thing would have been beyond the ageing

malevolence of the King's accumulative mind.'[45] (But that 'accumulative' gives the game away.) The biographies show the emergence of a style and vocabulary that comes to full flowering in *The Descent of the Dove*, by then purged of mannerisms, and effortlessly articulate.

Perhaps the most considered account of the common theme of the biographies appears in *Bacon*, which, if not the most graceful (it has its *longeurs*), is certainly the weightiest and most rewarding.[46]

> There is, it seems, a law in things that if a man is compelled to choose between two good actions, mutually exclusive, the one which he chooses to neglect will in course of time avenge itself on him. Rightly considered, this is a comfortable if chastening thought, for it implies that the nature of good is such that it can never, not even for some other mode of itself, be neglected. If ever it is, for whatever admirable reasons, set on one side it will certainly return. No virtue can be followed at the expense of another virtue without injury to the actor. But if that personal harm is a consequence of impersonal justice, the condition of man is not without nobility, so only that his imagination is strong enough to see and understand, love and embrace, the suffering which it involves.[47]

Here is an explicit identification between the Impossibility and its own resolution, one that is at the same time a definition of tragedy. It leads directly to Williams's most important work.

IV

The production of Williams's play *Thomas Cranmer of Canterbury* at the Canterbury Festival of 1936 provided his first piece of genuinely public recognition. Since the production of Masefield's *The Coming of Christ* in 1928 the Festival had been an important occasion for the presentation of verse plays with Christian themes, foreshadowing the post-war renaissance of this kind of drama at the Mercury Theatre, London and the achievements of Christopher Fry, himself a friend of Williams. The play preceding *Cranmer* had been Eliot's *Murder in the Cathedral* (1935) and Williams was to develop still further Eliot's experiment towards combining an authentic Christian drama with a sense of contemporary relevance.

The problem of relevance in a society of dwindling belief is partly a question of language. The capacity of religious language for extending the imagination is pre-empted by pious associations: it has an inbuilt, predetermined resonance. Eliot's achievement in *Murder in the Cathedral* lies in the presentation of a historic religious conflict in such a way that the issues were seen as being valid for his own time. This comes about through his stress on the central controlling truth of the Incarnation, evident in the representational nature of Becket's martyrdom, which is here interpreted as

a *figura Christi*, a sacramental action, itself and other than itself, that confirms or fulfils in a moment of time the redemptive function of the real and archetypal sacrifice of Christ and that prefigures at the same time the final fulfilment of the eternal pattern.[48]

The word 'pattern' is central to Williams's thinking, and illuminates his particular contribution to religious drama. Although his early plays are pseudo-Shakespearean and unaffected by the rhythms and syntax of his more *avant-garde* contemporaries, one discerns in the masques performed at Amen House an apprehension of a timeless present indicative of Williams's essentially metaphysical cast of imagination. Dramas in time, the enactment in a linear progress of human affairs and their temporal consequences, actually slowed down, and thus clogged up, the darting force of his perceptions: *The Witch*, the first of the *Three Plays*, is a case in point. Ornamental language, top-heavy metaphors, are essentially materialistic; they draw attention to themselves, not to the reality they are supposed to indicate. So too with archaic diction. All the 'doth's and 'thereof's and 'wot's and 'sooth's spell out for their readers that this is 'poetry'. Williams was aware of what was wrong; but the awareness appears to have come to him less through sensitivity to the literary climate of his time than through pondering the matter of the Incarnation. How was knowledge of God to be reconciled with the knowledge of men?

There were to be two paths to a solution. One was the realisation of timelessness; the other was the experience of contradiction. The realisation of timelessness is foreshadowed in another of the *Three Plays, The Rite of the Passion*; the exploration of contradiction, as has been seen, was begun in *The Chaste Wanton*. *The Rite* might be described as a nonmusical oratorio, in which the performers recite their parts and the action is produced through what they say rather than through what they do. Conceived as part of a three-hour service of Good Friday devotions, it suggests, both in its presentation and its content, the existence of a timeless world of absolute realities to which the characters conform, and to which and in which their personalities are relative. This is underlined by the pairing of characters, Peter with Caiaphas, James with Pilate, John with Herod, in addition to the more obvious apposition of Gabriel to Satan. But more than apposition is implied: 'contraries are not negations', and already one detects the seeds of Williams's later understanding of the mutuality of good and evil in human experience. In *human* experience: Williams's later plays make explicit that no ultimate dualism is implied. But the abandonment in this early work of even a relative dualism witnesses to the eschatological emphasis in Williams's theology. For him all things are seen in relation to their place in an ultimate pattern which controls, and is exhibited in, the contradictions and diversities of human life.

In *The Rite of the Passion* the opposing forces exist side by side rather than in strife or, as in the later plays, in apparent indissolubility. And this is reflected in the verse, which merely states its propositions, limply. When Satan proclaims

> I am thy shadow, only known as hell
> where any linger from thy sweet accord[49]

the idea is fatally debilitated by the feebleness of its expression.

The invitation to write a festival play must have seemed heaven-sent, if Williams's dubiety about ecclesiastical pretensions will allow the expression. Probably fired by Eliot's example, he wrote a play which, while following the historic progress of Cranmer's career, did so in a way that made it a portrait of humanity's relationship with a Creator who is simultaneously and painfully a Redeemer. But this theological point of view arose, in part at least, as the solution of a dramatic problem. How to infuse a religious drama with a contemporaneity that would not renege on that drama's initial premises? How to make the past truly present, true both to its own contemporaneity and to ours? Williams's solution is to abolish time, place and external events. The play is about Thomas Cranmer, from the year 1528, when he was still at Cambridge, until his martyrdom in 1556; but the action does not take place through a series of set dramatic pieces. It moves with speed, one scene dissolving into another cinematically. External events are conveyed through a stylised symbolism in the manner of Bertolt Brecht; and the characters are representative less of qualities or humours than of capacities and attitudes. The play is no sedate or sonorous costume piece. Instead of regular stresses and elaborate metaphors Williams writes a vigorous rhythmical verse which varies the beat of the decasyllabic line with one strung on five irregularly placed stresses inlaid with rhymes. In this play he attempts a marriage between poetic and colloquial idiom. His speed and concentration, however, are almost his undoing, for the language is too knotted and succinct; there are not enough concessions to the naturally sluggish ear.

The central theme is that of human integrity and its precise worth in the context of the idea of God.

> Thomas, all your life you have sought Christ
> in images, through deflections; how else can men see?
> Plastic, you sought integrity, and timid, courage.
> Most men, being dishonest, seek dishonesty;
> you, among few, honesty, such as you knew,
> in corners of sin, round curves of deception;
> honesty, the point where only the blessed live,
> where only saints settle, the point of conformity.[50]

The speaker is the enigmatic figure of the Skeleton, the *Figura rerum* or shape of things. He derives from Satan in *The Rite of the Passion*, there designated 'dark viceroy of the Holy Ghost'; and his function was to be developed through similar figures in succeeding plays. These reflect Williams's current interest in the writings of Kierkegaard, and are the outcome of his preoccupation with the springs of action and the nature of tragedy where men and women can only truly act when their fortunes conflict with their natures, so that they are compelled to deny their self-sufficiency. Man exists in dialogue with his circumstances; and in

Cranmer the fact of this opposition between fortune and nature, the Impossibility, is personified in the Skeleton, the divine providence, that adverse fate which is Christ's back. What such kindred figures as the Accuser and the Flame do more generally in later plays, the Skeleton does here for one man. This play is an interior drama, and the subordinate characters are only seen in relation to the consciousness of the central figure. It is not the interaction of personalities that interests Williams, but the hounding of a man into salvation.

As an exhibition of how God takes man at his word it provides a good example of its author's ironic spirit. The chorus is made up of the singers who comment upon events through the medium of Cranmer's own prose. They open with the prayer 'that we may so pass through things temporal that we finally lose not the things eternal' – a prayer which is to be answered. The entry of the Skeleton follows upon the words 'Thy Kingdom Come', and the Chorus greets him with the Messianic salutation 'Blessed is He that cometh in the name of the Lord.' He answers Cranmer's offering of himself to God with the warning that

> Populous with prayers is the plain of Paradise,
> skirring after the men who prayed, whose cries
> beseech heaven to refrain; heaven hears not twice.[51]

Cranmer's desire can only be attained through his own integrity – and by the surrender of that integrity to God.

> . . . I must divide
> his life to the last crack and pull his soul
> – if it lives – through the cracks . . . .[52]

It is Cranmer's just desert, for he is an idolater of words. The Skeleton mocks at all his efforts after righteousness, scourging him to his heavenly doom with sardonic laughter, in which the rhythms of the Eliot of *Sweeney Agonistes* may be detected.

> . . . I am the way,
> I the division, the derision, where
> the bones dance in the darkening air,
> I at the cross-ways the voice of the one way,

crying from the tomb of the earth where I died
the word of the only right Suicide,
the only word no words can quell,
the way to heaven and the way to hell.[53]

Later it comments that

The price of heaven or hell or the world is similar –
always a broken heart, sometimes a broken neck.[54]

It declares itself:

I am the delator of all things to their truth.[55]

It accosts Cranmer:

You believe in God; believe also in me;
I am the Judas who betrays men to God.

When Cranmer refuses to accept this, it asks,

You will choose the rack instead of the cross?
I am sorry, friend; it takes longer.[56]

The years pass, and Cranmer, clinging to his honesty of purpose,
is moved to protest,

Have I erred? Let them show me then where I have erred.

The Skeleton replies,

In thinking, though it was important for you to be right,
it mattered at all in the end whether you were right.[57]

Driven to despair, Cranmer cries,

Where is my God?

Mocking, it echoes,

Where is your God?

Then, after a pause, it adds,

> When you have lost him at last you shall come into God.[58]

The final renunciation made, Cranmer asks,

> Can life itself be redemption? all grace but grace?
> all this terror the agonizing glory of grace?

Then the Skeleton reveals itself.

> I am Christ's back; I without face or breath,
> life in death, death in life,
> each a strife with, each a socket for, each,
> in the twisted rear of good will, backward-running speech,
> the derision that issues from doctrines of grace
> through the division man makes between him and his
>   place.
> Christ laughs his foes to scorn, his angels he charges
> with folly; ah, happy who feel how the scorn enlarges!
> I am the thing that lives in the midst of the bones,
> that (seems it) thrives upon moans, the thing with no face
> that spins through the brain on the edge of a spectral
>   voice.
> Rejoice, son of man, rejoice:
> this is the body of Christ which is given for you;
> feed on it in your heart by faith with thanksgiving.[59]

Here Ezekiel is echoed in terms very different from the slow sonorities of Eliot's *Ash Wednesday*, but the swinging measures nowhere suggest frivolity. *Thomas Cranmer* involves its audience at a level beyond that treated by Brecht; its drama is enacted within them.

Religious drama was a perfect medium for Williams's essentially intellectual imagination. The artificiality of the conventions of theatre enabled him to employ embodied abstractions, and to clothe his pictorial, associative method of thought in appropriate forms of character and action. In the plays that succeeded *Cranmer* he experimented freely. In the same year he undertook a Nativity play, arguably a more challenging task than writing for the Festival: as he said in an address to the play's Colchester

audience in October 1937, 'Which do you find more *interesting*
... the Nativity or the latest murder?' A Christian dramatist is
faced with the problem that, while a play's form must arise from
the author's imagination, the form of religious drama is predetermined by the author's beliefs.

Seed of Adam is a spirited attempt to revivify traditional
religious imagery. Within a timeless world of action Williams
brings together Adam and Eve, Joseph and Mary and the three
kings. Two of the latter represent commerce and philosophy; the
third, the Negro, 'represents the experience of man when man
thinks he has gone beyond all hope of restoration to joy'.[60] By a
neat piece of dovetailing, Adam is combined with Caesar
Augustus. He is powerless to return to Paradise; nor do his
children even wish to do so, until the coming of the Third King.
When the latter arrives he makes himself known, greeting
Augustus sardonically as 'the old Adam after all!'

> You saw me
> when you breathlessly slid down the smooth threshold
> of Paradise gate? and saw the things that were hid
> as God warned you you would? did you know
> I was the core of the fruit you ate?
> Did you remember, ungrateful that you are,
> how you threw me away, with such a swing
> I flew over Eden wall, dropped,
> and stuck between two stones?
> You did not see; you did not look after me!
> Smell and taste for you; let the core go to hell.[61]

The King is accompanied by Mother Myrrh, a negress symbolis-
ing Hell. Hell is Heaven's antithesis and thus, in Williams's
emerging sense of salvation through reversal, Heaven's complement. It is a state of negation so intense as to beget its opposite,
just as Mother Myrrh's attack on Mary results in the Saviour's
birth. She and the Third King together are another manifestation
of the Skeleton. The essentially schematic nature of Williams's
imagination fuses Nativity and Redemption in a single vivid piece
of symbolism.

Seed of Adam, going beyond *Thomas Cranmer* in its supra-
temporal personifications, becomes a vehicle of multisignificant
references. Thus the first two kings are not merely iconographical

representations: they also embody the life-experiences involved in the capacities they symbolise, and their attendant choruses give voice to these. For one, Paradise 'is bought for a penny / and slept off'; for another, 'wise men have recognized / it is only our mothers' forms rationalized'. For both, 'tomorrow everything begins again'.[62] The human setting for the Incarnation is thus not so much the historical moment as the timeless need.

The verse attempts a similar timelessness. The imagery is a blend of Islamic, English and biblical references. The 'folk' element is pervasive. At his best Williams achieves a convincing fusion of physical and mental experience, as in Mary's description of her encounter with the Archangel.

> As I came from the fair I looked back; there
> I saw it all in a sheath and a shape of flame,
> having an eagle's head that turned each way
> as if it were guarding something and looking for something.
> Its eyes burned at me; the noise
> of the hurly-burlies and the hurdy-gurdies,
> the ball-spinners, the silk-sellers, the rum-peddlers,
> the swings, and the songs, rose to a whirring voice,
> the air was a hum of sound; I heard it come
> as if the fair all rose in the air and flew
> on eagle's wings after me; I ran
> through the fear and the laughter and the great joys.
> I came by the vineyards to my father's roof;
> there it held aloof a little.[63]

The vitality of this, both in its rhythms and in the emergence of the Archangel from the sounds and activities of everyday life, shows the thrust of an imagination that is riding its theme for victory.

And yet this passage is preceded by a speech from Joseph loaded with all Williams's earlier pomposities.

> Do not with descent, O altitude, even of mercy,
> sweeten the enhancèd glance of those still eyes
> which to my lord's house, and to me the least,
> illumine earth with heaven, our only mortal
> imagination of eternity,
> and the glory of the protonotary Gabriel.[64]

Seed of Adam, fine achievement though it is, still labours under Williams's tendency to cram his text with words, to make his idea bring forth the verse rather than to let the verse carry the idea. It was a hazard necessarily attendant on this particular undertaking. The majority of Nativity plays were of the kind usually designated 'beautiful and reverent': they were not required to make people think. Williams was bent on overcoming such mummified complacency, and this particular play, with its blithe disregard for convention, its swinging rhythms, its irony and verve that almost teases its audience out of thought, triumphantly obliterates the simper of lethargic piety.

The subsequent plays, although less forceful and inventive, make full use of *Seed of Adam*'s innovatory breakthrough from the framework of time and place, and of the personifying and dramatic use of the divided consciousness. But they also lay stress on the authentic life of the symbol, and are more naturalistic than the earlier plays because more truly sacramental in approach. *Judgement at Chelmsford* is the most conventional of them. A pageant play written for the twenty-fifth anniversary of the Essex diocese, it had its proposed London performance postponed because of the outbreak of the Second World War. This was disappointing for Williams, with whom the play was a favourite. He wrote it under the pseudonym 'Peter Stanhope', the name of the dramatist in *Descent into Hell*. *Thomas Cranmer* and *Seed of Adam* had made him suspect in some Church circles; he was unconventional and daring, qualities as rare as they are desirable in a religious dramatist. Because of this he was labelled 'obscure', and suspected of unorthodoxy. At Canterbury, after the performance of *Cranmer*, one clergyman wrote to the press alleging blasphemy. The boys and girls of Canterbury, he complained, had sat in the Chapter House and heard God's majesty insulted.[65] It must have been galling for the author. He was to be a frequent victim of those whom he stigmatised with tempered irritation as ' "the weaker brethren", those innocent sheep who by mere volume of imbecility have trampled over many delicate and attractive flowers in Christendom'.[66]

Judgement at Chelmsford is a history of the diocese presented, through a conflation of time and eternity, not only as 'a judgement of the diocese (a dual concept already anticipated in Williams's biographies), but also as a spiritual drama, the diocese representing the individual soul. As John Heath-Stubbs observes,

the play's retrospective action, from Hell through Purgatory to
Paradise, owes much to Dante.[67] *Judgement at Chelmsford* also
had much in common with *Thomas Cranmer*, the same process
of salvation-through-exposure being deployed; but it is,
inevitably, more leisurely and more historically precise, with
passages of charming comedy and caustic satire. It is easily the
most accessible of the plays. The role of the Skeleton is taken by
the Accuser, who meets the personified diocese at the gate of
Heaven. He is 'the dweller on the threshold of love'[68] (a nice fusion
of celestial and demonic associations) whose task is to exhibit
Chelmsford to herself.

> I stand
> at the right hand of all men in their hour of death;
> but also they may see me at any hour. Their breath
> catches, their blood is cold, they remember their sins.
> They see what they have made of their lives.[69]

He is the universal life-illusion.

> God made me to be the image of each man's desire –
> a king or a poet or a devil – and rarely Christ.
> Most men when at last they see their desire,
> fall to repentance – all have that chance.[70]

His role is to be a devil's advocate within the self, a conception less
mythical than existential.

The liveliness and good cheer of *Judgement at Chelmsford* is
also found in three shorter plays, written in the early 1940s for the
Oxford branch of the Pilgrim Players. Of these, *The Death of
Good Fortune* is like a masque, the characters, with the exception
of the Blessed Virgin and the allegorical figure of Good Fortune
himself, being personifications, such as the Lover, the Magician,
the Girl. Good Fortune reigns in the city, giving everyone his
desire; only the Girl rejects him, knowing as she does that life is
empty and vain, and that to talk of 'good luck' is mockery. Mary
agrees with her, but knows something more: she therefore
pronounces Good Fortune's death sentence. In the face of disaster
the King advocates resignation, but the Lover opposes him, for
'Love must live.' Mary then raises Good Fortune from the dead,
and thus exhibits his true meaning.

> Good Fortune, you have your fortune;
> yours is the only fortune; all luck is good.[71]

The phrase, originating with Boethius, has been called 'the intellectual return to Eden'.[72] It echoes the discovery made at the end of *Thomas Cranmer*, 'Can life itself be redemption?' *The Death of Good Fortune*, slight though it is, makes a surprising impact on account of the dramatic consequences of its intellectual logic. Has the Virgin Mary ever caused anyone's death on stage before – or since? Nevertheless the interest lies in idea rather than in action.

The House by the Stable (1939) and its sequel *Grab and Grace* (1941) are more persuasive. The figures of Pride, Man, Hell, Grace and the rest are appropriately realised as types and fully alive as individuals, so that the plays' message is organically, not arbitrarily, presented. *The House by the Stable* portrays Pride's first expulsion from Man's house through his half-hearted sheltering of Joseph and Mary. Gabriel is dignified, slightly pompous, bewildered by Mary's friendliness towards Man, and unmercifully teased by the urchin Grace. Man himself is well-meaning and rather slow on the uptake; likable amid all his inconsistencies, he has enough natural goodness to respond to the promptings of Grace. *Grab and Grace* deals with the second step after conversion (the expulsion of Pride disguised as Self-Respect) in terms of knockabout farce. Faith is a sophisticated young woman, Pride a slithery, gushing cheat. The whole range of characterisation constitutes an imaginative theology.

The verse carries the theological overtones with ease. A good example occurs in Man's embarrassed account to Pride of his new friend, Faith.

> She was a friend of Immanuel, the child born
> the night you went ... O well, Pride –
> I beg your pardon; it is old habit in me –
> we need not go into all that now.
> There was a misunderstanding of what he meant
> and a tussle – you, my dear, will understand
> there was something to be said on my side;
> but anyhow – it was all rather unfortunate – he died.[73]

Such verse has a suppleness that retains its lilt while responding to the demands of idiomatic speech.

Terror of Light, a Whitsun play of 1940, only exists in a prose version, but was to have been rewritten in verse. It is a pity that it was not, for the prose is uncertain in tone, often lapsing into the stilted or the chatty. Possibly Williams had been aiming for the kind of popularity (but also scandal) enjoyed a year later by Dorothy L. Sayers's broadcast sequence *The Man Born To Be King*. Verbally, his play anticipates hers; but we also find Williams parodying himself. 'Oh Augustitude pray for me', says John to Mary Magdalene. Elsewhere the language is flat and over-definitive: Thomas speaks of 'being put completely into one's own identity'. Williams was clearly tired when he wrote the play, and falls back on his earlier definitions.

Nevertheless *Terror of Light* has its impressive moments. One of them is the redemption of Judas. He is said to have 'gone down the wholly negative way, where there is nothing but God'.[74] The refusal of intermediaries, of co-inherence, leads to the total fusion of nature with fortune: 'he became himself'. But a way of return is defined by the Blessed Virgin.

> Judas has betrayed my Son and his own place; very well – his place shall be given to Matthias. Matthias shall be a substitute for Judas; very well, – but Judas shall be glad of substitution and love it, and in degree as he loves it where can he be but in the substitution? Miracle of healing! His exclusion shall become his inclusion.[75]

This awareness of the all-comprehending power of the Creation–Redemption is the theological perspective towards which all Williams's writings on the Impossibility have been pointing.

The Three Temptations is a radio play, performed in 1942. Freedom from the requirements of stagecraft suited Williams's tendency to effect mythic fusions; and the resulting alignment of Herod, Caiaphas and Pilate with Christ's three temptations in the wilderness is subtle and suggestive. The compression shows how essentially spatial Williams's imagination was: he sees the events of time as so many facets of eternity. The austerity of his moral viewpoint is now absolute. Men shall have what they have chosen. 'Hell / is always there for the craving, and the having is easy.'[76] (The echo of Ira Gershwin's 'Summertime', though presumably unintentional, is curiously effective.)

Williams's last play, *The House of the Octopus* (1945), is also his most naturalistic. As one reviewer wrote, 'in it the results of his work in various literary fields are so successfully rallied that the play stands to his entire output much as the final note or chord of a piece composed in accordance with the principles of mode, not of key, stands to the foregoing musical elements; it designates their relative positions, and reveals their deeper significance'.[77] This play represents the full maturity of Williams's thought on the question of human integrity and its relation to the providence of God: on its inception he had approached Margaret Sinclair, who had commissioned the play for the United Council for Missionary Education, with the request, 'Will it be all right if I make the missionary the villain of the piece?' (Her ready permission finds graceful acknowledgement in the Preface.) Technically this is Williams's best play, alike on account of its dramatic qualities, its clarity, and the dynamic expression of its theme; and it throws a searching light upon a certain type of religious temperament. It was evidently too searching for comfort, since it is said that at one performance by the students of a northern theological college the missionary was praised in the synopsis for his courage and devotion. Williams might, or might not, have appreciated that.

The setting is an island in the Outer Seas, where Anthony the missionary has established a small native Christian community, centred round their newly built church. Led by his desire to be a saviour to his flock, he compromises with the power called P'o-l'u, already invented by Williams for his Arthurian poems, and here suggestive of the despotism of Hitler's Germany or Stalin's Russia. However, Williams declared it to represent a spiritual threat rather than any earthly power. Anthony is portrayed with considerable irony. He is all for courage and unflinching loyalty, encumbered with a sense of his own responsibility – one of those people Williams stigmatised as being in 'a state of high anxiety to defend and protect, and generally stand up for, Almighty God'.[78] He accordingly condemns without mercy a convert whose fear of death causes her to apostasise. In spite of this the girl, Alayu, is killed by the soldiers of P'o-l'u – a piece of ruthlessness fully in keeping with the premises of modern warfare. Her fellow Christians who saw her die can never feel the same as Anthony, who did not.

SIRU: . . . We in these isles
         live in our people—no man's life his own –
         from birth and initiation. When our salvation
         came to us, it showed us no new mode –
         sir, dare you say so? – of living to ourselves.
         The Church is not many but the life of many
         in ways of relation. This new birth
         was common to Alayu and to us; no sin,
         no death through sin, no death in sin,
         parts us. It is sin, you say, our Lord redeems
         in his Church; how if he now redeem this?
ANTHONY: If indeed she had repented before she died –
SIRU: Sir, we lay there our hands on our mouths.
         See, because of her death we live more strong
         in his clear goodness – much less doubt,
         less fear; this is God's way –
         to cause his day to dawn in sheer blood.
         It is she, let me say, as well as you, to whom
         we owe now all that we know of grace.[79]

The temptation of this second Anthony is presented with a skill
that matches Eliot's in *Murder in the Cathedral*. The Imperial
Marshal knows what he is about.

                I have studied
         all my life, my dear Prefect, the religious mind.
         Every pious man – and, of course, woman –
         has one – just one – surface where religion and he
         are so delicately mixed in his soul as to be
         indistinguishable; he is never quite sure –
         and does not (believe me!) ever want to be sure –
         whether his religion or he is being soothed
         into a lascivious spiritual delight.[80]

The priest's dictatorial inner nature being shown as itself an
expression of P'o-l'u, his repentance is the more effective: indeed,
in its use of political issues Williams's drama of redemption
through self-knowledge compares favourably with Eliot's esoteric
treatment of the theme in *The Family Reunion*.[81]
   Like all Williams's plays *The House of the Octopus* is a drama
of purging by illumination, Divine Providence being symbolised

by the Flame, a personifying of one of the fiery tongues of
Pentecost, who appears whenever invoked, however casually. He
has the character of an underlying law that is at the same time an
active power in relationship with men. To Anthony he shows
himself in apparent hostility, as much 'Christ's back' to the
recalcitrant missionary as the Skeleton is to Cranmer; and it is he
who sums up the play with the statement of inescapable reconciliation.

> Yes; you may be right,
> but to be right in the Devil is to be wrong in the Spirit,
> and yet, even in the Devil, right is right.
> Blessed and praised and glorious for ever be he
> who will have us right all ways, not only one.[82]

Such flexible, simple verse is Williams's nearest approach to the
naturalistic manner of Eliot's later plays: it is also in its very
expression the embodiment of the sacramental vision governing
all his later work.

4 The Novels

I

Charles Williams was not primarily a novelist and such fiction as he wrote was eccentric to traditional forms. The majority of English novels are naturalistic, faithful to observed reality and imagined within the confines of tangible experience; yet ever since the rise of the Gothic novel in the late eighteenth century there has existed another tradition, one that explores the byways of spiritual experience, either through a portrayal of the occult or through a literary method that may be designated visionary or poetic. The Gothic novel itself was concerned primarily with the heightening of emotional or imaginative experience, either through terror or through aesthetic appreciation; or through both, as in what is arguably the masterpiece of the tradition, Ann Radcliffe's *The Mysteries of Udolpho* (1794). The nineteenth-century novelists, however, have little to offer compared with the philosophical insights into the fusion of spirit and matter that we find in the greater Romantic poets; only *Wuthering Heights* (1847) stands out as a truly comprehensive vision of both spiritual and physical reality. For the rest, the spiritual is either thinned into idealistic aspiration or erupts demonically through the occult, or in psychological disturbance or in crime. The Victorian novelists were on occasion able to make something of wider significance out of such 'sensational' material. Dickens did so, in his play on supernatural dread in *Bleak House* (1851) and *Little Dorrit* (1857), while Le Fanu's *Uncle Silas* (1864) draws on distorted spirituality or indirectly conveyed sexual repression for its effect. This particular use of supernatural motifs to provide a kind of spiritual anthropology was brought to perfection in some of the shorter tales of Henry James. But ultimately both the appeal and the success of such stories depend on unbelief, and their premisses are not to be taken at their own valuation. The logical outcome of this use of the tradition is the popular ghost story, for, however enjoyable as relaxation even such learned and skilful tales as those of Montague Rhodes James may be, they do not in the last resort take the experience of the supernatural seriously. But in Charles Williams's formative years a considerable number of writers were doing so. Algernon Blackwood and Walter de la Mare were the most accomplished; but more influential on Williams were, it seems, the diverse but broadly Christian novels of Arthur Machen, Evelyn Underhill and G. K. Chesterton.

Arthur Machen is one of those minor writers of genuine originality who, largely ignored by academic criticism, maintain an enduring hold upon their readers. He made his name in the 1890s with a number of tales of the occult, collected in *The House of Souls* (1906). But, in addition to 'shockers' such as 'The Great God Pan', the book contains two stories more representative of the tradition out of which Williams wrote. 'A Fragment of Life' is a portrait of a city clerk who lives the drabbest of married lives in London's suburbia, an extreme instance of that limitation which was Williams's own lot. Gradually he is overtaken by a visionary awareness of a world of glory underlying the one of which he is normally conscious. Williams was to provide his own gloss on this theme in his last two novels, but Machen's story has a very un-Williams-like conclusion: the clerk discovers the hidden country when he takes up the inheritance of an old house on the Welsh border, the landscape Machen so powerfully evokes in his visionary novel *The Hill of Dreams* (1907). Machen's outlook is a kind of unsystematised Neo-Platonism; and throughout his writing career he was a vociferous champion of that literature which was based on what he designated 'ecstasy', by which he means the realisation of this underlying or overarching world of spiritual reality. His most forceful and persuasive presentation of his case is in *Hieroglyphics* (1902), a literary manifesto which, while owing as much to the Aesthetic movement as to the seventeenth-century Neo-Platonists, has marked affinities with Williams's remarks on the power of literature in his early novel *Shadows of Ecstasy*.

The House of Souls also contains another story which anticipates Williams's fiction. 'The White People' is recounted by a girl innocently caught up in devil-worship. Machen, like Williams, is no sentimental supernaturalist. For each man he posits not only a beneficent 'shadow companion' witnessing to the glory of the immanent spiritual world, but also a 'muddy' companion ready to pull down and destroy those who venture improperly equipped across the spiritual borderline. The dangers of occult investigation are frequently symbolised by this 'watcher on the threshold', a supernatural presence powerfully evoked by Bulwer Lytton in *Zanoni* (1842) (a novel Williams admired) and who reappears in *The Necromancers* (1909), Robert Hugh Benson's novel attacking spiritualism. Benson, a member of a prolific literary family, and a popular Catholic apologist, shows a sharp satirical awareness of the crankier spiritualist experiments of his time, and anticipates Williams in his resolute outflanking of their claims with the more powerful rituals of orthodoxy. This particular account of trafficking with the dead has certain features in common with Williams's *All Hallows' Eve*; but one has only to read the two novels alongside each other to appreciate the greater depth and sophistication of the latter.

Benson's work clearly owes much to the novels of his friend Evelyn Underhill, a close friend also of Arthur Machen, and a well-known exponent of mystical theology. Williams's rather unenthusiastic comments on her novels in his Introduction to her *Letters* is a shade surprising in view of the fact that they clearly influenced his own. The title 'Many Dimensions', for instance, comes from phrases used in both *The Grey World* (1904) and *The Lost Word* (1907);[1] while the latter novel also speaks of 'the descent of the Dove'.[2] *The Column of Dust* (1909) makes use of the hymn 'Christians Awake' in a manner anticipating *The Greater Trumps*;[3] and its theme, that of the invasion of the material world by a spirit which takes up its habitation in a human body, anticipates Williams's portrayal of the interaction of living and dead in *Descent into Hell* and *All Hallows' Eve*. Indeed, Evelyn Underhill is a writer whose work is a key to much that is now strange to us in Williams's imagination, for in her first novel she examines the relation of mystical vision to the world of everyday experience. The stress undergone by those who find themselves possessing a double sense of reality is made matter for satirical comedy as well as tragedy; readers familiar only with her religious writings will be surprised by some brisk, even tart, turns of phrase. Not only the crude incomprehension of the unimaginative materialist but also the pretentious meddling of the would-be 'spiritual' are objects of her mockery, a ridicule, however, that is never savagely administered. In Williams's novels something of the same process goes on, as in his delineation of his characters' reactions to the supernatural invasions that dominate several of the plots; but his writing is more urgent and original than hers. Evelyn Underhill's novels suffer from her inability to infuse any real drama into the situations she has imagined. Her portraits of spiritual reality have therefore to rely on what is, perhaps as a result, an emphatic, over-florid style.

The Column of Dust, however, as Williams concedes, has a theme of genuine power and dramatic possibilities. The occult experiments of a bored woman living alone with her illegitimate child draw into her mind and consciousness a spirit-being through whose eyes the human world is seen in a new perspective. The novel is thereby provided with the somewhat static satire that we find in its predecessors; but this is now combined with the discovery of the Holy Grail ('Graal' in Underhill's, Machen's and also Williams's spelling) in a makeshift shrine in the Cumbrian fells. The dying keeper hands the Grail over to the troubled Constance; the result is the healing not only of her own disaffected nature but also of her spiritual tenant.

There is much in this odd, uneven, but interesting novel that anticipates Williams's work. The opening chapter describing the consciousness of 'the Watcher' as he hovers on the edge of Constance's awareness suggests similar passages from *Descent into Hell*:

> he saw the many worlds and planes of being, which, from the standpoint of eternity, are perceived under an aspect of great and serene simplicity, interpenetrating one another; and the world of matter, turbulent and many tinted, crossing them all.[4]

The Watcher's appreciation of the beauty of the created world neatly aligns the visionary experience of Traherne and Blake with the author's own understanding of its significance: he calls it 'a gloss upon eternity'. Art for him is 'a dream about the dream'.[5] The Grail itself is presented, in keeping with the theories of Machen and of A. E. Waite,[6] as the focus of a secret religion. Williams, although he borrows much of the machinery of this Grail story for *War in Heaven*, transports the idea of a secret focus of power to the Stone of Solomon in *Many Dimensions* and the Tarot cards in *The Greater Trumps*; but in all three novels we find guardians and initiates. The guardian of the Grail in *The*

Column of Dust insists on the unity of every aspect of love, a belief which underlies all Williams's finest work.

> 'Right through existence, from beginning to end, and in every relation, one always as a matter of fact loves in the same way.'
>   Thinking of the foolish enthusiasms of the past, she said, 'No! I hope not!'
>   'Oh yes, but we do', he answered. 'Why, isn't that just our job, to get the little loves right, so that the big love may be in order too? *"Ordina quest' amore, O tu che m' ami!"* Friend, lover, toy, ambition and sacramental divinity; we really turn the same face to them all.'[7]

The citation (used by Williams also),[8] the faintly reductive language and didactic tone, are characteristics of Evelyn Underhill's fictional technique: her novels are discussions rather than dramas, and lack (for better or worse) any real sense of the activity of evil. Their quest is for a deeper understanding of the good. In this they have affinities with the most positive aspects of Williams's work, both in aim and in specific instances. The Watcher's reaction to the imperial procession in the London streets anticipates Nancy's vision of the policeman as the Emperor in *The Greater Trumps*: 'he saw Sovereignty, the ruling and governing Idea, behind its poor image, and hardly perceived the shabbiness of the symbol through which he gazed'.[9]

The semi-magical world evoked by Evelyn Underhill and Arthur Machen certainly influenced Williams more than the fantasies of his celebrated contemporary G. K. Chesterton. Chesterton, like Williams, devoted a multifaceted literary career to the expression of Christian belief; and Williams's early poetry does, in its proclamatory certainties, owe a good deal to Chesterton. But, where fiction is concerned, only *War in Heaven* really bears any resemblance to Chesterton's work, which derives more from H. G. Wells than from the Neo-Platonic tradition, not only in the way in which the extravagant events are made to impinge, often humorously, on the everyday world, but also in its didactic qualities. Chesterton's fantasies, entertaining though they are, proceed from certainties: they are not exploratory. Williams may have sought to emulate their lightheartedness in his early work, but he gradually shook off an influence that was in its very nature, if not in its beliefs, alien to his particular viewpoint.

That viewpoint develops as the result of his own experiments within the metaphysical literary tradition. Williams's novels embrace various schools within the genre, *War in Heaven* (1930) being occultist in the manner of Robert Hugh Benson and of 'Sax Rohmer', author of the popular Dr Fu-Manchu thrillers; while *Many Dimensions* (1931) is the kind of time-fantasy made popular by such books as J. W. Dunne's *An Experiment with Time* (1927) and P. D. Ouspensky's *A New Model of the Universe* (1931), and concurrently treated in fiction by John Buchan in *A Gap in the Curtain* (1932). *The Place of the Lion* (1931) and *The Greater Trumps* (1932) are parables in the fantastic mode, esoteric spiritual fables of the same genus, though hardly of the same literary attainment, as T. F. Powys's *Mr Weston's Good Wine* (1927). Both reflect Williams's knowledge of Cabbalistic lore. *Descent into Hell* (1937) is closer to the visionary, multidimensional novel of the Underhill type, while the final book, *All Hallows' Eve* (1945), combines a similar approach with a return to occultist elements, the two aspects welded together by a greater stress on human relationships than one finds in the earlier books.

Indeed, it is this stress on ordinary humanity which distinguishes Williams from the general run of occult novelists: that, and his strongly intellectual slant. Machen tends to be polemical. He writes as an avowed Catholic, a crusader, in this resembling Chesterton; Evelyn Underhill, on the other hand, plays strongly on emotion, and her novels are at times heavily incantatory. De la Mare remained agnostic as to the interpretation of those supernatural experiences which he, more convincingly even than Machen, Underhill or Williams, could describe. His attitude is enquiring, being concerned with man's condition on the frontier between two worlds, either of which he can portray as hostile. Inconclusiveness is of the essence of his style. Williams, however, concentrates on achieving precision. He works from the Neo-Platonic premiss that the world of sight and touch is the expression of a spiritual reality, but elaborates it by a method well described as 'an effort to fuse different levels of experience: theological, supernatural, psychological', and as 'a new twentieth-century form, an equivalent for [*sic*] the great medieval allegories'.[10] As much as Evelyn Underhill he seeks to reveal a path of salvation out of the confused knowledge of the two worlds: to that extent his novels are gnostic parables. But he has a more developed sense of evil than she exhibits, and is thus able to solve the dramatic problem that inevitably constrains the visionary novelist with Neo-Platonic leanings. A dynamic is required; but if dualism is rejected it is hard to find one. Machen, indeed, does have a dualistic imagination; but this produces a schism in his work, the sensationalist black-magic elements consorting uneasily with the affirmative visionary passages. If Machen separates good and evil, Evelyn Underhill tends to evade the issue; although *The Column of Dust* strikes a deeper note of personal responsibility and human inadequacy than do its predecessors, any truly disturbing tension between the two modes of experience and the dangers attendant on them are only faintly realised. But Williams does succeed in treating evil satisfactorily in relation to the positive aspect of his vision, and thus in generating drama. He achieves this by fusing the concepts of good and evil in an overall concept of divine providence as both creative and redemptive, one whose control of the action is necessarily total. The contradictory experience of the Impossibility is here set forth in a more general context.

Williams's novels are also interesting in that they constitute an enquiry into the nature of the supernatural in itself. *Shadows of Ecstasy*, the first of them, stands alone: it is a philosophical thriller rather than a metaphysical one, and is characterised by a prevailing scepticism. *War in Heaven* examines the distinction between magic and religion, while *Many Dimensions*, *The Place of the Lion* and *The Greater Trumps* use specifically mythological material to explore the nature of power, and the relation between human freedom and divine providence. Williams here attempts a reconciliation between the magical and the religious, employing the mode of the metaphysical thriller to construct a parable on the controlling nature of love. In his hands the supernatural romance becomes affirmative, transforming the darker aspects of occultism into a vision of potential joy.

In his two final novels he moves from the metaphysical to the visionary. The focus becomes closer, so that he seems to be looking at this world in order to discern the spiritual dimension breaking through it. In the earlier novels, on the other hand, the supernatural takes the initiative, forcing itself upon the characters' attention. It is invasive, challenging, catastrophic. But Williams focuses less on the nature of the invasion than on the human responses it evokes. In order to demonstrate the individuality of spiritual and physical experience, he presents the forces let loose by the Tarot cards and the other means of entry as being themselves governed by spiritual laws, laws which can be apprehended and maintained by those who will lay themselves open to them. The occult elements are therefore subordinate to the proposition that love, in so far as human beings can learn to understand it, is what upholds and sustains the universe. The influence of Dante is obvious here, an influence of more importance in Williams's work than his knowledge of magic; indeed, his portrayal of the latter only serves to refute its claims to offer any worthwhile powers to its practitioners. The common theme of the novels emerges as being the discovery that love in all its forms is both the mainstay of human life and its ultimate purpose.

As Williams presents it, such a discovery involves little dynamic moral struggle. For him, love and strife are not, as in Empedoclean cosmology, in eternal opposition; rather, love is a reality that makes itself known as power even in the assertion of its opposite. One way of putting the matter would be to say that it means, to use Williams's own phrase, the voluntary choice of necessity. A good deal of passive acceptance is involved in it, but this is an acceptance of everything that happens as being, however inconceivably, an occasion for love and joy, regardless of personal preference or esteem. The achievement of such an attitude is the measure of salvation. In each novel the characters are presented with an unexpected supernatural invasion which threatens the existing order. Because it decisively and irresistibly challenges their self-centredness, their attitude towards it becomes a gauge of their attitude to any fact outside themselves. Some ignore it, others (Williams's none-too-holy fools) remain blissfully unaware of it; others fight it or attempt to exploit it; the blessed accept it as a manifestation of a still greater power into whose hands they have already committed their lives. The novels are concerned with encounter and response, with the tension between being and becoming. The 'bad' characters (so to call them) are those who only wish to become more themselves – would-be supermen such as Gregory Persimmons in *War in Heaven*, frustrated egotists such as Dora Wilmot in *The Place of the Lion* – and those who do not even want that, but merely to stay as they are forever, Lawrence Wentworth in *Descent into Hell* being the most obvious example. Each type acts in accordance with his or her nature. Thus, Gregory, who all his life has tried to dominate and control other people, endeavours to dominate and control the Grail – an absurdity, as his chief opponent, the Archdeacon, realises; Sir Giles Tumulty in *Many Dimensions*, whose life has been governed by callous curiosity, can only see the Stone of Solomon as matter for experiments. In *Shadows of Ecstasy*, the self-absorbed Rosamund totally rejects the new powers offered her by the African invasion.

In contrast to such characters Williams portrays a number of others who are either at peace with themselves, and thus able to find in the new crisis nothing they have not known and accepted long ago – characters such as the Archdeacon, or Sybil in *The Greater Trumps*; or else those who, through a knowledge arising from love for someone or something outside themselves, accept and even cherish the supernatural intruder, and in so doing restore the world to its proper balance. Through such a plot device Williams suggests that to live by the dictates of love is to live in accordance with the fundamental laws of the universe. It is a belief easy neither to maintain nor to set forth: the novels are more like imaginative confessions of faith than effective demonstrations, but they do depict what in Christian terminology is known as the divine call, the response of the elect soul, and the experience of redemption.

Williams himself tended to avoid that terminology, being well aware of the limiting imaginative associations of time-honoured but time-worn religious phrases. In an address given to the Church Union School of Sociology, he pointed out that the Church's prophetic voice is often hampered by sincere men 'who blanket their message by making heroic efforts to talk in a way nobody listens to'.[11] Williams's dislike of religious cliché means that there is little or no formal Christian language in his novels, even though they are founded on the principles of Christian spirituality. Williams uses his own vocabulary, referring to the Godhead in terms of its particular aspect for the point at issue – for example, as the Mercy, the Permission, or the Omnipotence – a style of address that shows his respect for Islamic spirituality. Christ he usually refers to as Messias, while the Holy Ghost becomes Our Lord the Spirit. The aim, as always in his writing, is accuracy.

II

Shadows of Ecstasy stands apart from Williams's other novels.

Originally called 'The Black Bastard' and written in the 1920s, it was not accepted for publication until 1933. Although fifth in the series, it is in fact better read as a prelude, for it sets out the themes and treats of issues which the later books enact. As a supernatural thriller it is the least of the novels. The story of an attempt made by a white superman-adept called Nigel Considine to harness the energies of Africa and to create a new civilisation in the West, based on the powers of the imagination which post-Descartian man has suppressed, it is a confused, inchoate affair: not for one moment are the events convincing. But the theme is full of interest, and might have been appropriate for a Gothic novel of the late Romantic movement; the central character has a Byronic air.

The character most closely resembling the author is Roger Ingram, a teacher of literature whose concerns are the same as Williams's own: he could well have written *The English Poetic Mind*. He sees himself as 'an embalmer'.

> I embalm poetry ... with the most popular and best-smelling unguents and so on, but I embalm it all right. I then exhibit the embalmed body to visitors at so much a head. They like it much better than the live thing, and I live by it, so I suppose it's all right.[12]

The words have a timely reference.

Against this, Considine offers a new hope. He is the spokesman for a self-transcendence which is Nietzchean in inspiration. (At other times his injunctions recall the contemplative philosophy of Walter Pater.) When an attempt to resurrect a dead man fails, he urges his followers to

> look as masters. Don't lose a moment; change this into victory within you. Death here shall be life in you; feel it, imagine it, draw it into yourselves; as with all experience, so with this. Live by it; feed on it and live.[13]

The echo of Christ's words at the Last Supper underlines, by way of ironic contrast, the predatory nature of the aspiration.

Considine's technique of applied ecstasy anticipates ideas explored by John Cowper Powys in *Maiden Castle* (1937); but Powys's adept in that novel is presented, characteristically, with a homeliness and humour alien to Williams's gaudier imagination. The power of withheld sexual energy is an idea which interested both men. Williams's subsequent view of the matter, to judge from his discussion of the Early Christian *subintroductae* in *The Descent of the Dove*,[14] was more cautious, and infused with something of Powys's scepticism.

Power, whether exercised or withheld, is the real subject of this novel. Considine's claims are questioned by three of the characters, whose reasons for doing so are held in interplay. The Anglican priest, Ian Caithness, opposes him from the standpoint of Catholic orthodoxy. Williams neatly diagnoses his position.

> The nature of his intellect and the necessities of his office had directed his attention always not towards things in themselves but towards things in immediate action. He defined men by morality; it was perhaps inevitable that he should define God in the same way. ... He was always trying to avoid Dualism, and falling back on the statement that Omniscience might permit what it did not and could not originate, yet other origin (outside Omniscience) there be none. It is true he always added that it was a mystery, but a safer line was to insist that good and evil were facts, whatever the explanation was. True as this might be, it had the slight disadvantage that he saw everything in terms of his own good and evil, and so imperceptibly to resist evil rather than to follow good became the chief concern of his exhortations.[15]

This passage looks ahead to Williams's theological books; but it is marred by such stilted affectations as that 'there be none', and the too-heavy playfulness of 'slight disadvantage', vices of style that betray a lack of self-assurance.

Sir Bernard Travers is a more effective portrait. His delicate irony is largely Williams's own.

> Dante was to him no more ridiculous than Voltaire; disillusion was as much an illusion as illusion itself. A thing that seemed had at least the truth of its seeming. ... A thing might not be true because it appeared so to him, but it was no less likely to be true because everyone else denied it.[16]

Sir Bernard voices an absolute relativity, the point of view that informs all Williams's subsequent writing. It finds its most precise and effective expression in *The House of the Octopus*.

> Will God dispute over words? no; but man
> must, if words mean anything, stand by words,
> since stand he must; and on earth protest to death
> against what at the same time is a jest in heaven.[17]

This is the essence and the justification of what Williams elsewhere calls 'the quality of disbelief'.

Such discriminating scepticism is likewise a mark of Roger's wife, Isabel. It is she who puts her finger on Considine's weak spot – that, instead of having the faith to trust himself to death, he seeks to master it: the contrast with the attitude of Christ is obvious. Her exchange with Sir Bernard on the subject of love is characteristic of Williams's use of dialogue at its best, simple and unpretentious, and lucidly analytic.

> [Sir Bernard] said to Isabel as tenderly as possible:
> 'Why did you tell Roger to go?'
> 'Because I wanted him to, since he wanted to', she said. 'More; for I wanted him to even more than he did, since I hadn't myself to think of and he had.'
> Sir Bernard blinked. 'I see', he said. 'But – I only ask – isn't it a little risky ... deciding what other people want?'
> 'Dear Sir Bernard, I wasn't *deciding*,' she said, 'I was wanting. It isn't quite the same thing. I want it – whatever he wants. I don't want it unselfishly, or so that he may be happy, or because I ought to, or for any reason at all. I just want it. And then since I haven't myself to think of, I'm not divided or disturbed in wanting, so I *can* save him trouble. That's all.'
> 'O quite, quite', Sir Bernard said. 'That would be all. And is that what you call quiet affection?'
> Isabel looked a trifle perplexed. 'I don't call it anything', she said. 'There isn't anything to call it. It's the way things happen, if you love anyone.'[18]

Isabel is 'adult in love': beside what she possesses in herself Considine's aims look meretricious.

Shadows of Ecstasy is a testing-ground not only for Williams's belief in the power inherent in great imaginative writing, but also for his belief in the need for law. The book reflects the restiveness of both emotional and social frustration; but it also looks ahead to the political ideas of Williams's Arthurian poems, to the idea of voluntary obedience especially. Isabel's attitude to Roger is one example. Elsewhere Williams comments more specifically:

> beauty cannot be manifested unless the mind assents. Without that assent, beauty itself must be tyranny; but with that grave acceptance there is no government that is not beautiful, for love is not only the fulfilling but the beginning of the law.[19]

In such a view one sees Williams's remoteness from both left- and right-wing writers of the time. (There are, however, affinities here with the hierarchical concepts to be found in the work of Yeats.)

For all its wealth of ideas, its wit and passages of beauty, the novel is uneasy with itself. Sir Bernard's scepticism gets into the very fabric of the narrative, and his diagnosis of Roger's state is applicable to the book as well. 'He's fanatic enough to believe passionately and not sufficiently fanatical to believe that other people ought to believe.'[20] The novel is testing scepticism as much as it tests belief. The attitude to Considine is ambivalent, not to say uncertain; and this ambivalence is reflected in the tone. The dialogue oscillates between the pretentious and the larky, but the descriptive prose can reach poetic heights, as in the account of Roger's journey to Considine's house by the sea. The uncertainty of the artistry reflects the uncertainty of the ideas. But the novel includes two prophecies of what is to come. One is Sir Bernard's understanding of Isabel's love for Roger as itself a resolution of the Impossibility. The other is the novel's own pointing to the ones to follow:

> was all the war, were the armies and munitions and the transports but the shadow of the repression by which men held down their more natural energies? . . . But things forgotten could rise; and old things did not always die.[21]

III

That *War in Heaven* should have found a publisher is easy to understand: it is an entertaining and fast-moving mixture of black magic, theological speculation, easy satire, plot and counterplot, which adds up to a palatable brew. The action is precipitated by the discovery that the Holy Grail has lain hidden for centuries in an English country church – a good example of Williams's mischievous irony and a reflection, perhaps, of current occult beliefs as reflected in the supposed burial of the Holy Grail at Glastonbury.[22] The struggle for its possession between those who wish to use it and those who seek to preserve it becomes the occasion not only for detailed accounts of necromantic practices, but also, and more importantly, for a further examination of the true nature of power. *War in Heaven* is indeed a key work for appreciating Williams's understanding of the supernatural.

Gregory Persimmons, a publisher who dabbles in the occult, and the acerbic experimentalist, Sir Giles Tumulty, together with their companions in trying to control the Grail, are shown as pursuing a course as futile as that of Milton's Satan. 'Only Destiny can defy Destiny.' Gregory is likened to 'a clerk at a brothel', Sir Giles to a fly in a chalice. They have no understanding of the supernatural since they cannot recognise it as being precisely that – super-natural. On the other hand, their chief opponent, the Archdeacon of Fardles, in whose church the Grail is found, treats it with what seems to its less initiated supporters to be levity. As he says, 'You staunch churchpeople always make me feel like an atheist.'[23]

The Archdeacon is the Galahad of this particular Grail quest, and bears a certain resemblance to Chesterton's Father Brown. His own belief is the reverse of bigoted, even while he asserts the grounds from which bigotry can spring. 'No-one can possibly do more than decide what to believe.'[24] But the recognition that such is the case is the true safeguard against bigotry. In the words of Prester John, the Guardian of the Grail, 'Believe certainly that this universe also carries its salvation in its heart.'[25]

This contention is supported by some of Williams's most persuasive prose. The Archdeacon is contemplating the Grail as it stands a prisoner in Gregory's house.

By long practice he had accustomed himself in any circumstances . . . to withdraw into that place where action is created. The cause of all action there disposed itself according to that Will which was its nature, and, so disposing itself, moved him easily as a part of its own accommodation to the changing wills of men, so that at any time and at all times its own perfection was maintained, now known in endurance, now in beauty, now in wisdom, now in joy. There was no smallest hesitation which it would not solve, nor greatest anxiety which it did not make lucid. In that light other things took on a new aspect, and the form of Gregory, where he stood a few steps away, seemed to swell into larger dimensions. But this enlargement was as unreal as it was huge; the sentences which he had altered a few days back on denying and defying Destiny boomed like unmeaning echoes across creation. . . . It was a useless attempt at usurpation, useless yet slightly displeasing, as pomposity always is. In the universe, as in Fardles, pomposity was bad manners; from its bracket the Graal shuddered forward in a movement of innocent distaste. The same motion that seemed to touch it touched the Archdeacon also; they came together and were familiarly one. And the Archdeacon, realizing with his whole mind what had happened, turned with unexpected fleetness and ran for the hall door.[26]

The passage is a good example of Williams's methods. The language has a formal, precise ring, carefully definitive in its theological content, then widening out to incantatory reiteration. The thoughts of the Archdeacon and the comments of the author fuse definitively as Gregory is evoked by name, only to separate with the comment on pomposity, which in turn leads up to the apparently objective account of the Grail bowing into the Archdeacon's outstretched hands. The actual moment of capture is thus rendered a happening in the spiritual as much as in the physical dimension. But the controlling force is intellectual, not pictorial.

The same is true of much of the dialogue: the whole novel is shot through with a sense of theology in action. The Archdeacon asserts that

'There is no use in . . . weighing one thing against another. When the time comes He shall dispose as He will, or rather He shall be as He will, as He is.'
'Does He will Gregory Persimmons?' Kenneth said wryly.
'Certainly He wills him,' the Archdeacon said, 'since He wills that Persimmons shall be whatever he seems to choose. That is

not technically correct perhaps, but it is that which I believe
and feel and know.'
  'He wills evil, then?' Kenneth said.
  ' "Shall there be evil in the City and I the Lord have not done
it?" ' the Archdeacon quoted.[27]

The fact that the word from the quotation translated 'evil' means
'misfortune' rather than metaphysical evil is (or is not) more relevant for the theologian than the critic. That particular uncertainty pinpoints the unusual quality of Williams's literary
endeavour..

War in Heaven is less a tale of black magic than one which
affirms the resolution of discord: black magic is only a manifestation of that 'zone of madness which encloses humanity'.[28]
However tranquil the world of Williams's saints may be, it exists
on the further side of that chaos. This is brought out in the
portrait of the publisher's assistant Lionel Rackstraw, a portrait
of Charles Williams in his middle years as Roger Ingram is of his
younger self. Lionel's disenchantment is so total that he is beyond
Gregory's power to disturb. Indeed, the true pessimist
transcends himself, for only by rejection can the world be totally
affirmed. The paradox is another instance of absolute relativity.

But *War in Heaven* is a novel whose theme is at odds with its
method. The wild lurches between Wodehouse-like farce and
spiritual intensity; the stylistic jumble of facetious chatter with
the plum-in-the-mouth utterance Williams sees fit to give to his
people when engaged in serious matters (both Gregory and the
Archdeacon can be equally out of character when it comes to
talking about their deepest concerns); the intrusion of some
heavy-handed humour (*vide* the grossly overdrawn 'liberal'
clergyman, Mr Batesby) − all work against the appreciation of
that underlying singleness of will which the book proclaims. The
misadventures of the Grail and its frequently ignominious
fortunes are appropriate to its uncertain status as a symbol, and
to the Archdeacon's awareness of the necessarily relative value of
even the most sacred object; but the scenes of black magic have a
compelling power that renders the book imaginatively dualistic.
The uncertainty of the central symbol and its passive role in the
plot is at once the novel's weakness and its message. The book is a
conundrum which Williams's next three novels attempt to resolve
through symbols of unquestionable centrality and power.

IV

Nowhere is the intellectual quality of Williams's imagination more apparent than in *Many Dimensions*: its central symbol dominates the plot by virtue of the ingenuity of its presentation. The pattern of the novel resembles that of its predecessor. It concerns the discovery of an object of immense spiritual power; attempts by the selfish, the ambitious and the greedy to secure it for their own ends; and its ultimate restoration to its rightful place by a human being content merely to serve it. This time the supernatural focus is a stone from the crown of Solomon, which can multiply itself indefinitely, can move its bearer about in space and time, and which is discovered to be both the First Matter from which the physical world derives ('the Centre of the Derivations') and the true fulfilment of human desire. The coincidence demonstrates the centrality of the Incarnation in Williams's theology, and he portrays the Stone as a type of the Divine Logos or Word. But in using a religious symbol of this kind he returns to pre-Christian imagery, for the Stone resembles the Logos as understood in the Wisdom literature of the Old Testament and Apocrypha, rather than the Incarnate Logos of the Fourth Gospel. In accordance with these associations Williams also makes use of the devotional phraseology of Islam, in such terms as 'Under the Mercy' and 'Under the Protection', which in their impersonality prevent any equation between the Stone and the God of familiar personal, or casual agnostic, piety. The tenor of *Many Dimensions* is more theological and exploratory than that of its predecessor, and its Islamic imagery is appropriate: this novel is concerned with Divine Unity, and in it Williams relates Christianity to other religions and traditions, demonstrating in the process its all-inclusiveness. The Hajji Ibrahim maintains that 'He who divides the Unity is a greater sinner than he who makes a mock of his brother.'[29] But in Williams's presentation of coinherence the two sins are the same.

The book's moral austerity likewise is Islamic: there are no merciful interventions by a personalised God, and the profoundly mysterious nature of the Stone reveals itself in depth below depth as the plot unwinds. Its effect on those who come in contact with it is wittily presented in the account of the government's embarrassment; in the suave but slightly sinister figure of the Home Secretary, Mr Garterr Browne; and in the conflicting motives of those who seek to exploit the Stone for their own ends. Since the supernatural movements of the Stone are swayed by the behaviour of its wielders, it puts itself completely at their disposal, and events resolve themselves with logical inevitability. The book explores the relation between predestination and free will.

The Stone, being the origin of all matter, manifests itself as body to body, mind to mind, spirit to spirit: far from the Stone being in time, time is in the Stone. An image of visible eternity is being proffered. Spiritual laws likewise are seen at work in the Stone. Lord Arglay, the Chief Justice, attempting to rescue the victim of an experiment with the Stone, who is trapped in the past, makes no attempt to impose his will on the man, but merely offers him to the Stone, which alone has power to rescue him; while his young secretary, Chloe Burnett, experiencing the lost man's desolation in herself, becomes the means of drawing him back into the present through a substitution similar to the more explicit exchanges in Williams's two final novels. On the other hand, Sir Giles Tumulty[30] is frustrated in his attempt to read Lord Arglay's mind in the Stone by his own hatred of the Chief Justice; and this betrays him into self-cancelling presuppositions concerning that mind. The Stone does not lend itself to the imposition of one personality upon another. Again, when Sir Giles tries to dominate Chloe he is only successful in so far as her own nature makes her vulnerable. Beyond that he cannot go, and it is sufficient for Lord Arglay to assert the authority of his own relationship with Chloe for her to be restored.

The significance of Lord Arglay resembles that which Christianity accords to the Judaic Law: he shelters and protects a Messianic figure, Chloe Burnett. The letters of the Tetragrammaton (the not-to-be-spoken letters of the name of God), which are in the Stone, are perceived on her forehead by the Stone's Moslem guardian. Her hostility towards Sir Giles is immediate and instinctive, and incurs his own; her love affair with a young estate-agent is swamped by her devotion to the Stone, a devotion in its turn nurtured by her relationship with her employer. She alone among the characters gives herself entirely to the Stone. The resultant ravaging of her lesser affections is the point at which she is, unconsciously, able to rescue the man lost in his own past. Her moment of self-offering is thus the moment of salvation – for another. This self-offering makes a deeper inroad upon her nature in a moment of supreme danger. When one of the guardians of the Stone tries to recover it, she refuses to use it for her own protection, even for what she is tempted to believe is its own good:

> she would use it; after all she was using it to save it. She was doing for it what it could not do for itself. She was protecting it. Not being a reader of religious history Chloe was ignorant what things have been done in the strength of that plea, or with what passionate anxiety men have struggled to protect the subordination of Omnipotence. But in her despair she rejected what churches and kings and prelates have not rejected; she refused to be deceived, she refused to attempt to be helpful to the God, and being in an agony she prayed more earnestly. The God purged her as she writhed; lucidity entered into her; she turned upon her face, and with both hands beneath her pillow holding the Stone, she lay still, saying only silently in her panting breath: 'Thy will, . . . do . . . do if Thou wilt; or' – she imagined the touch of the marauder on the calf of her leg and quivering in every nerve added – 'or . . . not.'[31]

The Stone saves her, for she has placed herself within the Stone. The biblical quotation and the objectifying of abstract qualities serve to underline the Christian ethos of the passage. Chloe's refusal to use the Stone is a refusal of what Williams in his Arthurian poems was to designate the blasphemy of the Dolorous Blow.

Later, Chloe offers the Stone to itself, under the direction of the Chief Justice: it is too great a burden for mankind to carry. She makes herself a way of return, interceding as she does so for all those who have trafficked with it, until she herself has to all intents and purposes become the Stone. It is characteristic of Williams that he should envisage the End of Desire as being the unmanifested essence of 'the holy and glorious flesh' rather than as some remote and infinitely different spiritual state. It is a far cry from his choice of epigraph for *The Silver Stair*, the lines from Yeats's *The Shadowy Waters* concerning a love 'of a beautiful, unheard-of kind / That is not in the world.'

At its deepest level this novel is a closely worked-out parable of Redemption. For example, the Moslem guardians of the Stone are helpless because, through their denial of the potential salvation of matter, they are incapable of Chloe's wholehearted acceptance of the way of return. Again, the Chief Justice's disbelief is contrasted with the cynically 'realistic' unbelief of the Home Secretary, who is convinced that no one must be allowed to believe in the Stone, and who disproves its power by producing a fake one. Equally well conceived is the death of Sir Giles, which comes about through his demented hatred of Chloe. Demanding angrily of her, 'I wish I could get at you', he is granted his desire; but, since Chloe is 'within' the Stone, he too is drawn into it. The End of Desire gives him itself and destroys him in its intolerable light. The light in the Stone is its final mystery, for it is a point of the light which is the spirit sustaining the physical universe, and the protection of all those who commit themselves to it. The central image of *Many Dimensions* is thus one of an absolute inclusiveness.

V

The Place of the Lion works less through images than through a myth, one peculiarly suited to Williams's imaginative gifts. Its symbolism is drawn from Neo-Platonism and from medieval angelology. Williams makes use of the Cabbalistic teaching that strength, subtlety, beauty and wisdom are not mere abstractions, but absolutes existing in their own spiritual world. In this novel the archetypal world, by means of the experiments of a spiritual adept, is opened upon this one, so that angelic powers are let loose to walk the earth. They manifest themselves as gigantic animals, those which conform to their particular natures: the Lion of Strength, the Serpent of Subtlety, the Butterfly of Beauty and the Eagle of Wisdom most prominent among them. They absorb into themselves all kindred types and even those human beings in whom they are the dominating element, so that those who idolise strength turn into and are finally devoured by the Lion, the subtle and cunning are absorbed by the Serpent, and so with everyone according to his nature. In some, the annihilation is joyous, in others horrible. Damaris Tighe, who spends all her time writing about the work of the great medieval schoolmen, without pausing to consider the truth of what she is studying, sees the Eagle of Wisdom as a huge stinking pterodactyl; while her father, an over-zealous but disinterested entomologist, is granted a vision of beauty that slowly and blissfully kills him. Those who try to use the principles of life for their own aggrandisement are in turn used and devoured by them. Others try to shut their eyes to facts and collapse in terror. But, as in *Many Dimensions*, the world of balance and order is restored, in this case by Damaris's lover, Anthony, who, choosing to know the truth at whatever cost, finds himself riding the Eagle, and thus restores the Angelicals to their own world.

Anthony's choice is dictated by love for his friend Quentin and by love for Damaris, both of whom are in mortal danger from the power let loose, the one through fear, the other through her intellectual arrogance. Having promised Damaris to do anything possible to help her to obtain her degree, Anthony remains loyal to that promise, even though it means trying to govern the principles of Creation: in Williams's spiritual cosmology scale is an irrelevance. Once taken, his choice works itself out according to the universal law of Redemption as Williams here first articulates it. Damaris, having been frightened into sanity, is the means of saving Quentin from the Lion. She knows his fear, he knows her blindness, while Anthony is being directed how to close the breach in the created order. The restoration is a network of substitution and exchange.

The chapter called 'The Place of Friendship' is a moving exposition of what Williams elsewhere describes as 'this dearest mitigation of human existence'.[32] It emphasises the mutual indwelling of the material and the spiritual; so too does the fact that it is empty, newly built houses which collapse before the power of the Angelicals, rather than those strengthened by human association. Again, the field where Damaris saves Quentin from the power of the Lion is the place where she had previously rejected his attempt to save her. What for her becomes the place of repentance, for him becomes the place of salvation. The place of the Lamb, it is also the place of the naming of the beasts, the new Eden from which Anthony and Damaris return to the world, hand in hand.

Damaris herself, obsessed with her own cleverness, devoid of imagination and without interests apart from self-appointed ones, is an embodiment of the unfeeling intellect: 'Shakespeare's not my subject', she says. To her Abelard and St Bernard and St Thomas are 'merely the highest form in a school of which she was the district inspector'.[33] Her awakening comes through a singularly dramatic confrontation with the Impossibility.

It seemed to be perched there, on the window-sill or the pear-tree or something. Its eyes held her; its wings moved, as if uncertainly opening; its whole repulsive body shook and stirred; its beak – not three yards distant – jerked at her, as if the thing were stabbing; then it opened. She had a vision of great teeth; incapable of thought, she stumbled backward against the table, and remained fixed. Something in her said, 'It can't be'; something else said, 'It is.'[34]

Anthony's comment, following his rescue of her, is accurate and ruthless.

'You saw what you know . . . and because it's the only thing you know you saw like that. You've been told about it often enough; you've been warned and warned again. You've had it whispered to you and shouted at you – but you wouldn't stop or think or believe. And what you wouldn't hear about you've seen, and if you're still capable of thanking God you'd better do it now. You, with your chatter about this and the other, your plottings and plannings, and your little diagrams, and your neat tables – what did you think you would make of the agonies and joys of the masters?'[35]

This is Williams's case against all arid intellectualism, literary or ecclesiastical or whatever. Poetry and ideas are living realities, as dangerous to play with as the Lion which breaks into the world of men in a Hertfordshire garden.

This and such other heightened moments as Anthony's vision of the Eagle, the burning of the adept's house, and the appearance of the Unicorn, do not stand apart from the book as a whole, for the thoughts and feelings of the characters play far less part than in any of the other novels except *War in Heaven*, and the plot moves forward without interruption. This unity of tone emphasises stylistically the book's main theme – the power of intellect, imagination and human love to behold a unity in created experience, to cherish and adore it, and to make it real. What Williams calls 'the Mercy' protects its creation, through the bonds of matter, from its own awful powers. The narrative method underlines this. Close, brooding, thunderous heat permeates the action, and the characters move in a world of threatened dissolution. Plot, themes and literary treatment coalesce in an artistic unity that makes *The Place of the Lion* the most technically flawless of the novels, and thus a more satisfyingly integrated fable than its predecessors.

VI

Just as heat is the pervading element in *The Place of the Lion*, so the pervading element of *The Greater Trumps* is cold. Much of the action takes place in an isolated country house during a raging snowstorm on Christmas Day, a microscopic drama dominated almost to breaking-point by its central symbol, the Tarot pack, most ancient and mysterious of playing cards. Williams draws on his knowledge of the Caballa for his account of them, and, as with the Grail and the Stone, uses them as a symbol of the creative power of God. He relates them to a group of magical golden figures, similar to those portrayed on the greater trumps, figures whose perpetual motion corresponds to the ever-lasting dance which is the rhythm and pattern of the universe. When the original cards and the images are brought together, the fortunes of the world can be read, for the relation between them constitutes the true knowledge of reality.

The fortuitous reassembling of cards and images provides the mainspring of the plot. The figures are hidden in the house of Aaron Lee, latest of a long line of gipsy guardians, now 'civilised'. His grandson, Henry, finds the cards in the possession of Mr Lothair Coningsby (a Warden in lunacy – both his name and occupation are pleasing but superfluous jokes), whose daughter Nancy he is engaged to marry. Through her, by using the spiritual energy of their mutual love, he plans to possess and rule the cards – the blasphemy against love degrading him to the level of the false magicians of the earlier books. The cards have magical properties controlling the four elements. Following their owner's refusal to part with them, Henry unleashes on him the forces of rain and wind, only to lose the cards in the storm, which as a result breaks out of his control. But Nancy, who loves without calculation, restores the remaining cards to the images and thus re-establishes the balance of nature.

The novel is a drama of vain desire and the nature of the reconciliation between such desire and its only possible fulfilment. The separation of the cards from the images symbolises the separation between reason and knowledge, and provides yet another myth of that condition (also imaged in the stricken state of Israel, of the Fisher King, of Balder and of Osiris) described here as 'the mystical severance [which] had manifested in action the exile of the will from its end'.[36] It is an image of the Fall.

The union between the human will and its destined and unavoidable end is indicated through the figures of Nancy and her aunt Sybil. The latter is Williams's most elaborate portrait of achieved sanctity: she lives in a condition of joyous calm, ironic, affectionate, secure, beholding 'the primal Nature' (the nature of co-inherent triune Godhead) 'revealed as a law to the creature'.[37] Williams was always chary of using the name of God in his work, for so all-embracing a synonym blunts imaginative response; and his account of Sybil's spiritual journey is the more convincing for the omission.

Sybil's anti-type is Joanna, the embodiment of emotional frustration. An old gipsy, convinced that she is the divine Isis (though in Williams's world such identifications usually have some justification), she vainly searches for her dead child, craving the Tarot cards as a means of satisfying her own warped will to love, warped since it is an example of the inevitably thwarted human urge to love on one's own terms rather than to accommodate one's self-will to its predestined end.

Nancy, on the other hand, is awakened in time to make that accommodation: her vision of romantic love as being the start of a vocation recalls the similar awakening of the Duchess of Mantua, Williams's 'Chaste Wanton'.

> 'But I can't', [Nancy] exclaimed, 'turn all *this*' – she laid her hand on her heart – 'towards everybody. It can't be done; it only lives for – him.'
>
> 'Nor even that', Sybil said. 'It lives for and in itself. You can only give it back to itself.'[38]

This sense of vocation is brought to life by Nancy's horror on finding that the beloved Henry is trying to kill her father – the Impossibility again. Sybil sends her to Henry in order to reaffirm their love, and to unite its mystery with the mystery of the Dance, by giving the cards back to the images and thus quelling the storm. But they must do this together; only in so far as they are lovers have they power rooted in exchange. Henry himself is lost in the mist which surrounds the images and comes to a knowledge of his real self through a vision of the perpetually falling tower of Babel, itself one of the greater trumps. Assenting to his defeat, he is purged to share again the mystery of love.

The Greater Trumps is a closely knit book, in which the symbol of the dance recurs repeatedly. The magical golden images mark the different capacities of man and the facts which those capacities exist to encounter: again the unity of inward and outward is stressed. But the symbolism is not fully worked out, for the speed with which these novels were written tells badly on *The Greater Trumps*. Nowhere does Williams have such a rich and suggestive complex of imagery, and nowhere does he throw it away so carelessly. He displays an impatient imagination, and there is a disproportion between the profoundity of the theme and the frequent frivolity of its expression. 'This also is Thou: neither is this Thou' is not an easy maxim to sustain in literary performance, and in this novel Williams appears to have been overwhelmed by his material.

VII

Descent into Hell appeared in 1937, but was written in 1933. Eliot's instinct in publishing it was sound: this is the best of Williams's novels, and a substantial step forward in his fusion of idea with literary expression. The supernatural is no longer presented as invasive; rather, it provides the substructure of the novel; and only at the end does it erupt into the action. The coincidence of means and ends towards which the earlier novels had been pointing is here presented absolutely.

The technique employed is foreshadowed in Williams's solitary short story, 'Et in Sempiternum Pereant',[39] which describes an opening from the world of time into eternity. Christopher Arglay, on a country walk, sees an empty cottage from which smoke is pouring without any fire to cause it: he has come across an opening on to the Pit. It is characteristic of Williams that he should give such a spot a rural setting; and characteristic that it should also be a place from which ascent is made into Heaven. Arglay encounters a lost soul hastening to its own destruction, intercedes for it, and saves it: the momentous consequences of human action is once again Williams's theme. The story is a vision of the protective fragility of matter such as inspires many of the poems in *Windows of Night*; but the description of this symbolic gate to Hell is done with greater skill than is shown there, so that the solid realities of this world apparently dissolve into the aura of the next.

Descent into Hell is written out of a similar awareness. The picture it gives of its small area of human life is translucent, not opaque: everything is seen double, in its temporal guise and in its eternal reality. In the words of Mary McDermott Shideler,

> Nothing which ever is ever ceases to be, and everything that is now in process of happening has already been completed. . . . Eternity and nature have in common the double present, temporal and eternal, where the two worlds intersect.[40]

Outside Williams's own work, *Descent into Hell* has no parallel in English fiction, though the novels of Evelyn Underhill come close to providing one. But none of them affords such a sense of the interpenetration of worlds: in them the two modes of existence are presented in alternation. *Descent into Hell*, however, being the fruit of that concern with the union of opposites which was haunting Williams so obsessively at the time he wrote it, clinches the spiritual logic of the earlier novels, so that the two worlds, natural and supernatural, are now merged.

The novel's theme is once again beatitude and damnation, but seen this time as a moral dimension. The difference between the two conditions is measured by the willingness to acknowledge derivation from others and responsibility for them – in short, to acknowledge co-inherence. And there is a parallel alignment. Sanctity is shown to involve the love of fact for its own sake, damnation the preference of illusion. These two related antitheses form aspects of one design; and it is through their relation to this design that all the characters in the novel are made known. Knowledge here means a final assessment; consequently, the below-the-surface drama which reveals the design is a spiritual enactment of the Last Judgement. The Judgement is seen as taking place out of time, hidden within temporal realities. It is made known through the senses of the spiritually aware, who, at different times, hear the sound of the final trump; one of them, standing by a cemetery gate, even has a momentary vision of opening graves. But this imagery is uncertainly maintained.

There is no equivalent of the supernatural events of the early novels.

The ostensible drama which unites all the characters is the production of a play, a pastoral in verse by an eminent poet, Peter Stanhope, who is given the status of T. S. Eliot and the consciousness of Charles Williams: he is more priest than playwright. The novel opens with a preliminary discussion between author, producer and players, and ends with the actual performance itself, skilfully dovetailed into the Day of Judgement. Against the background of rehearsals the protagonists play out their several roles. The below-the-surface drama of Judgement is made up of four separate stories: the progress of Margaret Anstruther into beatitude and the descent of Lawrence Wentworth into Hell, and the first step taken in each direction by Margaret's niece Pauline and Wentworth's protégée Adela Hunt. And there is a fifth drama. Cutting across these several movements towards Judgement is the figure of an anonymous suicide who, having anticipated Judgement, retraces his steps from damnation into the free acceptance of fact and of exchange. The novel is a ghost story of a serious kind, in the sense that the ghostly element lies not in psychic phenomena but in psychic experience; this takes place in the fourth dimension, presented as an extension of the three we already know. A few other novelists have attempted something of the kind – Evelyn Underhill most deliberately, but also John Cowper Powys during Williams's own writing life, and Phyllis Paul[41] in the decade following his death; but none of them has made the consciousness of the 'ghost' a substantial part of the work of fiction itself.

The structure of *Descent into Hell* is multidimensional. On one level it tells how a play is produced in a respectable modern housing-estate thirty miles from London; how an old lady dies and how her granddaughter is freed from a nervous obsession; and how a distinguished historian and an undistinguished young woman undergo different kinds of nervous collapse. On a deeper level these events react on each other and take place in an eternal world, being conditioned by the law of the spiritual universe which encompasses the material one the characters consciously inhabit.

The novel's focal point is Peter Stanhope's play. In this respect it differs interestingly from two others of the period which also centre on such productions – Powys's huge *A Glastonbury*

Romance (1932) and Virginia Woolf's *Between the Acts* (1941). In the former, John Geard's pageant provides a turning-point in the action, and furthers one's knowledge of the characters. It is a means to an end, its function interpretative but external. In *Between the Acts* the pageant is the occasion for the novel and itself a comment on it, not so much on the action as on the author's record of it. In the one book it is the performance which matters, in the other the content of the pageant. In *Descent into Hell* what matters is the quality of the pageant's verse. The players only exist to express the poetry, itself the symbol of a greater creation and an everlasting drama. In this light the satire of the opening chapter strikes a warning note. Williams describes a producer and cast so oblivious of their true function that they quite cheerfully manhandle the author's work in his presence, imposing on it their own theories, fancies and ambitions. Pauline alone is concerned with the poetry as such; the others are more interested in elocution.

No less important is the novel's setting, the modern residential estate of Battle Hill. Williams's description of it is an account of the several dimensions of the novel. The hill is a hill of skulls, the scene of countless massacres and battles.

> The whole rise of ground therefore lay like a cape, a rounded headland of earth, thrust into an ocean of death. Men, the lords of that small earth, dominated it. The folklore of skies and seasons belonged to it. But if the past still lives in its own present beside our present, then the momentary later inhabitants were surrounded by a greater universe. From other periods of its time other creatures could crawl out of death, and invisibly contemplate the houses and people of the rise.[42]

This spiritual terrain pervades the action of the novel. Pauline is plagued by a visitation from it in the shape of the footsteps of what she knows from momentary glimpses to be her own image. Williams gives the *Doppelgänger* theme a Christian interpretation. As in such well-known tales as Poe's 'William Wilson' and Henry James's 'The Jolly Corner', the image represents a rejected self; but here there are no sexual or guilt-ridden connotations. Pauline's terror is more a matter of existential dread. The act of abstract self-realisation is in that moment of contemplation an actual division of the self. Absorption in outward events and personal relationships can maintain a spurious internal unity, but the incipient severance remains. Few people seek to be totally alone, but many live as though in fact they were: Pauline is redeemed from the terror of solitariness into a knowledge of co-inherent derivation.

The agent of her salvation is Peter Stanhope. He offers to bear her fear so that she can be free from it, and thus be more ready to face whatever fact is causing it. Similar acts of deliberate substitution were undertaken by Williams himself, both in his own life and in those of such friends (the word 'disciples' is perhaps, and again is perhaps not, too strong) whom he encouraged to do the same. Their incidence in fiction is rarer than their incidence in life; but it is possible that Williams was influenced both in his writing and in his life by the treatment of the subject, not only in Kipling's tale 'The Wish House', but also in R. H. Benson's last novel, *Initiation* (1914), a book that in turn owes much to those of Evelyn Underhill. It is the story of a Catholic landowner whose life is apparently destroyed, first by the breaking of his engagement to a sensitive but ruthlessly egoistic young woman, and then by the onset of a fatal disease inherited as a result of the excesses of his father – the shadow of Ibsen's *Ghosts* stretched far. Benson traces the growth of his acceptance of this apparent disaster as the revelation of the will of God. At the beginning he is still not what the saintly Mr Morpeth calls 'initiated':

> it's quite plain, surely, that there is one class of persons on one side and another on the other. The one accepts what happens, so soon as it really has happened; and the other does not. The one knows that the past is inevitable, and the other is not sure. The one is not surprised at things, and therefore does not resent them; he is behind the scenes, so to speak, and understands what it is all about, even if he cannot quite make out the details; and the other looks on from the stalls, and knows nothing except what he sees.[43]

There is a marked similarity here to the kind of distinctions drawn in Williams's novels between those who are 'adult in love' and those who are not. Later on, Nevill Fanning's aunt recalls an assurance given by him to his father on the latter's deathbed:

'... he seemed to think that Nevill would suffer for him somehow ... that ... that it was sure to be so. Well; but Nevill took him up, and said that he only hoped he would. Of course he didn't mean it. I don't think any of us knew what we are saying. ... But it was a fine thing to say, wasn't it? ... But do you think that kind of thing really does happen – people offering themselves for others?'

'Why, yes', he said, as gently as ever. 'The Old Law even said that it would be so; and the New Law underlines it, surely. ... The sins of the fathers are visited upon the children. That is in Nature, as we say. And the New Law says that the children ought to be ready to accept it willingly. This is the whole idea of Atonement, is it not?'

It seemed very simple, put like that, thought Anna.

'But ... but you don't think in this case – ' she began, suddenly a little afraid.

He spread his hands in a small gesture.

'Who in the world can tell?' he said. 'We know the principles of things: but no more. In any case it will be all perfectly well.'[44]

It is not only the echo of Julian of Norwich that evokes a kinship with Williams's thought and writing. But Benson's method is more naturalistic than his: to come to *Descent into Hell* after *Initiation* is to realise how essentially abstract and fabulous (in the strict sense) Williams's novels are.

Later on, as the shadow falls on Nevill Fanning, Morpeth renews the assurance of a good beyond good and evil as we know them:

some men might call this a curse. Well, we may call it that, if we will; so long as we remember that a curse is but the shadow of a blessing – that He Himself was made a Curse for us, who is our Blessing. That is all that the shadow is, Mrs Fanning: it is the shadow of Our Father's hand.[45]

Anna's final conclusion is that the line between good and evil is the line 'between the acceptance and the non-acceptance of destiny' – in other words, the choosing or not choosing of necessity.

Turning back to *Descent into Hell* one finds the same

principles in operation, but presented in a more detached and matter-of-fact tone. Stanhope knows that his action will not prevent the *Doppelgänger* from appearing, for it is Pauline's destiny to encounter it; but Pauline's knowledge of her destiny can be freed from dread by his spiritual companionship. All that is needed is her consent. In answer to her incredulity he asserts the apostolic command to bear one another's burdens, declaring that this involves something deeper and more practical than unselfishness and sympathy. It is part of the divine economy; when she objects that it is not right that another person should bear her burden, he laughingly rebukes her.

> If you want to disobey and refuse the laws that are common to us all, if you want to live in pride and division and anger, you can. But if you will be part of the best of us, and live and laugh and be ashamed with us, then you must be content to be helped. You must give your burden up to someone else, and you must carry someone else's burden.[46]

He duly bears her fear in his own heart, and this knowledge of exchange frees her from the burden of self-consciousness. Hitherto she has applied herself with a fundamentally resentful vigour to providing company for her grandmother.

> The girl was in fact so patient with the old lady that she had not yet noticed that she was never given an opportunity to be patient. She endured her own nature and supposed it to be the burden of another's.[47]

There is irony even in substitution; but, once she has submitted to Stanhope, and given up her insistence on bearing her fear herself, she enters upon a totally different life.

> The central mystery of Christendom, the terrible fundamental substitution on which so much learning had been spent and about which so much blood had been shed, showed not as a miraculous exception, but as the root of a universal rule ... as supernatural as that Sacrifice, as natural as carrying a bag.[48]

It is because of this divine centre, source, and mover of exchange that Pauline is able in her turn to bear the fear of an ancestor, a

Protestant martyr burned at the stake on Battle Hill. In this moment of clarity and fully accomplished action she turns and at last sees her own image face to face, to find it no longer an image of fear but one of glory.

> It had been her incapacity for joy, nothing else, that had till now turned the vision of herself aside; her incapacity for joy had admitted fear, and fear had imposed separation. She knew now that all acts of love are the measure of capacity for joy; its measure and its preparation, whether the joy comes or delays.[49]

Such a vision is the result of her act of exchange – in the words of Stanhope's play, she is 'only the perception in a flash of love'. Through Stanhope she has been liberated into the freedom of the City where all facts are known and loved in joy. Her relationship with the poet resembles that of Chloe Burnett with the Chief Justice in *Many Dimensions*, a relationship of teacher and disciple united in a common devotion to the mystery conveyed by the one to the other, whether it be organic law or the doctrine of substituted love, the second being itself an example of the first. Pauline, accepting subordination from and through Stanhope, is released to know and to love not only things outside herself, but ultimately everything outside herself.

The alternative to such freedom is described by Williams under the name Gomorrah.

> Haven't you seen the pools that everlastingly reflect the faces of those who walk with their own phantasms, but the phantasms aren't reflected, and can't be ... There's no distinction between lover and beloved; they beget themselves on their adoration of themselves, and they live and feed and starve on themselves, and by themselves too, for creation ... is the mercy of God, and they won't have the facts of creation.[50]

Once again Williams reverts to the city for his imagery. His account of Gomorrah is an indictment of self-indulgent fantasy, in its way the most penetrating thing he wrote. It centres on the character of Lawrence Wentworth.

Wentworth, an authority on military history, has a hatred for a fellow scholar which is more than professional rivalry: 'he identified scholarship with himself, and asserted himself under the disguise of a defence of scholarship'. Accordingly, his very scholarship becomes imprecise, his presentation of evidence unfair. 'In defence of his conclusion he was willing to cheat in the evidence – a habit more usual to religious writers than to historical.'[51] Wentworth has a recurring dream of a descent down an unending length of rope. The dream reflects his own deliberate and secretive descent into Hell, a descent furthered by his desire for Adela Hunt and by his self-tormenting resentment of her relationship with her lover. Jealousy leads him to play the voyeur and to indulge in unreal sexual fantasies. 'He desired hell.' The small letter denotes Williams's interpretation of Hell as a state rather than as a place.

Wentworth's desire is implemented by envy of his rival's success and by a surrender to delusion that renders him impotent to embrace reality. Too lazy and absorbed in his self-created phantom-ridden Eden, he cannot be bothered to correct the faulty historical details of the play's costumes. His sole desire is solitude. He shuts himself up in his house. He rejects the real Adela and eventually the phantom Adela, being unable to bear anything that is not himself. He is last seen at a dinner, barely conscious, existing supernaturally in Hell. The function is described through the eyes of a dying man, its horror only lightened by the irony of his doom at the hands of his well-meaning rival. Wentworth, who now shrinks from every personal contact, has to endure his endless chatter raining down upon him like the fire upon Gomorrah.

But *Descent into Hell* demonstrates that, if Williams was pessimistic about human nature, he was not so about human fate. It is here that the novel differs from *Windows of Night*: it lies on the far side of Williams's confrontation with the Impossibility, and darkness is not the prevailing impression. In addition to Stanhope and Pauline the book portrays Margaret Anstruther, who is as near to Heaven in her activity as Wentworth in his torpor is close to Hell. The contrast between them is underlined by their attitudes to death. Wentworth is a deliberate moral and intellectual suicide, whereas Margaret, knowing that her death is near, goes out to welcome it. No less remarkable than Williams's account of Wentworth's self-drugged dreaming is his portrait of her life of prayer.

In the time of her novitiate it had seemed to her sometimes

that, though her brains and emotions acted this way or that, yet all that activity went on along the sides of a slowly increasing mass of existence made from herself and all others with whom she had to do, and that strong and separate happiness – for she felt it as happiness, though she herself might be sad; her sadness did but move on it as the mountaineer on the side of a mountain – that happiness was the life she was utterly to become. Now she knew that only the smallest fragility of her being clung somewhere to the great height that was she and others and all the world under her separate kind, as she herself was part of all the other peaks; and though the last fragility was still a little terrified of the dawn which was breaking everywhere, she knew that when the dawn reached the corner where she lay it would, after one last throb of piercing change under its power, light but the mountain side, and all her other mighty knowledge would after its own manner rejoice in it.[52]

In its blending of abstractions with concrete imagery this account of spiritual experience challenges comparison with similar passages (similar in method though not in point of view) in the later novels and tales of Henry James.

Equally convincing is Williams's account of the suicide's life after death. It is governed by an interior logic. The world the dead man sees is his own world, but his perceptions have sudden microscopic clarity. Moreover, his progress obeys the same spiritual laws as those of the other characters. The one world is merely a province of the other. The unfinished house in which the workman kills himself is Wentworth's house of suicide where the dead in body lives in his soul and the dead in soul lives in his body. Wentworth descends into Hell; but the power which works in and through Margaret harrows the place of the dead to save the man who has despaired of life. The suicide is a victim of injustice and neglect, and so, being a victim of others even more than of himself, he is not irreclaimable. He does not so much wish to die as not to live as he has been living – a common state of mind. Having killed himself, he is no longer subject to the normal temporal laws, and thus exists contemporaneously with Wentworth, whose spiritual rope is the one with which the workman hangs himself: Margaret and Pauline encounter him later in time. *Descent into Hell* is a ghost story written from the point of view of the ghost, and the two women are inexplicable presences to the dead man. But they are presences to heal and save.

> The silence in that place became positive with their energies, and its own. The three spirits were locked together, in the capacity of Margaret's living stone. The room about them, as if the stillness expressed its nature in another mode, grew sharply and suddenly cold. Pauline's mind took it as the occasional sharp alteration of a summer evening; she moved to go and turn on the electric fire, for fear her grandmother should feel the chill, and that natural act, in her new good will, was no less than any high offer of goodness and grace. But Margaret knew the other natural atmosphere of the icy mountain, where earthly air was thin in the life of solitude and peak. It was the sharp promise of fruition – her prerogative was to enter that transforming chill. The dead man also felt it, and tried to speak, to be grateful, to adore, to say he would wait for it and for the light. He only moaned a little, a moan not quite of pain, but of intention and the first faint wellings of recognized obedience and love. All his past efforts of good temper and kindness were in it; they had seemed to be lost; and they lived.[53]

This is Williams writing at his maximum intensity, with a compression that is itself an instance of spiritual experience being commingled with material. The passage continues with an extension of that premiss into theological terms which dares credulity to the utmost.

> But that moan was not only his. As if the sound released something greater than itself, another moan answered it. The silence groaned. They heard it. The supernatural mountain on which they stood shook and there went through Battle Hill itself the slightest vibration from that other quaking, so that all over it china tinkled, and papers moved, and an occasional ill-balanced ornament fell. Pauline stood still and straight. Margaret shut her eyes and sank more deeply into her pillow. The dead man felt it and was drawn back away from that window into his own world of being, where also something suffered and was free. The groan was at once dereliction of power and creation of power. In it, far off beyond vision in the depths of all the worlds, a god, unamenable to death, awhile endured and died.[54]

Nowhere does Williams more boldly express his belief in the inter-penetration of physical and spiritual. The hill of Golgotha, Battle Hill and the mountain on which Margaret moves are one with the place of exchange where hangs the central mystery of Christendom. (It is in such imaginative theological readings of experience that Williams's supreme originality is found, and which lift his work far above the customary commentaries that most purely pious or intellectual formulations amount to.) The place of the Cross being encountered, the workman is free to return to the place of suicide and then to make his way back to the city, to the London of his former life, to the acceptance of even his joyless past as fact, therefore as joyful fact.

Margaret's work for the suicide reveals the contrast between the activity of the spiritual city and the stagnation of Gomorrah. Wentworth, sitting in stupor behind drawn curtains is one image; Margaret, lying helpless in her bed, but subduing her will and capacities to the power which works in her, is the other. She is the centre of a complicated web of exchange. Aiming to carry Pauline's burden when the latter's newly found faith is under trial she instead finds herself carrying the burden of the suicide; Pauline, aiming to carry Margaret's burden, carries that of her ancestor, which is her own born by Stanhope. So, out of time, Stanhope bears the suicide, and Margaret bears Stanhope, and Pauline both Margaret and her ancestor, and each one the other, all being part of the act of substitution and exchange on Golgotha.

Illusion, the condition of Gomorrah and the fruit of elocution and self-delusion, is summed up in the Cabbalistic myth of Lilith, the demonic first wife of Adam.[55] She patters about the Hill, and is welcomed by Wentworth, to whom she becomes tangible in his sexual fantasies. Her footsteps are a continuous refrain, heard in Pauline's flight from the *Doppelgänger*, and in the suicide's flight from his past.

[Margaret] heard those feet not as sinister or dangerous, but only – patter, patter – as the haste of a search for or a flight from repose – perhaps both. . . . She had heard, in old tales of magic, of the guardian of the threshold. She wondered if the real secret of the terrible guardian were that he was simply lost on the threshold. His enmity to man and heaven was only his yearning to enter one without loss.[56]

That last speculation admirably sums up the difference between Williams's occult novels and those of a writer such as Benson: his attitude is always positive, grounded in intellectual faith rather than in psychological excitement. Wentworth's descent into Hell is more disturbing than any tale that relies for its effect on fright.

But, not content with the symbolism of the footsteps, Williams chooses to incarnate Lilith in the ambiguous figure of Lily Sammile (the name, perhaps, a combination of the Cabbalistic evil angel Samael with the kind of unthinking cheery optimism which he particularly despised). She is a supernatural being who mixes on normal everyday terms with the other characters, one whose sentimental chatter is unreal in altogether the wrong way, and quite inappropriate in a book where natural and supernatural interfuse. Wentworth embodies Gomorrah far more effectively than she does.

Indeed, with the exception of Wentworth's final collapse, the book ends on a note of anti-climax. Once Margaret is dead and the suicide is on his way to the City, and Pauline has met her own image, the plot disintegrates. The opening of the graves and Pauline's visit to Lily Sammile read like an afterthought; they belong to the world of the earlier novels. Nevertheless, in *Descent into Hell* Williams came near to writing a masterpiece, and its particular fusion of several orders of reality constitutes, together with similar achievements in *All Hallows' Eve* and the Arthurian poems, his most distinctive contribution to literary mythology. The weakness of the novel remains the same as in its predecessors: the cursory nature of the character portrayal. One has only to think of the major novels of George Eliot, Conrad or Lawrence to know the difference in mature imaginative insight between them and Williams's diagramatic presentations. But the word 'diagram' is one which Williams himself used frequently about art, and his work is relative to that of the greater masters in the same way that theirs is to the complexity of life itself. Such concentration on determining the pattern of the web was fully in keeping with the imaginative powers that were his and no one else's.

VIII

Descent into Hell is the logical climax of Williams's early novels.

His treatment of occult themes had been moving towards an all-inclusive vision that may be termed multispatial. The debate in *Shadows of Ecstasy* as to the nature and true terms of romantic experience finds its conclusion in the affirmation of unity set forth initially and dramatically in the four succeeding books, and acted out and set forth definitively in the final one. Parallel to the more selective exploration of division-in-unity leading to unity-in-division carried out in the criticism, biographies and plays, Williams uses prose fiction to enlarge his vision in more general and more widely referential terms.

His final novel, *All Hallows' Eve*, is distinguished by a much firmer grasp of the lives of ordinary people – not, it is true, in dramatic terms, of description or composition, but in focusing on day-to-day living and the dependence of the personality upon innumerable small objective happenings. Its theme is the same as that of *Descent into Hell*: the choice of fact or illusion, beatitude or damnation, made through the readiness, or not, to practise exchange. In the previous novels this choice is laid before living people; here it is seen operating among the dead. The choice is also presented as a return from exile into the redemptive life of the City of God, a theme already touched on in *The Greater Trumps*.

Outwardly the City is London, and underlying the London of the living is the London of the dead. But the City is more than either of these – it is the archetypal London; and behind that the providence of God within which men and women live before and after death, and which manifests itself in terms of their environment in this life, known after the manner of eternity. It is a world suggestive both of the vestibule to Hell and of Limbo in the *Inferno* of Dante; and like them it is a place where choice is made known.

It lay there, as it always does – itself offering no barriers, open to be trodden, ghostly to this world and to heaven, and in its upper reaches ghostly also to those in its lower reaches where (if at all) hell lies. It is ours and not ours, for men and women were never meant to dwell there long. ... One day perhaps it will indeed break through; it will undo our solidity, which belongs to earth and heaven, and all of us who are then alive will find ourselves in it and alone till we win through it to our own place.[57]

Williams's description of the City of the dead is in its kind the
finest thing he wrote; and it compares interestingly with Elizabeth
Bowen's transfiguring account of wartime London in 'Mysterious
Kôr'.[58] As the book proceeds, the provenance of the City becomes
more evident. An earlier essay on 'The Image of the City in
English Verse' defines it as 'the sense of many relationships
between men and women woven into a unity'; another, 'The
Redeemed City', envisages the Way of Exchange as the perfect
expression of the City's life.[59] In the latter, Williams foreshadows
the theme of this novel in describing the everlasting conflict
between the City and what, after Voltaire, he calls 'the Infamy',
that tyranny which is the denial of all exchange.

The Infamy is here incarnate in the person of Simon the Clerk,
a Jewish sorcerer modelled on the character of Simon Magus and
also, perhaps, on Williams's own image of what his spiritual
authority over others could become: Simon is the other side of
Peter Stanhope, his quest for power furthered by his appeal to the
human tendency to deny derivation from, and fellowship with,
others. A type of anti-Christ, he seeks to impose himself upon the
City; but the City has no truck with self-imposed power. Inevitably his own work recoils upon him, when 'all he could do . . .
was only done to himself'. He has chosen to defeat death by
appealing to men's fear of death and pain, but it is a victory only
in so far as he has successfully avoided death. In so doing,

> he had refused all possibilities in death. He would not go to it,
> as that other child of a Jewish girl had done. That other had
> refused safeguard and miracle; he had refused the achievement
> of security. He had gone into death – and the Clerk supposed it
> his failure – as the rest of mankind go – ignorant and in pain.
> The Clerk had set himself to decline pain and ignorance. So
> that now he had not any capacities but those he could himself
> gain.[60]

Simon shares the fallacious ambition of Nigel Considine in
Shadows of Ecstasy. His failure reveals the inviolability of Divine
Law. In the words of one of Williams's commentators, he is
defeated 'not by counteracting his black magic with white, nor by
the supernatural rites of the Church, nor by the energy of prayer,
but by the eternal principles of the universe, which is so organised
that there are limits beyond which no evil can go – limits set by

the essential nature of evil as derivative from good'.[61] Indeed, Simon in his very ineffectiveness highlights the fact that in Williams's world the evil characters are stripped of apocalyptic grandeur, both through the trivialising nature of the occult excitements, or else through the analysis of what constitutes Gomorrah. The moral evil, when presented in terms of the positive power of sanctity, shrinks into insignificance. It is the stress on holiness and on order which makes Williams stand apart from those writers of his time who see evil in terms of apocalyptic dissolution. Lawrence's *Women in Love* (1920) and Mann's *Death in Venice* (1912) come readily to mind in this connection.

Although the overriding concept in *All Hallows' Eve* is death, it is presented in what are essentially more judgemental terms, as a condition either to be accepted and therefore overcome, or to be avoided and thus invoked. Two girls, Lester and Evelyn, killed together when an aeroplane crashes near Westminster Bridge, find themselves in a strange, silent, empty London. Both of them are 'young in death', and both conditioned by choices made in their previous lives. Their condition at the outset is one of waiting, and Williams evokes with haunting power the emptiness involved in a total freedom from obligation; then the working of the City compels their true natures of assert themselves, so that Lester's path eventually takes her, through her inherent virtues and willingness to give herself in exchange, 'upwards' to Purgatory, while Evelyn, self-absorbed and futile, is incapable of anything but Hell.

Lester's progress is carefully described. At the beginning she feels helpless and bewildered: 'She had never much thought about death; she had never prepared for it; she had never related anything to it. She had nothing whatever to do with it, or (therefore) in it.'[62] But 'she had been a reasonably intelligent and forceful creature', though more interested in things than in people; and already her past begins to assert itself and to determine her new activity. This process increases with her capacity to love her husband in the same way – that is to say, as he is and not solely in relation to herself. It is one aspect of choosing necessity. An act of courtesy in Lester's past is productive of one now, to the frightened and snivelling Evelyn, inevitably less able to deal with this new existence. Evelyn has no interests outside herself: Lester, on the other hand, takes a delight in things for their own sake, so that the City gradually becomes less shadowy to her and more real. Lester's role is to frustrate the work of Simon, who is opposed to the entire meaning of the City. Fulfilling it, she passes beyond the knowledge of those left on earth into the place of purgation.

In these early days of death Lester is not completely separated from her husband. The portrait of the young lovers is drawn as much from Richard's side as from Lester's.

> Rash, violent, angry, as she might have been, egotistic in her nature as he, yet her love had been sealed always to another and not to herself. She was never the slave of the false *luxuria*. When she had served him – how often! – she had not done it from kindness or unselfishness; it had been because she wished what he wished and was his servant to what he desired. Kindness, patience, forbearance, were not enough; he had had them, but she had had love.[63]

The unflinchingly moral approach of this passage is reminiscent of George Eliot in its seriousness, if lacking her particular detached compassion. It is a world away from the tone of most late twentieth-century fiction. Through the acts of the City the lovers are reunited for a time, are able to exchange pardon and to reaffirm their mutual fidelity. Their later, inevitable separation is a further instance of the work of the Impossibility. It is characteristic of Williams to end the novel on such a note.

If this 'newly visioned life' is one theme of the book, so the other is the 'creeping death that was abroad in the world'; just as no other of Williams's novels has so vivid a sense of the natural goodness of the world triumphing over death, so none of them has so overpowering a sense of evil. Though the book's predecessors contrast two states of being – light and darkness, fact and fantasy, exchange and self-absorption – in *All Hallows' Eve* it is the world of the living which is unreal, the world of the dead which is alive. The figure on which the plot hinges is Simon's daughter Betty. By putting her into trance he sends her spirit into the timeless world so that she can tell him of the future: but there she makes contact with Lester, her former schoolfriend. The exchange of love and forgiveness between them allows Lester to substitute herself for Betty, and thus to defeat Simon in his hour of approaching triumph. The novel is a dramatised meditation on death and Judgement.

If the total impression left by *All Hallows Eve* is less satisfying than that of *Descent into Hell* this is because, until the triumphant eruption of Divine Law at the close, the world of magic and the world of love are pitted against each other almost as though the difference between them were less of kind than of degree. The detailed account of occult rituals, effective though they are, lend an esoteric air of the wrong kind, being reminiscent of such thrillers as *The Brood of the Witch Queen* (1918) by 'Sax Rohmer'[64] But in all other respects the novel ranks with Williams's finest achievements. Every detail relates and interlocks to produce a sense of inevitable moral justice. The book's profound exploration of the subconscious, and the objectifying of it in terms of the City, is the climax of the technique employed in all the novels; more successfully than any of them, it expresses the facts, moods and desires of daily life in terms of their metaphysical origins, and its language is essentially religious language. The operations of the City are presented with interior logic. This is partly the result of a carefully worked-out plot (the literary mechanics of the City) and partly because the supernatural element is so convincing. The final manifestation of the Hallows in floods of drenching and purifying rain is a far more appropriate climax than the miniature Doomsday in *Descent into Hell*. On a more everyday level there is a characteristic touch when the patient courtesy of a railway porter becomes a vehicle of 'golden-thighed Endurance, sun-shrouded Justice',[65] and, again, when Lester's restraint with an importunate lover is made the means of her first active step within the City. Even Simon and Evelyn are compelled to practise exchange, if only the exchange of their denial of the City. The City thrives between all its members, by its own choice. 'How it throve was theirs.'

This final novel expresses Williams's fullest consciousness of the all-embracing relevance of love. The whole purpose of living being to love, to love truly is to be reconciled with every aspect of life. There is a pointed expression of this in Lester's vision of the Thames as she trudges the streets in a loathsome magical body of Simon's making.

The Thames was dirty and messy. Twigs, bits of paper and wood, cords, old boxes drifted on it. Yet to the new-eyed Lester it was not a depressing sight. The dirtiness of the water was, at that particular point, what it should be, and therefore pleasant enough. The evacuations of the City had their place in the City; how else could the City be the City? Corruption (so to call it) was tolerable, even adequate and proper, even glorious. These things also were facts. They could not be forgotten or lost in fantasy; all that had been, was; all that was, was. A sodden mass of cardboard and paper drifted by, but the soddenness was itself a joy, for this was what happened, and all that happened, in this great material world, was good.[66]

This is the end-product of that resolute theological exploration of the nature of good and evil which had engrossed Williams in all his novels. The vision is persuasive because it had been earned.

5 The Arthurian Poems

I

In writing his own version of the Arthuriad Charles Williams followed the literary tradition in which he had grown up. Matthew Arnold, William Morris, Tennyson and Swinburne had all made distinctive contributions to the Arthurian literary myth, as had such lesser Victorian poets as Robert Stephen Hawker: the Arthuriad was indeed the accepted 'Matter of Britain'. But, whereas for the Victorian mind the legends carried primarily emotional overtones, what distinguishes Williams's version is its intellectual rigour and complexity. In Tennyson's hands the Matter of Britain had, as in the very different case of Malory, expressed the chivalric ideals of the day. Whatever their limitations of verbal energy and intellectual content, *The Idylls of the King* are coherent and consistent in their moral outlook. Tennyson's Arthuriad embodies the High Victorian standards of loyalty, chastity and spiritual dedication, without questioning or modifying them; and Williams characteristically puts his finger on the poems' shortcomings when he points out Tennyson's neglect of the imaginative possibilities inherent in the lines concerning Lancelot, 'his honour rooted in dishonour stood, / And faith unfaithful kept him falsely true'.[1] The words provide a clear instance of the Impossibility. And, since the love of Lancelot for Guinevere is the tragic matrix of the *Idylls*, this point is the more telling. Certainly Williams's own endeavour in part grew out of a desire to develop the implications latent in Tennyson's wasted opportunity. 'It is the *weight* of the myth which we have to recover; no myth has been more dreadfully thinned by familiarity.'[2]

The other Victorians put the Arthuriad to more occasional use. For Swinburne and Morris, and to a lesser extent for Arnold, the poems are occasions for describing human passions more acceptable in the world of legends than in that of contemporary reality.

The Arthuriad afforded scope for the expression of moral paradox – certainly to that extent *The Defence of Guinevere* and *Tristram of Lyonesse* are closer to the twentieth century than are the *Idylls*. But it is doubtful whether their influence on Williams was as great. For him, it is the Grail myth which holds the chief interest: he transmutes the sexual passion of the later Victorian poems into spiritual fervour. Moreover, in his own work he reverses the usual referential terms: for example, Galahad is called 'the alchemical infant'; he 'burns', while the passion of Morgause and Lamorack is portrayed in terms of stone and cold.

Williams's first and unpublished version of the myth was called 'The Advent of Galahad': the title indicates the centrality of the Grail. Such poems of the sequence as got into print[3] are subordinate to their own metrical and rhyme schemes, carried along on a Swinburnian torrent, padded and repetitious. In *Taliessin through Logres*, however, the influence of Hopkins becomes apparent: enjambment, internal rhymes, alliteration, irregular stress metres, above all, the deployment of monosyllables and a judiciously arcane vocabulary. Williams's editing of Hopkins's poems obviously has much to do with this; but the verse forms of *Taliessin* also reflect an increasing complexity of thought. Their difficulty in part rests on a concentration of ideas that expresses itself in what frequently amounts to verbal shorthand. It is as though Williams was reluctant to allow his language to expand for fear of being unable to nail his meaning.

Such a suggestion points to the peculiar character of the poems and to their potential limitation. Their inspiration is doctrinal; they are expressive less of the thing-in-itself than of the thing-in-its-origin-and-purpose. In articulation and technique they propose a series of relationships: between romantic love and religion, defeat and victory, poetry and mathematics, virginity and chastity, manual work and contemplation, choice and obedience, morality and aesthetics; and between all these human capacities and the central power in which they inhere and without which they have no meaning. In theme and treatment they are an example of co-inherence.

Williams's Arthuriad is frequently described as incomplete. It would be more accurate to describe it as unfinished. Both collections of poems are entire in themselves and have their own character; C. S. Lewis's arrangement of them in chronological order,[4] conflating the contents of the two books, although helpful as an exposition of their underlying ideas, does less than justice to their author's sense of design. Williams's notes and letters confirm that more poems needed to be written to further his own understanding of the myth; and he was certainly planning a third collection to centre on the Dolorous Blow; but the two books we have are self-sufficient, their contents dictating their form. *Taliessin through Logres* is not a narrative poem, but a series of reflective and dramatic pieces varying in mood, and dealing with the human impact of the myth rather than with the unfolding of a story. The latter is assumed to be familiar.

The book is precisely named. It is concerned with the relationship of the poet to the ideal kingdom – say, to the potential incarnation of the absolute in the material world. In an early poem Williams had described what might be called the 'Platonic' concept of Logres, that spiritual Britain which William Blake called 'Albion'.

> This is the heart of England; it is found
> Only by such as set their souls to find
> The harbours and great cities that abound
> Beyond the waters of the temporal mind.[5]

This conventional expression of a traditional idea is energised in the later poems not only stylistically but also thematically. By 'Logres' Williams denotes the Arthurian kingdom which is established to be the fulfilment, indeed epitome, of the laws of the Empire of which it forms a part. The latter is conceived both as Byzantium (iconographical model of the Divine Order) and as a collection of provinces representative of various human capacities, capacities which are called the 'themes' of the Empire: in its blend of intellectual and musical associations the term is apt. The Empire is the embodiment of a controlling pattern, as part of which the lesser designs become apparent: these are the story of the wounded King and stricken land, of Arthur's necessary but doomed attempt to build the ideal kingdom, and of Galahad's achievement of the Grail through substitution and exchange. Williams uses the Arthuriad as 'a mythopoetic vehicle that [serves] to give full and ordered expression to his conception of the relationship of civilization and religion'.[6] It symbolised for him the nature, failure, and perpetual redemption of Christendom.

In *Taliessin* the story has several layers of meaning. The primary one is the establishment of the kingdom, its failure, and the Grail quest. What distinguishes Williams's treatment of the myth is his use of the historical context to extend its significance. His Logres is a province of the Empire, which has its secular government in Byzantium, and the seat of its spiritual government in Rome. By the Empire is to be understood not only Byzantium but also the perfect social order and, indeed, the entire creation in its unfallen state; it also represents the human body and the subject-matter of great verse. Thus, through its relation to the Empire, the story of Logres is also concerned with the ideal society, the poetic mind, and the redemption of the body: the use of the myth ensures the co-inherence of Williams's preoccupations in a complex of associative imagery. But, if the poems give the effect of a colourful and elaborate tapestry, their texture has the glowing hardness of mosaic. They declare their meaning rather than embody it.

The poems in *Taliessin through Logres* are arranged round six principle themes. After the 'Prelude' comes a group of five poems describing the establishment of the Arthurian kingdom and the vocation of the poet within it: these deal with the calling and coronation of Arthur, and his victory against the heathen on Mount Badon; and with Taliessin's vision of the Divine Order in Byzantium and his return to his native land in order to communicate it. The second group consists of three poems celebrating romantic experience as an insight into an underlying order: the 'Song of the Unicorn' portrays the poet's relation to his world, 'The Fish of Broceliande' the lover's to his, and 'Taliessin in the School of the Poets' the human body as an index of the Divine Glory. There follow three poems exploring contradiction and defeat, through failures in poetry ('The Death of Virgil') and romantic love ('The Coming of Palomides', together with the latter's demonic counterpart, 'Lamorack and the Queen Morgause of Orkney'). The next three show one of Williams's central beliefs in action. 'On the King's Coins' expounds the doctrine of exchange, 'The Star of Percivale' and 'The Ascent of the Spear' its method of working. Exchange points the way back from the fatal knowledge of Virgil, Palomides and Lamorack. The

superbly poised, but extremely difficult, 'The Sister of Percivale'
is a poem of transition from one world to another, and ushers in
the three which describe the nature and effect of Divine Grace as
known in the life of Galahad. These are 'The Son of Lancelot',
'Palomides Before his Christening', and 'The Coming of
Galahad'. The cycle closes as it had begun, with five poems
corresponding in theme to the earlier ones, but in reverse order.
In each of them the establishment of the earthly kingdom is trans-
muted into its heavenly fulfilment, Galahad's Logres substituted
for the King's. Thus, 'The Departure of Merlin' reverses 'The
Crowning of Arthur'; 'The Death of Palomides' echoes the victory
on Mount Badon in what Williams would call a mood of defeated
irony; 'Percivale at Carbonek' shows Galahad's entry into Sarras
as the final consummation of 'The Calling of Arthur'; while
Taliessin's vision is fulfilled in 'The Last Voyage' and his home-
coming made eternal in the final poem, 'Taliessin at Lancelot's
Mass'. The sequence is an interrelated whole.

II

The 'Prelude' is terse, epigrammatic and precise. It outlines the
establishment of Logres; its decline under rulers who, anticipating the years of the Enlightenment, 'nourished the land on a
fallacy of rational virtue'; and the overthrow of the Empire by
Islam and the stern dictates of a puritan morality that denies the
holiness of matter and thus, implicitly, the Incarnation. The
poem is an austere indictment of the contemporary intellectual
climate, and establishes the political, social and religious
relevance of those that follow.

'Taliessin's Return to Logres' is an illustration in verse of the
argument of *The English Poetic Mind*. Its three-stress lines echo
the galloping of the poet's horse as it speeds through the oak trees
creaking in the wind, through the wood of Comus, of Keats's
nightingale, of Dante's suicides, of Lancelot's coming overthrow,
of all the delusions of the senses. Taliessin is protected overhead
by the seven golden stars of the Divine Providence of the
Emperor, and by the corresponding flashes of the golden sickle of
the Druids. The stars relate to St John's vision in the Apocalypse
of the ascended Christ, an image to be connected in 'Mount
Badon' with poetry; they suggest the seven gifts of the Holy Spirit,

as well as the perceptions of the poet. The sickle, which in the ancient Druidic rites gathered the sacred mistletoe, is blent with the mysterious arm, always for Williams, 'love's means to love', heavenly perceptions actualised through poetic vision. The sickle arm is the poetic image itself.

> As I came by Broceliande
> a diagram played in the night,
> where either the golden sickle
> flashed, or a signalling hand.

A *diagram*: the poetry must be accurate if it is to negotiate the dark wood of chaotic impulses, visions and sensations, and reach the King's camp. The function of poetry resembles that of the Arthurian kingdom: it is to manifest and incarnate the 'glory of substantial being' which is the glory of the Emperor. This poem relates to the poet's inspiration and to his craft: both are necessary for the establishment of Logres. The threefold falling of the Hallows recalls Williams's own development, through the first vision of romantic love when 'chaos behind me checked': the knowledge of division and despair when 'the wood showed the worst', and deliverance at the sombrely merciful hands of 'the dark viceroy' on emerging into enlarged vision and securer power. The whole poem is a blend of the intellectual, the theological and the personal.

As for Yeats, so for Williams, Byzantium is an image of intellectual order, and Taliessin's 'Vision of the Empire' captures something of the aloof formality of that patterned civilisation, though without the piercing particularity of Yeats's evocations. Like the Stone of Solomon in *Many Dimensions*, the throne of the Emperor is the centre of the derivations, and the 'phenomenal abating' of the identities of creation into 'kinds and kindreds' is presented as the translation by scribes of the imperial *fiat* into the several dialects: the imagery is typical of Williams in its vitalising of abstractions. The poet Taliessin is one who moves 'from the exposition of grace to the place of images' – that is to say, from God known in himself to God known in his creation, a reversal of normal devotional practice. Poetic insight, Williams suggests, contemplates its object's true identity (Hopkins's 'inscape') and is the result, conscious or not, of having stood in the presence of the Emperor. It sees the material world as invested with the glory of its source.

In this light four 'themes' or provinces of the Empire are apparent: Caucasia, Logres, Gaul and Rome. Since the Empire corresponds to the human body, these provinces have their physiological connotations. Caucasia is the province of the senses. To express this anatomically Williams chose the image of the human buttocks, one whose dignity has been compromised by centuries of robust jocosity, so that even calling it 'the lost name, the fool's shame' fails to rescue the usage from a sense of contrivance: 'the rounded bottom of the Emperor's glory' is not one of Williams's happier phrases. None the less the image is consistent, since it is on Caucasia that all the other capacities rest. Of these, the head, which houses the brain, is set in Britain, the place of the prophetic intellect and of Merlin, 'time's metre'. Gaul signifies the breasts, which provide the 'trigonometrical milk of doctrine': the mathematical ascription is both characteristic and appropriate, for doctrine is the measurement of the Divine Glory. Rome provides the hands, their several capacities for creation and suffering described in an extremity of complex allusions. Here 'strength articulated itself in morals' and something more than morals, 'a single sudden flash of identity, / the heart-breaking manual acts of the Pope', a phrase that relates the cult of the Sacred Heart of Jesus to the Last Supper.

Next, the desire of men to know good and evil is portrayed: it is the desire to view the acts of the Emperor in contention, an image which Williams was to develop when expounding the doctrine of the Fall in his theological writings. Those who nourish this perverse desire are in 'the hollow of Jerusalem', for Jerusalem is the place of generation and self-assertion. As a result the Emperor becomes known in reversal as the Emperor of the Antipodes.

> Phosphorescent on the stagnant level
> a headless figure walks in a crimson cope,
> volcanic dust blown under the moon.
> A brainless form, as of the Emperor,
> walks, indecent hands hidden under the cope,
> dishallowing in that crimson the flush on the mounds of
>   Caucasia.

The precision of the buttock imagery here tends to make the passage distractingly anatomical, following an otherwise creatively suggestive portrayal of something pathetic and perverse that might have been created by Jean Genet.

Into this disordered world comes Merlin, summoning Arthur to establish a kingdom of justice. 'The Calling of Arthur' portrays the tragic state of Logres, ruled by the last effete survivor of an overspent civilisation. The ironies of such a situation are caustically presented.

> The waste of snow covers the waste of thorn;
> on the waste of hovels snow falls from a dreary sky;
> mallet and scythe are silent; the children die.
> King Cradlemas fears that the winter is hard for the poor.

The poem ends on a mounting note of triumph, the words hacked out as though by the stroke of an axe. The last line is an instance of that sudden impression of length and amplitude of which Williams was a master. 'In Logres the king's friend landed, Lancelot of Gaul.' Lancelot symbolises the perfect harmony in man which is to be overthrown.

In the magnificent 'Mount Badon', victory reveals itself in the mastered poetic line. Taliessin, like Joseph in *Seed of Adam*, is captain of horse in the wars. Watching the battle of Mons Badonicus and searching for the weak place in the enemy ranks, in a trance he sees Virgil searching no less intently for the right phrase. The two images coalesce.

> Civilized centuries away, the Roman moved.
> Taliessin saw the flash of his style
> dash at the wax; he saw the hexameter spring
> and the king's sword swing; he saw, in the long field,
> the point where the pirate chaos might suddenly yield,
> the place for the law of grace to strike.

The interchange of terminology is carried into the two succeeding stanzas, where the images of poetry and war are assumed into the controlling image of the risen Logos from St John's Apocalypse. In great splendour of rhythm and phrase the poem blazes forth into a conclusion celebrating the joint victory of poetry and the Arthurian kingdom.

> The tor of Badon heard the analytical word;
> the grand art mastered the thudding hammer of Thor,
> and the heart of our lord Taliessin determined the war.

The *heart*: we are a world away from the introverted cerebralism of most twentieth-century poetry about poetry.

'The Crowning of Arthur' follows. By a number of deft strokes Williams conjures up a picture of crowded magnificence, banners lit by torchlight, flutes sounding through the smoke. Lancelot brings Guinevere to the king.

> So, in Lancelot's hand, she came through the glow,
> into the king's mind, who stood to look on his city:
> the king made for the kingdom, or the kingdom made for
>   the king?
> Thwart drove his current against the current of Merlin:
> in beleagured Sophia they sang of the dolorous blow.

The King's preference of himself to the pattern of the Empire coincides with the Islamic conquest of Byzantium, and the destruction of concord between spirit and body. It also constitutes a preference for Gomorrah. At the moment of choice all is concluded. Logres is overthrown, and the King's 'organic motion', his 'mind's blood', is faithless to him in the adultery of Lancelot and the Queen.

The next three poems celebrate the romantic properties of the body. The 'Song of the Unicorn' describes the difficulties and possibilities inherent in the romantic nature. As Williams had suggested in his life of Bacon,[7] the poet of romantic love is not necessarily an effective lover: his awareness is so intense that it inhibits, with the result that a woman may well prefer the huntsman to the unicorn of poetry (or any art or ideal): 'she cannot like such a snorting alien love'. But if she will consent to mother the unicorn's voice which speaks the mythological language of the fourth dimension, then there will emerge that glory of substantial being which is the 'twy-fount, crystal in crimson, of the Word's side'. The poem, which forms one long breathless sentence, expresses an impatient longing for perfection.

The 'twy-fount, crystal in crimson' is seen in another aspect in 'The Fish of Broceliande', spoken by Bors, type of the average householding man, to his wife Elayne. The fish is the lover's glimpse of the beloved's true self, only to be known by a 'twy-nature' – both the united life of the lovers and the two natures of Christ who gives his life for the world, and whom the early Christians symbolised in the Catacombs by a fish. The vision can lead to ways of affirmation or rejection: the poem anticipates much that Williams was to write later on the romantic vision. Behind Logres lies Broceliande, the elemental creation, the forest of infinite possibilities.

> Though Camelot is built, though the king sit on the throne,
> yet the wood in the wild west of the shapes and names
> probes everywhere through the frontier of head and hand;
> everywhere the light through the great leaves is blown
> on your substantial flesh, and everywhere your glory frames.

This poem is a good example of the unevenness of Williams's verse. The imagery is precise, clear and entirely original, and expressed in a masterly cadence; but the poem is marred by grammatical tangles, by such bathos as 'wild west' and such clumsy tongue-twisters as 'that Nimue the mistress of the wood could call it by'. However, it escapes the bloodless irony that emasculates so many twentieth-century poems – 'the stemming and staling of great verse' of which Williams makes Taliessin sing in 'The School of the Poets'.

   This, the third of these 'romantic' poems, defines the majesty of the human body and the work of poetry. On the floor of the school of the poets (a characteristic concept) is a mosaic of Phoebus Apollo, god of poetry and physical beauty, bestriding the Empire. Over this figure falls the shadow of Taliessin. His young disciples are 'searching the dark of Phoebus' style' – the line is an example of Williams's use of the embodied pun. Taliessin instructs them: the body must be not only hymned but also measured, for poetry studies precision and is the expression of Byzantium in earthly images; 'but best they fathom the blossom / who fly the porphyry stair'. The stair leads to the Emperor's presence: 'fly' means, but does not at first suggest, 'fly up'. It is the way of prayer. This coincidence of height and depth imagery is theologically appropriate. Taliessin goes on to sing of the failure even of great verse to encompass the eternal. It is in the treasure-house of the human body that true Incarnation occurs.

   There follow three poems of failure, of which 'The Death of Virgil' is the most straightforward and accessible. Virgil's poetry, though useless by itself to save him, does so through an act of substitution by those unborn generations who were to be nourished by it, an idea nourished by Williams's own earlier writings on the timeless world entered by the readers of great poetry. 'The Coming of Palomides', on the other hand, illustrates the failure of romantic love. The steady pulse of its rhyming couplets forms an appropriate medium for the cocksure young Saracen knight, an embodiment of self-sufficiency like some bright young executive fresh from university. A Moslem convinced of the permanent division between spirit and matter, he is a type of all 'rational virtue' which likes a tidy moral universe. Piercing the mists that wreathe the mysterious island in the north he comes to Logres: 'there I saw an outstretched hand'. The hand belongs to Queen Iseult. Its beauty suggests the ideal world of mathematics, where facts exist in abstract harmony. Now this harmony has become palpable.

> Blessed (I sang) the Cornish queen;
> for till today no eyes have seen
> how curves of golden life define
> the straightness of a perfect line,
> till the queen's blessed arm became
> a rigid bar of golden flame
> where well might Archimedes prove
> the doctrine of Euclidean love,
> and draw his demonstrations right
> against the unmathematic night
> of ignorance and indolence!

This vision appeals to heart and brain alike, a 'passion of substantial thought'. The Queen's arm bent on the table forms two sides of a triangle; in turn it forms the third to Palomides's mind and body. In the mathematical symbol he visualises the ultimate harmony to which this moment points, something beyond morals and beyond magic; but the vision fades. He is disregarded and grows jealous, so that

> division stretched between
> the queen's identity and the queen.
> Relation vanished, though beauty stayed;
> too long my dangerous eyes delayed
> at the shape on the board, but voice was mute;
> the queen's arm lay there destitute,
> empty of glory . . . .

It is a common experience, as is its sequel:

> I heard the squeak of the questing beast,
> where it scratched itself in the blank between
> the queen's substance and the queen.

This is the traditional fate of those who fail in the Grail quest.
The blatant beast suggests the sexual urge debased to an itch.

'Lamorack and the Queen Morgause of Orkney' conveys a
further stage in the tyranny of such desire.

> Her hand discharged catastrophe; I was thrown
> before it; I saw the source of all stone,
> the rigid tornado, the schism and first strife
> of primeval rock with itself, Morgause Lot's wife.

The burning cities of the plain are resolved into a figure of deadly
cold. In the second part of the poem Morgause commits incest
with her brother Arthur, and the result is Mordred, who over-
throws the kingdom.

> Through the rectangular door the crowned shape went its way;
> it lifted light feet: an eyeless woman lay
> flat on the rock; her arm was stretched to embrace
> his own stretched arm; she had his own face.

It is a further instance of Gomorrah. Moreover, the use of the
word 'shape' suggests the Emperor of P'o-lu, and also 'the
crowned form of anatomised man' in 'The School of the Poets'.
The image reinforces the reading of the fall of Logres as inherent
in Arthur's choice of status at the expense of function.

Three poems of restoration follow. The second Bors to Elayne
poem, 'On the King's Coins' evokes the tenderness of husband
and wife.

> When you saw me a southern burst of love
> tossed a new smile from your eyes to your mouth,
> shaping for that wind's while the corn of your face.

Here is a good instance of that creative use of metaphor which
upholds the tension between temporal and eternal in Williams's

understanding of romantic experience. But from exchange
within domestic love the poem turns to the world of the King's
court and to the nature of man. A way of return to harmony is
always in operation; it lies in the awareness

> that the everlasting house the soul discovers
> is always another's; we must lose our own ends;
> we must always live in the habitation of our lovers,
> my friend's shelter for me, mine for him.

That idea is now to be formalised with the setting up of the King's
mint. But, though money may be a medium of exchange, it is a
symbol merely; and symbols, when they escape the intellectual
control of verse, dictate their meaning. 'When the means are
autonomous they are deadly.' This poem, with its contemporary
political reference, is a good example of Williams's fusion of
image and idea in a discursive lyric, a mode of writing peculiarly
his own.

The two following poems deal with conversion in the context of
exchange. The slaves at court represent those in bondage to their
own passions and instincts, and in 'The Star of Percivale' the
liberation of one of them comes about through the beauty of
Taliessin's singing. That song, however, is elicited by the sound of
Percivale's harp. Percivale is the figure of integrated imagination,
the harmony of rational thought, and in 'The Vision of the
Empire' 'the phosphor of Percivale's philosophical star' is
contrasted with the obscene phosporescence of the Antipodean
Emperor. Here his star presides over the slave's conversion:

> between string and string, all accumulated distance of sound,
> a star rode by, through the round window, in the sky of
>   Camelot.

The multidimensional sense-impressions implicit in the line are
appropriate to a poem concerned with aesthetic experience.

'The Ascent of the Spear' is the second step in the slave's
conversion: the poem may reflect the relationship between
Williams and certain of his admirers. The slave is found by
Taliessin in the stocks. With gentle mockery he leads her to
confess the folly of false dignity. She is released from the tyranny
of self-respect; free to love and to do what she likes, she agrees to

be released. It is a neat and characteristic irony.

Up to this point the poems have concentrated on the workings of the Empire as manifest in Logres: the implications of romantic experience have been explored in differing forms and modes, and in all of them the technique has either been appropriate to, or has itself embodied, the complex physico-spiritual experiences the poems describe. 'The Sister of Percivale' marks a turning-point: following it, the poems are concerned with the remedial operations of the Divine Grace, the eternal no longer merely perceived but known in action. This poem is the most concentrated in the series and contains an elaborate interplay of symbolism. Taliessin, lying on a wall, composing verse, has a vision of a slave's body that is akin to Palomides's vision of Iseult; it coincides with his first sight of Blanchefleur, vowed novice and a figure of self-sacrifice. The vision's meaning is enlarged by the symbolic patterns employed. Once again they are basically geometrical. Taliessin lies between two horizons. One is visible, 'the horizon of sensation' which 'ran north at the back of Gaul', the 'cross-littered land' from which springs the 'trigonometrical milk of doctrine'; the other, the western horizon towards Broceliande, is hidden. Instinctively but illogically one thinks of them as straight and parallel. But no horizon is straight – it is the limit of one's vision, semi-circular as one stands still. The scar on the slave's back 'lightened over a curved horizon' – the beauty of her body is as far as Taliessin can see, but it suggests the vision of the Empire itself. 'The horizon in her eyes was breaking with distant Byzantium.' She is drawing water at a well, and, as Taliessin sees the smooth curves of her stooping body, 'A round plane of water rose shining in the sun.' The circle, symbol of perfection, has appeared; and as it does so a trumpet sounds, another manifestation of perfection. This call comes from the hidden horizon, the horizon towards Percivale's duchy. A second blast and the departure of the slave are similarly coupled, and with the entry of Blanche-fleur 'hemispheres altered place'. Taliessin has seen something very like perfection in the slave's back, marked and scarred as it was. Now, he sees it in 'the rare face of Blanchefleur'. And

> horizon had no lack of horizon; the circle closed;
> the face of Blanchefleur was the grace of the Back in the
> Mount.

Blanchefleur and the slave are types of the active and contemplative life, and their unity is underlined by their exchange of horizons: the slave's is the Empire's law and doctrine, the novice's is
the mysterious physical hinterland of Broceliande. Together they
embody something not far from perfection, as is shown in the
three final stanzas, where the circle imagery is developed further.
The first two give Taliessin's account of his vision. The slave's
scars (marks of discipline and order) and the lightning which
first directed his attention to her (the poetic perception or flash of
grace), form the perimeter of a wheel. The wheel when spun
produces light; but the wheel which the slave turned at the well,
the reel which was 'spun to the height' to raise the water,
'generates the sphere' – both the spherical beauty of the slave's
buttocks (with their 'Caucasian' associations) and also the
remembrance that the supreme perfection to which the wheel
corresponds is the sphere, the circle with a third dimension. The
poem closes with an analytical meditation using geometrical
symbols to point the relation of human to divine perfection, concluding with a triumphant embodiment of absolute relativity.

> Proportion of circle to diameter, and the near asymptote
> Blanchefleur's smile; there in the throat her greeting
> sprang, and sang in one note the infinite decimal.

Like the salutation of Beatrice, it is almost, but not quite,
perfection.

Galahad makes his first appearance in 'The Son of Lancelot', a
title suggesting the co-inherence of grace and nature, always a
cardinal theme with Williams. The poem is among the most elaborate and impressive in the sequence. The scene is wintry, with
Europe given up to snow and wolves, and the Moslem at the gate.
Following Galahad's birth at Carbonek, Merlin, in the guise of a
white wolf (apt image of the ambiguous effects of grace), carries
him to Blanchefleur, now deep in the life of prayer and exchange
as a nun at Almesbury. At the same time the Emperor launches
his army against the invaders. Like 'Mount Badon' this is a poem
of victory, but of victory in defeat. Williams here makes good the
limitations of Tennyson's handling of the Lancelot story. Lancelot's position is a contradiction in terms: his love for Guinevere,
while arising from all that is best in him, is founded on treachery

to the King. Now he is himself betrayed. Williams considered the story of how Lancelot begets Galahad on the dedicated virgin Helayne, while believing her to be the Queen, 'one of the greatest moments of imagination ever permitted to man'.[8] The manner of Galahad's conception is a characteristic piece of celestial irony; while the providential use of a sin to effect its own conversion is further illustrated by the fact that Lancelot becomes a wolf at the mercy of his bodily instincts. Lost in Broceliande, hungering to devour the child of his humiliation, he is overthrown by the white wolf of grace. The white wolf is also an image of the body in its perfect functioning, akin in its different way

> to the nuns of infinite adoration, veiled
> passions, sororal intellects, earth's lambs,
> wolves of the heavens, heat's pallor's secret
> within and beyond cold's pallor —

who are to cherish Galahad. Just as in the previous poem the slave's back is contrasted with, and yet is complementary to, the face of Blanchefleur, so here there is a sense of reversal in the substitution of Merlin for Lancelot, Helayne for Guinevere, Blanchefleur for Brisen. The poem keeps moving from its central story to the wider background of the Empire, and thence to the relation of grace to free will. This densely packed discursiveness is a good instance of the essentially spatial quality of Williams's imagination, and of the working of his sense of co-inherence in poetic terms.

'Palomides Before his Christening', on the other hand, has a single focus. The jaunty metres which announced his coming are replaced by long five-stress lines that record a slow, weary drag across a barren mountain (an image already used in *Descent into Hell*).

> Bone lay loving bone it imagined near it,
> bone of its hardness of longing, bone of its bone,
> skeleton dreaming of skeleton where there was none.
> From the cave the greasy smoke drifted slowly outward.

A common spiritual state, its termination is no less convincing. Palomides merely becomes frightened, and his paralysis ends. Outside the cave 'the sky had turned round'. It is another case of 'truth from the taunt'. Palomides is contrasted with Dinadan, who takes loss lightly, and who realises that 'the missing is often the catching'.

Something of the catch which is involved in the loss appears in 'The Coming of Galahad', the most enigmatic and baffling of the poems. It takes the form of a conversation between Taliessin, the slave girl and Gareth of Orkney, who is performing his service as a scullion. Gareth and the slave between them represent the paradoxical nature of Christian freedom as Williams understood it. Gareth's choice of servitude is a type of voluntary obedience; while the slave, newly freed, remains in servitude to her own desires. They question Taliessin concerning the new life whose birth is signified by the repose of Galahad in Arthur's bed. To express the meaning of this new life Williams turns to Words-worth's image of the stone and the shell, mathematics and poetry, what he called 'the hard exploration of romantic states and the beauty of romantic states'.[9] These two must be fitted together, and this is achieved when Galahad takes his place in the Siege Perilous. The discovery of identity lies in the combination of heart and brain; this truth applies to poetry, philosophy, religion, law and romantic love. There arises, however, the question, which of these five is supreme, and how are they related? It is the test of co-inherence; but the old terms no longer apply.

> Felicity alters from its centre; but I – free
> to taste each alteration, and that within reach
> then and there; why change till the range twirls?

Another case of absolute relativity: Palomides's defeat is the obverse of this, for everything has become equally tasteless. But in the least action the stone of intellect can be fitted to the shell of poetry. In a symbol Taliessin apostrophises the slave's hand, and this in turn leads to a poignant image in which the false romanticism is revealed in the tormented jealousy of Guinevere.

> But I looked rather tonight at the queen's hand
> lying on her heart, and the way her eyes scanned
> the unknown lord who sat in the perilous sell.
> The bone of the fingers showed through the flesh; they
>   were claws
> wherewith the queen's grace gripped: this was the stone
> fitting itself to its echo.

The poem ends with the presentation of the themes as planetary zones, but the presentation is confusing. Williams lacks the confident lucidity of Yeats. Instead of the assured progression of such a similarly didactic piece as 'The Phases of the Moon', we have a gingerly piece of compression in which the poet seems to be puzzling out his meaning from an only half-communicated private mythology.

The concluding poems correspond to the five opening ones, and portray the withdrawal of Logres into its supernatural origins. 'The Departure of Merlin' reverses 'The Crowning of Arthur'. With the coming of Galahad 'the method of phenomena is withdrawn to Broceliande'. This is another poem of victory in defeat: the victory of grace is the victory of nature also. For good or evil the natural joys of the flesh find their origin in 'the heart's simultaneity of repose'. In 'The Death of Palomides' the leafy mysteries of 'the sea-rooted western wood' merge with a landscape of barren plateaux. This too is a poem of victory, the 'Victory in the Blessing'. Palomides has passed through all substitutes to the adoration of God as he is in himself. 'The Lord created all things by means of his blessing.' Such knowledge is attained at ruinous cost, but the loss of the Prophet, of Iseult, of the Questing Beast, leading to defeat and ironic conversion, has made Palomides discontented with all but pure being.

> If this is the kingdom, the power, the glory, my heart
> formally offers the kingdom, endures the power,
> joins to itself the aerial scream of the eagle . . .
> That Thou only canst be Thou only art.

It is a bleak poem, austere and consolatory.

Whereas 'The Calling of Arthur' portrays the establishment of the earthly kingdom, 'Percivale at Carbonek' depicts Galahad's entry into the heavenly one. But here too the interdependence of spirit and body is maintained; Galahad is still the son of Lancelot. At the gate of Carbonek, the sanctuary of heaven on earth, he remembers his father's betrayal to truth, his compelled falsehood to Guinevere, and asks Bors, Lancelot's kinsman, for forgiveness. It is promised, and on that note of exchange 'Carbonek was entered.' The poem hints at a resolution of tragedy beyond the understanding of the unbodied angels.

Doubtfully stood the celestial myrmidons, scions
of unremitted beauty; bright feet paused.
Aching with the fibrous infelicity of time,
pierced his implacability, Galahad kneeled.

It is one of the most moving moments in Williams's work.

But Carbonek is only the starting-point for Sarras, the
Heavenly City, and the goal of 'The Last Voyage'. Under the
image of the Ship of Solomon cleaving its way through the sea of
Broceliande, Williams suggests the in-Godding of man, when 'the
necessity of being was communicated to the son of Lancelot'.
Galahad, Percivale and Bors, who have achieved the Grail, go to
Sarras, bearing with them the body of Blanchefleur, who has
given her life's blood that another woman might live. Galahad,
the elect soul, is thus accompanied by the types of philosophy (or
intellect), human love and self-sacrifice. Man's apotheosis is
attained. And this voyage is the inevitable rush of power back to
its source, the return of Christ to the Father. The sky is filled with
'an infinite flight of doves' – the Empire is dissolving into these
birds, themselves types of the Holy Spirit, which are propelling
the ship; its progress is related to the work of poetry and the
sexual functions. In 'The Vision of the Empire' the Adam are
seen to rebel 'in the hollow of Jerusalem', the place of the genitals,
physical expression of man's power to assert and reproduce
himself, the place at once of supreme egotism, supreme self-
denial and supreme exchange. Now in this corresponding poem,
when the Empire is itself being transformed,

The wonder that snapped once in the hollow of Jerusalem
was retrieved now along the level of the bulwark
to where the hands of Galahad were reeved on the prow:
the hollow of Jerusalem was within the hollow of his
    shoulders . . . .

With a flashback to 'The Calling of Arthur' we are told that 'In
Logres the king's friend landed, Lancelot of Gaul.' But this
second landing encounters a very different situation. Logres has
become the historic Britain, through the exchange of death and
healing between Arthur and Pelles. The victory over Mordred has
been won, Pyrrhic victory though it be; the fruits of self-

aggrandisement have been destroyed, but they cannot be ignored as though they had never been. Logres is no longer Logres, the pattern of the Empire; it has become divided into the nation of poets and the nation of shopkeepers. From now on its true nature can only be achieved by exchange with that which is beyond it.

'Taliessin at Lancelot's Mass', a vibrantly rhythmic piece in which the anapaests of Swinburne are counterpointed with the stress patterns of Hopkins, provides an illustration. Lancelot is a layman; his Mass is the Mass of all believers. The full meaning of the life of exchange is revealed in a vision of perfect reconciliation between all the protagonists in the drama of the Round Table. Even the antipodean regions are redeemed. Now the King's poet 'rides to the barrows of Wales up the vales of the Wye' to sing of the new Byzantium, just as previously he had ridden through the dark forest to announce his vision of the old.

III

The second collection of Arthurian poems forms a commentary upon the first. In the Preface Williams describes them as 'incidental to the main theme'; but they develop the eschatological aspect of the myth. They portray the mission of Logres as it relates to the themes developed in *Taliessin*, those of the nature of the human body, the function of poetry, and the affirmation of images. The book consists of eight poems, all but 'The Meditation of Mordred' written in long, irregularly stressed stanzas. More diffuse than their predecessors, they are easier to comprehend.

The controlling image of the Third Heaven or 'region of the summer stars' (a phrase taken from Lady Charlotte Guest's translation of the *Mabinogion*[10]) derives from Canto VIII of the *Paradiso*; it is the sphere of Venus, where the earth's coned shadow comes to rest in space. Fused with this image is Wordsworth's notion of the 'mens sensitiva', the 'feeling intellect', as defined in Book XIV of *The Prelude*. Williams's Third Heaven is both the goal of lovers and poets, and their prototype; the poems reflect a tension between 'being' and 'becoming', and are strung, as it were, between Logres and the region of the summer stars. *Taliessin through Logres* charts a progress through the earthly kingdom: its sequel defines that progress in terms of its heavenly

fulfilment. Thus 'Taliessin in the Rose-Garden' relates the Third
Heaven to the romantic's awareness of his natural surroundings,
and 'The Departure of Dindrane' to the crisis of contradictory
knowledge. 'The Founding of the Company' constitutes the
charter for the Way of Exchange, and 'The Queen's Servant'
presents the reintegration of grace and nature in the redeemed.
The last poem, 'The Prayers of the Pope', is a portrayal of the
spirit of love as it confronts and bears, and thus defeats, the
enemies of Logres, the Empire and the City. Every happening in
the poems is seen in the light of the Third Heaven, which is for
Taliessin 'his' heaven, and therefore the ultimate point of
reference for his vision of the Kingdom.

The theme of the Third Heaven is intimately bound up with
that of the *Parousia* or Second Coming of Christ. Williams's interpretation of the Arthuriad here becomes a genuine vehicle of
theological expression, its meaning being related to three distinct
themes. In the first place it can be taken as a myth of the
Creation, Fall and Redemption – say, Logres, the Dolorous Blow,
Galahad; as such it is also a myth of individual salvation. But
Williams does not isolate the tale from its setting. It takes place
within an already existent Christendom, and so becomes a myth
of the Second Coming told in terms of the First. It is the story of a
proposed Parousia which is historically thwarted by the failure of
Logres and fulfilled by the voyage of the achievers of the Grail to
Sarras. The myth is presented as a paradigm of the fundamental
spiritual laws of human life, a model of how the Second Coming
operates in human experience. The themes of the Fall and
Redemption, both cosmic and individual, and that of the Second
Coming, cosmic and individual, are related in the commonality
of style and images. Thus Galahad in the first theme symbolises
both the Redeemer and also 'love's means to love', while in terms
of the Second Coming he represents the life in grace which
achieves the Grail. In the poetry these several meanings co-
inhere.

Logres itself is designed to be the recipient of the Hallows
borne 'from Carbonek into the Sun': the latter phrase is a more
specific presentation of the Second Coming, that of the manifested presence of the Hallows in the Empire – the hidden presence of
God made fully known. The secret first coming of Christ in
Bethlehem and Nazareth is now to be known as a full epiphany.
Thus, Carbonek is the place of the secluded Hallows, just as the

Hallows are obscured in ordinary religious experience, and Judgement and the Second Coming are seen in terms of a revelation of what lies hidden within quotidian reality.

A certain paradox, however, attends the achievement of the Grail. While the Company, the faithful remnant, are a pledge of the Second Coming and the ever-living link between Logres and Britain, the achievers of the Grail, Bors, Percivale and Galahad, are identified with

the chief of the images, and the contemplation of the images, and the work of the images in all degrees of the world.[11]

Bors, the type of the affirmative way and himself the chief of the images, returns to Logres. Moreover, the work of the images is the grand Rejection (Galahad) born of the grand Affirmation (Lancelot). Affirmation tempered with Negation – 'This also is Thou; neither is this Thou' – is the life which achieves the Grail.

IV

'The Calling of Taliessin' is a remarkable *tour-de-force*. In a haunted landscape between the wilderness of Logres and the wood of Broceliande the poet meets the twin shapes of Merlin and Brisen, 'time and space'. It is a moment of creation, when earth and the Third Heaven are in communication, the moment also of the poetic and all such romantic visions as prepare for the Second Coming.

Done was the day; the antipodean sun
cast earth's coned shadow into space;
it exposed the summer stars; as they rose
the light of Taliessin's native land
shone in a visible glory over him sleeping.
Rarely through the wood rang a celestial cry,
sometimes with a like reply, sometimes with none.
The trees shook, in no breeze, to a passage of power.

In a dream Taliessin sees the magical preparation for the making of Logres, which is to be the meeting of the Empire and Broceliande when Arthur will be united with Pelles, the wounded king. Logres is to be the perfect manifestation of earth in Heaven, and the union of all its capacities is symbolised in the power of the feeling intellect which translates the wilderness into a place of glory.

> Merlin and Brisen
> heard, as in faint bee-like humming
> round the cone's point, the feeling intellect hasten
> to fasten on the earth's image; in the third heaven
> the stones of the waste glimmered like summer stars.

Taliessin is commissioned to be the King's poet in Logres; he is to

> stand by the king,
> Arthur, the king we make, until the land
> of the Trinity by a sea-coming fetch to his stair.

Poetry is one pledge of the Second Coming, the fulfilment of earth in Heaven.

> I am more than the visions of all men and my own
>   vision,
> and my true region is the summer stars.

Taliessin's call is also a summons to freedom. Poetry in the pagan world is imprisoned within the cycle of birth and death, 'the changes of the cauldron of Ceridwen'; but in this new dispensation it is to be liberated by 'the doctrine of largesse', the doctrine of joyously superfluous creation, and the limitless exchanges, natural and supernatural, of the redeemed life. The act of poetic creation is ratified and confirmed in Heaven; there is an absolute to which it can conform, and an absolute way of conformity. That way is the way of exchange, and Taliessin's task is also to establish the Company which will be the faithful remnant in Logres.

'Taliessin in the Rose-Garden' celebrates Guinevere's 'lordly body', the 'feminine headship of Logres'; it is a vision of beauty in the flesh, sumptuously conveyed.

> Hazel-lithe she stood, in a green gown;
> bare against the green, her arm was tinged

> with faint rose-veins, and golden-flecked
> as the massed fair hair under the gold
> circlet of Logres; on one hand was the ring
> of the consort of Logres; deep-rose-royal
> it drew the rose-alleys to its magical square.

But Guinevere, in her adulterous love for Lancelot, is a source of division within Logres: and yet also, being a woman, she is a type of the whole natural creation, the feminine matter which, in Williams's cosmology, awaits the quickening of masculine form. Taliessin relates the wounded figure of King Pelles to the menstrual blood-letting of womanhood: nature reveals that of which theology, 'the divine science', also speaks.

> Flesh tells what spirit tells
> (but spirit knows it tells) . . . .

Taliessin's vision is the result of the tension between these two categories of one identity.

'The Departure of Dindrane' describes the way back to a true understanding of love. Dindrane (the 'Blanchefleur' of *Taliessin through Logres*) is, like Helayne, a dedicated virgin; Taliessin's beloved, she is leaving the court to take up her vocation as a nun at Almesbury. Hers is the Way of Rejection of Images, just as his is the way of their affirmation; but in their common choice of necessity neither way is exclusive. The parting is presided over by the unborn voice of Galahad, falling from the Third Heaven, hailing his father Lancelot, the Rejection honouring the Affirmation.

> It was toned to a sweetness of note disowned by the world
> while the world was self-owned . . . .

Because of this co-inherence of the two ways, there is in the last resort only one necessity to choose. This discovery is made by a slave girl, uncertain whether to accept freedom or to remain a servant in the poet's household. The sight of the union between the lovers, one going into voluntary obedience, the other remaining 'free', resolves her doubt:

> at once, in her heart,
> servitude and freedom were one and interchangeable.

The music of the poem, with its steady beat in time with the falling rain and the horses' hooves, reflects this resolution; the straight lances and the hazel rods, and the counterpointing of the imagery, convey a sense of vibrant tension tightened into resilience, the natural innocence of the uncut hazels submitting to the discipline of the cut hazel rod.

> before her eyes
> the hands of the great personalities linked as they rode,
> as they rode fast, close-handed, oath-bonded,
> word-in-the-flesh-branded, each seconded
> to the other, each in the crowd of Camelot vowed
> to the other, the two Ways, the Ways passing
> over and through the swelling heart of the hazel,
> all the uncut nuts of the hazel ripening to fall
> down the cut hazel's way; and it she.

She vows herself to the poet's household and thus to his Company. 'The Founding of the Company' describes its origins and purpose. To its ranks belong all those who behold 'the primal Nature revealed as a law to the creature'. Such a company has no real leader, and yet a leader is necessary. Dinadan, meeting Taliessin on the Feast of Fools, persuades him to accept the superfluous office. In the Company 'all luck is good'. The poem defines the exact place of authority in the redemptive kingdom

> Any may be; one must. To neighbour
> whom and as the Omnipotence wills is a fetch
> of grace; the lowest wretch is called greatest
> – and may be – on the feast of fools. The God-bearer
> is the prime and sublime image of entire superfluity.
> If an image lacks, since God backs all,
> be the image, a needless image of peace
> to those in peace; to you an image of modesty.

Absolute relativity again, applicable to all who seek to exercise authority.

These last two poems return to a vision of glory through discipline, obedience, exchange and defeated irony, all seen in the light of the Third Heaven. The protagonist of 'The Queen's Servant' is a slave in Taliessin's household. The poet gives her her freedom, and creates for her magical garments of roses and golden lambswool, a portrayal of the resurrection body in images of sensuous beauty, power and innocence. But the slave must first unclothe: a native of Caucasia, symbol of the body of flesh, she has not realised its true wonder. The body prefigures not only Byzantium, the perfect operation of divine order, but also Sarras, the Holy City itself.

> And so, in a high eirenical shire,
> are flashing flaunts of snow across azure skies,
> golden fleeces, and gardens of deep roses.
> There, through the rondures, eyes as quick as clear
> see, small but very certain, Byzantium,
> or even in a hope the beyond-sea meadows
> that, as in a trope of verse, Caucasia shadows.

With a complete change of tone 'The Meditation of Mordred' defines the infernal opposite of the Third Heaven. The epitome of self-centred worldly prudence, Mordred evokes P'o-l'u. Like Shakespeare's Iago, he has his wisdom – up to a point the wisdom of clear sight. But the precise nature of that clear-sightedness is revealed in his imagining of the Antipodean Emperor, in which, as C. S. Lewis points out, 'there is a sickening combination of extreme distance and extreme clarity'[12] – a peculiar property of nightmare. Mordred states the inevitable alternative when Logres fails and the Third Heaven is no longer desired.

> Here, as he in the antipodean seas,
> I will have my choice, and be adored for the having;
> when my father King Arthur has fallen in the wood of his
>   elms,
> I will sit here alone in a kingdom of Paradise.

The trite phrase pins him neatly.

The final poem summarises the others. The young Pope (the attribution is surprising but not illogical) is at prayer before the Christmas Eucharist at the time of 'the total Birth intending the total Death'. He sees the desolation of the Empire, one that inevitably suggests the havoc wrought in Europe by two world wars; the refrain of his prayer is 'Send not, send not the rich empty away.' For six consecutive stanzas the sufferings of Logres and the Empire are evoked and met by his prayers and reparation. The divisions within Logres spread outside it, the themes of the

Empire fall apart, denying each other in affirming themselves. The Empire is smitten by savage hordes from without, the body becomes the prey of its warring instincts: everything is known in schism. The Pope accepts that he is one even with these. 'We know how we have sinned; we know not how they.' An unholy magic invokes P'o-l'u and resuscitates the dead – hereditary terrors stalk the earth. The Pope receives this also, admitting co-inherence and gathering into himself the kind of universal catastrophe Williams describes in *The Place of the Lion*. Now, the Second Coming suspended, it is the hour of Mordred, of the man who sees no images anywhere and thus begets 'the falsity of all images and their incoherence'. In response the Pope appeals again to the all-Imaged un-Imaged, who himself shares in the life of his creation.

Although it is the hour of Mordred, the household remains. They are known to be Taliessin's enduring work and the human equivalent of the poet's achievement of significant relationships. What is true of the leader of the Company is true also of each member of it:

> We a needful superfluity,
> the air in which the summer stars shine,
> nay, less – the mode only of their placing and gracing.

The Pope commends them to the co-inherent Trinity, and as if in response Jupiter, planet of irony and defeated irony,

> rode over Carbonek; beyond Jupiter,
> beyond the summer stars, deep heaven
> centrally opened within the land of the Trinity . . . .

There follows the arrival and year's dwelling at Sarras of the achievers of the Grail. The tentacles of the octopods of P'o-l'u, fumbling round the base of the world, are caught in the stronger tendrils of Broceliande, the inherent goodness of the natural creation itself responding to and defeating the unnatural growths. It is one aspect of the harrowing of Hell: however deep the loss, however wide the division, there is still but one Creator and one creation.

> That Thou only canst be, Thou only
> everywhere art; let hell also confess thee,

bless thee, praise thee and magnify thee for ever.

The words of Palomides are here recalled in triumph.

V

Williams's next collection of poems was to have been called 'Jupiter over Carbonek': the legends continued to develop in his mind, and few modern poets can rival his mastery of so ambitious and wide-ranging a project. Some hint as to what might have been contained in this next instalment can be found in his unfinished 'The Figure of Arthur', which was posthumously published under the title *Arthurian Torso* (1948), together with a valuable commentary on the poems by C. S. Lewis. A study of the growth and interrelation of the myths of the Round Table and the Holy Grail, 'The Figure of Arthur' does not aspire to original historical research, relying heavily, as it does, on such authoritative studies as J. D. Bruce's *The Evolution of Arthurian Romance* (1923) and E. K. Chamber's *Arthur of Britain* (1927); but it contains an outline of the development of the legends as it occurred in Williams's mind, one elaborated further in his *Dublin Review* essay 'Malory and the Grail Legend' (1944).[13] Imaginative absorption in the legends had fused over the years with his theological and spiritual concerns.

Williams's account of the Grail legend is prefaced by a short history of eucharistic theology in keeping with his earlier critical books, the theology being presented as a product of the corporate imagination of Christendom – imagination being understood in Wordsworth's sense of 'reason in her most exalted mood'. Following A. E. Waite and Arthur Machen, Williams makes little of the pagan origins of the myth, dismissing the stories of 'vessels of plenty' and 'cauldrons of magic' as irrelevant: the creators of the Grail romances were intending reference to the actual cup used at the Last Supper.

> There is no need to suppose the poets and romancers were particularly devout; it is only necessary to suppose they were good poets and real romancers. . . . Cauldrons of magic – 'dire chimaeras and enchanted isles' – are all very well at first, but maturing poetry desires something more. It desires something more actual to existence as we know it.[14]

The dismissal is characteristic; and it also places Williams for once firmly among the poets of his particular time. In such a statement theology and modernism touch hands.

'The Figure of Arthur' is a study of the developing poetic imagination in which not only Geoffrey of Monmouth and Chrétien de Troyes have a part, but also Malory, and Tennyson, and Charles Williams himself. His own belief that with the entry of the Grail the myth becomes 'a kind of working out of a theme which is eventually discovered to be the Christian theme'[15] shows the same kind of detection of the imaginative roots of Christian doctrine as one finds in Chesterton's study of comparative religion, *The Everlasting Man* (1925); but his poems in turn illuminate the doctrines they discover. Williams is unusual among poets in that his inspiration was at once the awareness of a time-less world and a keen speculative consciousness of historical process: only Eliot and David Jones surpass him in this respect. The co-inherence of time and eternity is of the essence of his poetic vision; and its systematic exploration is the matter of his theology. As Williams practised them, the two disciplines are complementary.

6   Theology

Williams's theological writings are in many ways his most remarkable achievement. Whereas his other books belong to particular genres, these can be said virtually to create a genre. They are not scholarly dissertations, nor treatises proceeding along the lines of intellectual argument; nor are they devotional manuals, nor apologetics, nor exhortatory commentaries. Indeed, one of their attractions is precisely their freedom from any apparent design upon the reader. Although very much addressed *to* the reader, they assume as shared the experience they examine and elucidate.

Williams could be critical of religious writings. Reviewing a batch of devotional works for *Time and Tide*, he remarks that he is sure that his authors (a Catholic, an Anglican and a Free Churchman) 'have each his public and that their public will profit'. But the authors will have been less gratified by what follows.

> I am not quite sure how far they would convince any larger public, nor how far, setting aside the familiar readers, it is worth while multiplying such books. But that is the publishers' business, not mine.

He then makes some telling comments on how such books treat their subject-matter, suggesting that

> Why [William] Law's style is utterly right, when so many attempted simplifications are false has, I fancy, something to do with the nature of the Kingdom; which is that if one is anxious to write about God, one ought to be anxious to write well.

He proceeds to remark that the authors under review 'maintain, on the whole, a bearable level'.[1]

Williams certainly practised his own precepts. Each one of his theological studies is based on the presumption that spiritual beatitude is a state not only attainable but also the norm in terms of which all other modes of apprehension should be assessed. Such an attitude is the mark of an analytic visionary. Williams defines beatitude as the reward of those who are prepared to live in the belief that love not only has meaning as a concept but is also an authentically sustaining and activating force. His chosen method is to substitute definition for rapture, or, better, to raise definition into rapture. *He Came Down from Heaven* (1938), a short, pondered meditation on the Creeds and Bible, both in their literary forms and their practical implications, inaugurates the method; while *The Descent of the Dove* (1939) develops it by tracing the growth of belief in co-inherence in the outward life and inner experience of the Church. *Witchcraft* (1941) and *The Forgiveness of Sins* (1942) explore the negative aspects of this experience, and the Church's inbuilt powers of recovery. In addition, Williams wrote several essays on similar themes (most notably a sombre consideration of the doctrine of the Atonement, called 'The Cross'). These were reprinted by Anne Ridler in her collection of his shorter writings, *The Image of the City* (1958).

Williams's theological books are a curious blend of speculative theology, couched in the language of myth, with an acute feeling for its personal application. As in his poetry, he works through the personification of concepts. His style is thus allusive and oblique, and as a result his ideas call for aesthetic as well as intellectual assent. But, if his appeal as a writer is limited, his reading of Christianity compels attention. It is one that interprets theology as though it were poetry. Williams approaches disciplines through the medium of his own personal response; he never seems to speak at second-hand, and is free from that constant use of critical or biblical citations without which many scholars seem unable to proceed. Not so much a theologian of a systematic kind as an alert commentator, he interprets the doctrines of the Church as so many symbols for a multidimensional experience of life, and does so in a manner which enhances both their credibility and their imaginative impact.

II

Like many of Williams's books, *He Came Down from Heaven* was written in response to a request. (One could cite as a happy example of the workings of the City the fact that so much of his writing should to this extent derive from others).[2] The book sets out to define the meaning and implications of a belief in the transcendent significance of love, but is notably free from emotionalism or false sentiment. Love, so Williams's hypothesis goes, is the true meaning of the term 'Heaven'; and 'Heaven', so understood, is the matter of all his theological writing. But this particular book is also an analysis of how love is known in the corporate life of men and women both in and outside the Church.

Its dedication to his wife indicates its personal source. 'To Michal by whom I began to study the doctrine of glory.' 'Glory' to Williams meant 'love's radiance, which cannot be seen without us but we are not it.'[3] Williams's understanding of Christianity springs from, and in turn directs, his experience of romantic love. His theology was shaped by his experience as a poet, so that his view of life is determined by his vision of its consummation as a network of related images. In this first systematic essay on the nature of love he presents it as operating within the orbit of the divine. Taking human relationships at once more seriously and more lightly than is customary, instead of treating them as ends in themselves he presents them primarily as means to a fulfilment that transcends them; indeed almost, one might say, as poetic images.

He Came Down from Heaven, for all its impersonality, constitutes a spiritual testament. It is a closely packed book, proceeding from cautious enquiry to rhapsodic apprehension; and something like this movement is repeated in every chapter. Each one opens tentatively, making qualifications and defining terms. Then, as the theme develops, it quickens pace and ends in a blaze of rhetoric, moving from analysis to poetry.

The opening is unwaveringly affirmative. Heaven is defined as 'beatitude and the eternal fulfilment of the [Divine] Will, the contemporaneousness of perfection'. It is a state, a knowledge, an awareness, and it 'only exists because of the nature of God, and to his existence alone all bliss is related'. The coming of Christ is the manifestation of him in whom Heaven consists; in his earthly life God's will is done as it is in Heaven. The life of Christ is Heaven-on-earth and earth-in-Heaven; and the mythical pattern of that life (the Nativity, the Death, Resurrection and Ascension) 'perfection known in sequence' is the pattern of love's operation in the world. It is 'a pageant of the events of the human soul'.[4] Williams's interpretation is thus set forth in terms of spatial myth rather than through subjective, individualistic apprehension: his theology stems from the Catholic rather than from the Protestant tradition.

Such a view of the Incarnation shows a strongly developed eschatological sense. Williams's poetic imagination and his sense of craftsmanship dictate a language of pattern and design. Writing of the Divine Glory which is the manifestation of the presence of God, he points out that the word 'glory' 'usually means no more than a kind of mazy bright blur. But the maze should be, though it generally is not, exact, and the brightness should be that of a geometrical pattern'.[5] The emphasis on exactness is characteristic: it presupposes that the glory of God seen in the life and person of Jesus of Nazareth constitutes the fusion of earth and Heaven – what a less pictorial theological vocabulary would call 'the eschatological event'.

Williams's examination of the biblical account of that event is the work of a literary critic as much as of a theologian. He detects an interplay of themes resolved into a controlling theme which is 'the original nature of man, the entrance of contradiction into his nature, and the manner of his restoration'.[6] The mythological presentation of the theme commences with the Fall of man, 'the alteration in knowledge'. The doctrine of the Fall traditionally relates it to a misuse of free will, or, as Williams glosses the matter, 'the preference of an immediately satisfying experience of things to the believed pattern of the universe; one may even say, the pattern of the glory'.[7] A refusal of exchange, it involves the assertion of the 'I' at the expense of the 'we'. It is not an historical event, but a permanent human reality.

The dramatising of the crisis of dual consciousness in Williams's plays and novels clearly influences his reading of the Fall as an alteration in knowledge. Following his chosen method of commenting on the biblical account by way of discursive meditations, he points out that the denial of creaturehood involves a state of self-contradiction and moral distortion.

Since there was not – since there never has been and never will be – anything else than the good to know, they knew good as antagonism. All difference consists in the mode of knowledge. ... [Man] knows good, and he knows good as evil.[8]

This interpretation of the knowledge of evil as being the result, rather than the cause, of sin is an attempt to square that experience with the Christian doctrine of Creation. The Creation, being of God, is good; the cardinal sin of pride is a refusal to admit that derivation and obedience are good. All other sins are its result, and men and women, at odds with the laws of their being, find the good creation to be hostile. Moreover, these sins are themselves perverted and disordered virtues functioning wrongly and turned into means of delusory self-enhancement. A literary influence is apparent here. Williams's exposition of *Paradise Lost* in his books on the poetic mind reveals the debt he owed to Milton in his interpretation of the Fall, a debt clearly evident in his dictum that 'Hell is always inaccurate.'[9]

It may be objected that to speak of sin in terms of false knowledge and inaccuracy shows a gnostic tendency to reduce it from a disease to a mistake. But there is a distinction between the nature of sin, the condition of sin and the activity of sin. The nature of sin, as defined by the omnipotence of the good is inaccurate in the sense that sin disrupts the harmony of the created order: it is antagonism to the Father. The condition of sin is known in relation to the Incarnate Son as separation, blindness and hardness of heart. It is wilful self-exclusion from the community of humankind, and thus the knowledge of good as evil. The activity of sin (if activity be the word) is antagonism to God the Creator Spirit, and involves personal deliberation. Williams embodies it in two verbal formulations of his own, one active, the other passive. The former he labels 'the perversion of images', the latter is the state which, in *Descent into Hell*, he calls 'Gomorrah'.

With regard to the origin of evil Williams's approach to the problem is to work from Redemption backwards, rather than from Creation forwards. He begins with what is known, not with what is opined, so that his presentation of the Fall is directed by his consciousness of its reversal. If his method is inductive, his point of view is existential: it stems from the paradoxical experience of the good creation as evil, and of God the Creator as good. In his plays this dual consciousness is presented as a resentful and half-conscious awareness of Christ's presence as it is known by those co-inherent in sin. In both a spatial and a moral sense this is the opportunity of salvation. That Williams does not attempt to explore its metaphysical implications is less a limitation than evidence that his concerns lie more with moral theology than with dogmatics.

Commenting on the story of Cain and Abel, he points out that Cain 'could not guess that the very purpose of his offering was to make his brother's acceptable'.[10] Freedom implies choice, but every good demands its complement in order fully to realise its identity, and there is no full identity in a life of solitude. This suggests that the opposite of 'good' as known by man's limited understanding does not necessarily have to be what is meant by 'evil'. In the redeemed life as Williams defined it, Blake's dictum holds true: 'Without Contraries is no progression.'[11] In the tale of the Flood the relation of the one to the many is further clarified in God's covenant with Noah. 'Man becomes men.' Although the declaration 'At the hand of every man's brother will I require the life of man' is 'an exchange of responsibility rather than of joy', 'into the chaotic experience of good as evil the first pattern of order is introduced'.[12] This is developed in the covenant with Abraham, where Israel 'is to be exclusive and inclusive at once, like all modes of redemption, particular and universal'.[13] (The same quality might be posited of a poetic image.) With the call of Israel, the Chosen People, the knowledge of good as good emerges from the knowledge of good as evil.

Williams's account of the book of Job is characteristic. For him, it is the *im*patience of Job that is important, for it is a divinely endorsed refusal to accept any easy explanation of the existence of pain and suffering. The voice from the whirlwind may not give a particularly reasonable reply to Job's furious questionings, but a reply it is. 'A great curiosity ought to exist concerning divine things. Man was intended to argue with God.'[14] Such a declaration testifies to Williams's integrity, and derives from his interpretation of God's providence in his plays.

The revelation of God through the Law and the Prophets is a further vision of the 'inclusive–exclusive thing', the design and working of a new and separate community whose life is to be vicarious, and a means towards restoring joy and wholeness to a fallen world. The background of its struggle is the life-weariness of Ecclesiastes, 'a classical expression of utter boredom, though the boredom is set to such high counterpoint that its very expression is exciting'.[15] Here we are back in the world of Williams's literary criticism. He had made the same point about the poetry of Housman.[16]

Williams next turns his attention to the Old Testament prophets who 'are sent out from the visible mathematics of the glory to proclaim the moral mathematics of the glory'.[17] They call Israel to accuracy, and proclaim the condition of receiving the Divine Pardon. That pardon is effected by an act of substitution, historically enacted in the persons of Bar-Abbas (the name means Son of the Father, in other words, Everyman) and Jesus the Christ; it is maintained in the life of natural and supernatural exchange. Williams, like Gerard Manley Hopkins, subscribed to the teaching of Duns Scotus that there would have been an Incarnation even had there been no Fall. The distinction may be philosophically irrelevant, but in terms of myth it offers an interpretation of human life more affirmative than the traditionally held account of a prediluvian catastrophe which tends to suggest that, rather than controlling and encompassing time, God's purposes are governed and contained by it. Williams sees everything in terms of function and destiny, and interprets the Atonement in this light. The Incarnation having determined the Creation, the Divine Son proceeds to endure that Creation as, in the context of sin, inescapably a victim. Time being an element in Incarnation, this victimisation is declared in an historic event, and with the recognition of this comes the exchange known as conversion, as a result of which it is possible

> for mankind itself to know evil as an occasion of heavenly love. It was not inappropriate that the condition of such a pardon should be repentance, for repentance is no more than a passionate intention to know all things after the mode of heaven.[18]

That mode Williams defines as being

> to know the evil of the past itself as good, and to be free from the necessity of the knowledge of evil in the future; to find right knowledge and perfect freedom together; to know all things as occasions of love.[19]

Williams's exposition of the myth of Redemption eschews historical enquiry: for him, it is clearly as self-authenticating as a poem might be. It commands assent because it satisfies the imaginative intelligence.

The second part of *He Came Down from Heaven* deals with the application and relevance of Christian doctrine to certain aspects of daily life; and in it Williams analyses the theological connotations of three of his leading themes – romantic love, substituted love, and the City.

Williams's theology of romantic love is partly the fruit of his study of Dante; but his early poems, written before he came to read Dante, show that the doctrine was authentically his own. (Though he may also have been influenced by Patmore's *The Rod, the Root and the Flower* (1896), a great deal of which is congruous with his later thought.) Here he relates the doctrine specifically to the coming of Christ.

> The kingdom came down from heaven and was incarnate; since then and perhaps (because of it) before then, it is beheld through and in a carnality of joy. The beloved – person or thing – becomes the Mother of Love; Love is born in the soul; it may have its passion there; it may have its resurrection.[20]

Williams views sexual love as a pointer towards the redeemed life, for desire delivers men and women from the self-absorbed miasma of Gomorrah into the physical enactment of co-inherence and exchange. The same theory is found in Williams's early verse, which celebrates love as a vocation, leading on to the discovery, made in the early novels, that love itself is to be loved.

The cult of romantic love as expressed in the thought and songs of eleventh-century Provence was given a religious signification by Dante. Williams's interpretation finds powerful support in C. S. Lewis's influential *The Allegory of Love* (1933). It may be contended, however, that the whole ethos of the cult derived from the Catharist heresy, in which many of the Provençal troubadours were involved, and was a denial of the substantial goodness of the body. Thus the analysis of the Tristram romances by Denis de Rougemont in *Passion and Society* (1940) interprets them as voicing an ultimate desire for death, through the glorification of passion for its own sake – an interpretation for which Wagner's opera affords ample warrant. It is significant in this connection that Williams allows little room for the Tristram story in his own Arthuriad; but, while appearing to agree with de Rougemont in stressing the fatal error of being in love with being in love, he differs from him in vindicating the romantic phraseology of the troubadours, which for him was accurate.[21] Romantic love was ennobling, although

> like many other religious ideas, it was to become a superstition; on the other hand, it was to be, naturally but regrettably, cold-shouldered by the ecclesiastical authorities. It was to be an indulgence to the populace and a stumbling-block to the Puritans – using both words of intellectual states of mind. It was to save and endanger souls . . . . In fact, and in itself, it is a thing not of superstition and indulgence, but of doctrine and duty, and not of achievement but of promise.[22]

Williams takes the words 'falling in love' as meaning what they say. The lover 'falls' either slowly or swiftly into a state of dependence on another which brings him within the orbit of love, where self-sufficiency is abolished, and where he not only feels love but learns to exercise it. Following Dante, Williams suggests that such love may, through a devoted attention to its leadings, be identified with the divine creative Love which is its source. But what matters most is love's direction. Is it to be rendered in homage to its originator, and in a proper degree to its human occasion? or is it to be turned back upon the self, an exquisite emotion in which to luxuriate? The latter is what de Rougemont calls 'passion'. But for Williams, passion means the energy of love in response to a vision of beauty and truth which, however, needs proper understanding and direction. He had said as much in *The Greater Trumps*.

This doctrine has wider connotations which Williams only indicates. Falling in love is the equivalent in sexual terms of aesthetic vision. 'Vision' is the operative word. Every true lover sees for a moment like a poet – he beholds 'the physiological glory'. What matters most to Williams is the romance rather than the physical and psychic emotions, the 'wherefore' of this stirring of the senses and the mind. He is explicit enough as to what it meant. '[It] flashes for a moment into the lover the life he was meant to possess instead of his own by the exposition in her of the life she was meant to possess instead of her own. They are "in love".'[23] Or, as C. S. Lewis defines it with his customary succinctness, it is 'the recovery (in respect to one human being) of that vision of reality which would have been common to all men in respect to all things if Man had never fallen'.[24]

However transcendental his understanding of the falling-in-love experience, Williams was no sentimentalist. He warns against the folly of claiming for the beloved

> a purity as non-existent as the purity of the Church militant upon earth. Hers, or his, humanity is an extremely maculate humanity, and all the worship under heaven ought not to prevent her lover from knowing (with reasonable accuracy and unreasonable love) when she is lazy, lewd, or malicious. She has a double nature, and he can have double sight.[25]

He proceeds to define three basic heresies concerning the experience: the belief that the vision is going to last, and that if it fades it can be abandoned; secondly, that it belongs to the lover – this results in jealousy and possessiveness, 'a desire to retain the glory for oneself, which means that one is not adoring the glory but only one's own relation to the glory';[26] and, thirdly, that it is enough simply to be in love. Lovers exist for the function of love; hence they live not only 'for' but also 'from' each other.

In the penultimate chapter, 'The Practice of Substituted Love', Williams develops more systematically the idea he had already dramatised in *Descent into Hell*. It is, perhaps, his most individual contribution to the interpretation of Christian experience. The substitution of Christ for man is the foundation of the Kingdom, and exchange the manner of its operation, beginning with the recognition, however reluctant, of things and people as existing independently and not simply in relation to oneself. In his essay 'The Way of Exchange' Williams points out how, of many possible attitudes to this recognition,

> the good taste of the West (one can hardly call it more) had, until recently, made a general amalgam which it called, roughly, 'tolerance'. Tolerance meant, at worst, sullenly putting up with what one could not alter; at best, willingly accepting what one could not alter.[27]

'To tolerate' is, he remarked, generally considered to be an active rather than a passive verb.

The life of substituted love, or way of exchange, is both the acceptance of co-inherence and a pattern of behaviour which exemplifies it. The taunt 'He saved others; himself he cannot save'[28] is the definition of Christ's kingdom. The 'way of return to blissful knowledge of all things' calls for a new self to travel on it. For most men it is the case of 'the old self on the new way'. That way 'consists of the existence of the self, unselfish perhaps, but not yet denied. ... It aims honestly at better behaviour, but it does not usually aim at change.'[29] But love involves change; it is 'to live from a new root', and to be 'in Christ'.

> We are to love each other *as* he loved us, laying down our lives *as* he did, that this love may be perfected. We are to love each other, that is, by acts of substitution. ... All life is to be vicarious – at least, all life in the kingdom of heaven is to be vicarious.[30]

This is what in *The Greater Trumps* is named 'the Dance'. Men co-inhere in Christ and in one another as part of what Williams calls 'the web' – the criss-cross threads of human motive and action forming part of a divine pattern with Christ at the centre, in which all courteous and selfless actions have their place.

These only partly conscious acts, though purposeful, are limited. There are also the profound and deliberate acts of exchange described in *Descent into Hell*. Williams, who spoke from experience in the matter, stresses that three things are needed in order to undertake exchange: to know the burden, to give up the burden, and to take up the burden. Exchanges of this kind involve humility and intelligence, and are an extension into particular time and place of the formal intercession of the Church in the Eucharist, God's will being very much done on earth as it is in Heaven. In any case, the substance of the burden remains: in *Descent into Hell*, for instance, it is only Pauline's reaction to her fear that Stanhope carries; and so when she does meet her image face to face it is still her own experience. Not that it is necessarily easy to give up one's burden, for 'a pride and self-respect which will be content to repose upon Messias is often unapt to repose on "the brethren" '.[31] But Christ dies not only 'for' all men but also 'in' all men; the substitution is not arbitrary but organic. The life of Heaven-on-earth and earth-in-Heaven is a continuous exchange of love, symbolised by the image of the City, the life of the community in all its manifestations. It is the awareness of the good as good at all times.

The closing chapter of the book is an eloquent vision of the redeemed life in its social operation. In it, Williams shows the glory of God as being a glory in movement, and the revelation of a God who acts and who must be acknowledged to act everywhere and in everything. All facts of whatever kind are to be known for what they are.

It is this which has distinguished the doctrines of Christendom; nothing is to be lost or forgotten; all things are to be known. They can be known as good, however evil, for they can be known as occasions of love.[32]

This is the conclusion of the search for integrity: some such paradisal knowledge shines through all Williams's subsequent writings.

III

Williams's masterpiece is *The Descent of the Dove* and this despite the fact that the sub-title 'A Short History of the Holy Spirit in the Church' constitutes a theological solecism. The book is an historical commentary on the themes of *He Came Down from Heaven*, and a portrait of the Church reflected in its history, that history being interpreted as 'an operation of the Holy Ghost towards Christ, under the conditions of our humanity'.[33] Williams reads into the Church's history the expression of its nature – a similar treatment to that accorded the protagonists of his biographies and plays – in a tension between the fulfilment of its nature in acts of exchange and the tug of an individualism leading to sterility and incoherence. Because certain events reveal this tension more than others, the treatment of the historical material is selective.

The book's overriding concept is that of the co-inherence, both natural and supernatural, of men and women in each other and in Christ. Williams emphasises that the Christian doctrine of the Godhead, the doctrine of the Three-in-One, is itself a postulation of exchange within co-inherence. It answers affirmatively the questions, 'If there had been no creation could love be predicated of Godhead?' and 'Would Love have had an object?' The definition of God as Love is, in anything less than a Trinitarian theology, impossible to reconcile with his transcendence; for only such a formulation can accommodate a God who both sustains and endures what he creates. For this reason Williams regards the Athanasian Creed as being 'the definition of salvation': 'it lays down a primal necessary condition – that one shall believe in the existence of salvation and in its own proper nature'.[34] The experience of love-in-exchange is 'a new state of being, a state of redemption, of co-inherence, made actual by that divine substitution, "He in us and we in Him" '.[35] Williams notes many striking examples of the awareness of this state in the writings of the early Church, but he sees co-inherence equally manifest in St Augustine's doctrine of original sin; in the medieval practice of indulgences; and in the eighteenth-century cult of the Heart of Jesus and Mary. The width of understanding is remarkable. Itself the basis for the recognition of authority in the Church, co-inherence provides a key to the meaning of heresy.

> However right a man's ideas, they were bound to go wrong if he nourished them by himself. The value of dogma, besides its record of fact, is the opportunity it gives for the single mind to enter the Communion of Saints – say, of Intelligences.[36]

Although sympathetic to the great rebels from Montanus to Kierkegaard, Williams always remained loyal at heart to the traditional Catholic concept of Christendom.

His discussion of the Montanist controversy also brings to the fore the idea of the two Ways, which surfaces as he considers the 'rigorous' and 'relaxed' views of Christian ethics.

> The Rigorous view is vital to sanctity; the Relaxed view is vital to sanity. Their union is not impossible, but it is difficult; for whichever is in power begins, after the first five minutes, to maintain itself from bad and unworthy motives. Harshness, pride, resentment encourage the one; indulgence, falsity, detestable good fellowship the other.[37]

A bland *via media* is one answer to a question inevitably arising in a religion which does not include the Hindu concept of *dharma*, that sense that each person has an essential nature peculiar to himself, with his own direction and leading within the overall law of right conduct and natural piety. The Catholic doctrine of vocation, however, does reckon with this diversity in unity, and Williams's interpretation of it is characteristically influenced by his concept of coinherence as the necessary resolution of every paradox.

Some were called to a strictness, some to a laxity. It naturally happened that strictness, being more difficult, was regarded as superior. So, as far as difficulty is concerned, it is; but so, as far as vocation is concerned, it is not. Relaxation is no less holy and proper than rigour, though perhaps it can hardly be preached so. But the lovely refreshments of this world in some may not be without their part in the lordly rigours of the others; the exchanges of Christendom are very deep; if we thrive by the force of the saints, they too may feed on our felicities.[38]

So, later, he notes of St John of the Cross that 'even he, towards the end, was encouraged to remember that he liked asparagus; our Lord the Spirit is reluctant to allow either of the two great Ways to flourish without some courtesy to the other'.[39] The balanced sentence structure, the urbane tone betoken a confidence almost eighteenth-century in its grace.

This is the first time that the two Ways are defined in Williams's work with any elaboration. They represent two methods of living within the co-inherence. The more generally recognised is the Way of Rejection of Images, the ascetic life, the refusal of all that is not God in order that the soul may find its perfect happiness in him alone; the other, the Way of Affirmation, is scarcely recognised as a Way at all, and as a result there has appeared the false dichotomy of the dual standard, one for the avowedly 'religious', the other for the layman.

The two Ways, embodied in two of the supreme literary products of medieval Christendom, *The Divine Comedy* and *The Cloud of Unknowing*, are complementary. On the affirmative view every created thing is, in its degree, a valid image of God; on the negative view an image is but an image which, considered apart from its source, leads to delusion. Williams, however, maintains that 'rejection was to be rejection but not denial, as

reception was to be reception but not subservience'.[40]
Commenting on the Athanasian Creed, the charter of the
Affirmative Way, he remarks that 'All images are, in their
degree, to be carried on . . . all experience is to be gathered in.'[41]
It is a belief to which as a poet he was himself committed.

In spite of his insistence that 'the body has not . . . as some
pious people suggest, fallen a good deal farther than the soul'[42]
(that 'unofficial Manicheism' against which this book was written
to protest) he does not ignore the horrors and anomalies of
Christian history. His very first paragraph emphasises with
characteristically gnomic *panache* the contrast between Jesus and
his followers.

> The beginning of Christendom is, strictly, at a point out of
> time. A metaphysical trigonometry finds it among the spiritual
> Secrets, at the meeting of two heavenward lines, one drawn
> from Bethany along the Ascent of Messias, the other from
> Jerusalem against the Descent of the Paraclete. That measure-
> ment, the measurement of eternity in operation, of the bright
> cloud and the rushing wind, is, in effect, theology.[43]

The phrase 'against the Descent of the Paraclete' (the word may
be translated as 'Mediator' or 'Helper' rather than as 'Comforter')
links Williams's concept of the Church, the second Israel, with
one meaning of the word Israel itself: 'He who strives with God.'
This movement against the Spirit is the Church's experience of
tension between being and becoming, and Williams finds the
condition embodied in the person of Søren Kierkegaard, who
'caused alien and opposite experiences to co-inhere. . . . He lived
under a sense of judgement, of contrition, of asceticism; but also
(and equally) of revolt, of refusal, of unbelief'.[44] Kierkegaard's
predicament is a further example of the Impossibility.

Williams here puts forward another manner of knowing this
experience, the exercise of what he calls 'the quality of disbelief',
the recognition that man's knowledge is conditioned by his
nature, and must therefore always necessarily be relative. He had
already explored the contention in *Reason and Beauty*; now he
traces its growth as a common way of thought reacting against the
dogmatism which had caused the religious wars. One of his
masters is Montaigne, who made clear the difference between
believing in a thing and knowing it to be true. 'Man has always to

proceed by hypotheses' and even the Christian faith 'had first been a hypothesis and had been generally translated into the realms of certitude by anger and obstinacy and egotism'.[45] Such dogmatism provides a spurious authority but a common refuge for the intellectually careless or insecure. Intellectual insecurity, however, is a condition of human existence – almost, one might say, a necessity of it. To embrace that particular necessity is to exercise the quality of disbelief.

Williams sees Christianity as constituting the defeat of irony. Disillusionment is where one starts from, and there is, therefore, no call to take it too solemnly; in any case, by definition if not by popular consent, it is a fortunate condition to arrive at. Disbelief is something more than tolerance, and certainly something more than scepticism, 'a qualitative mode of belief rather than a quantitative denial of dogma'.[46] Elsewhere Williams speaks of 'the delicate tension of Catholic doctrine' that has 'had to maintain that eternity is at once, as it were, absolute and yet relative'.[47] Such an attitude is sanctioned by what he calls 'the superfluity of matter'. Everything but himself is necessarily superfluous to God, otherwise he would not be God. Life, however unwelcome, is a gift; and life in Christ is in one aspect nothing more (but also nothing less) than the art of receiving gracefully – the adverb is precisely meant. Williams asserts the superfluity of matter to be the condition of man's freedom: 'we need not love, but mightily decide that we will'.[48] It is the gaiety, almost the irresponsibility, of his presentation of beatitude which singles him out from other religious writers, Chesterton alone excepted: it is the light that offsets the darkness of his two last novels and his book on witchcraft. Always more concerned with the goodness of God than with the deserts of man, he could appreciate joy in a manner possible only to those who have plumbed joy's opposite.

Such serene clearsightedness makes for a book as illuminating as it is readable. It combines the excitement of the novels, the acute critical intelligence of *He Came Down from Heaven*, and the wit and historical perception of the biographies. Highlights include the balanced assessment of the theology of St Augustine, the analysis of the Faith and Works controversy, the typical acknowledgement to Voltaire. The aphorisms are legion. The prose, though condensed, is varied enough in speed and texture to meet the various calls upon it. No less striking is the masterly handling of the narrative, which neither gets clogged with superfluous particularities, nor subsides into the vagueness that denotes the amateur. Of all Williams's books this one is the most distinctive, varied and interesting. It provides a vision of syntheses underlying and not bypassing theological divisions, and witnesses, even more than does its predecessor, to his native understanding of beatitude.

IV

Williams's next book was written at the request of T. S. Eliot, the handling of its subject being determined by the author's phrase, 'the perversion of images'. *Witchcraft* describes a misuse of reality based on a misunderstanding of it. At the heart of the book lies the Church's failure to accept its own revelation of the omnipotence and omnipresence of love: the title is thus over-simple, and misleads. The Church with a tragic loss of nerve desired 'an opponent it could divinely hate'.[49] The tragedy, however, as happens in so many of Williams's writings, is overthrown by celestial irony, and with perfect justification from orthodox theology, the resurrection of Christ being a reversal of all values and the establishment of joy in sorrow. *Witchcraft* might have been more suitably entitled 'The Quality of Disbelief'.

Williams's interest in his subject is primarily psychological. This is not to say that he regarded it merely as an hallucination, but rather that for him it was essentially an aberration of the spirit. He had already portrayed its cause and effect in *War in Heaven* and *Descent into Hell*; now he analyses the impulse towards it in terms that are anything but esoteric.

> Most children and most youths take pleasure in fancies; the secrecy of those fancies is sometimes a part of them. That one's parents may be but foster-parents, that one's blood is particular, that one is predestined, that a hidden greatness looms in one's heart – such things are common imaginations. ... But if a religious heart and mind were, for some reason, oppressed and antagonized by the order of religion in the world, or if greed or curiosity sprang high, there might be every kind of opportunity to welcome and enjoy some other fancy, however preposterous – what fancies are not? – of a powerful, satisfying, and secret justification of oneself.[50]

This kind of insight is characteristic, as is the aside about fancies: the figure of Lawrence Wentworth comes to mind at once. Williams distrusted day-dreaming, the historian always going hand in hand with the poet. Thus witchcraft for him was first and foremost a refusal of co-inherence; it denied its spirit while seeking to manipulate it as a fact, in a preposterous search for power without love.

Williams was a master of compressed narrative. His account of the history of the Church and the witches is conducted with a sure eye for the essential. From a brief consideration of magic in the ancient world he proceeds to determine its relation to the changed perspectives inaugurated by the coming of Christianity. It is notable that by his use of such widely read documents as *The Golden Ass* of Apuleius and the Nativity story in St Matthew's Gospel, he stresses the importance of the imagination as it shapes human beliefs. Throughout the unfolding of the story, from the Church's acceptance of the urge to hate as well as to oppose the Devil, to the dissolution of belief in witchcraft that came with the more general weakening (though not obliteration) of belief in the supernatural during the nineteenth century, Williams preserves a strict detachment; his only outright conclusion is that, whether the witches were deluded or not, the Devil did most certainly appear in the treatment of them by their persecutors. As he wrote elsewhere, 'It is certainly better for man to disbelieve that such communion of evil can be, for man is not to be trusted with the belief.'[51] The mordant cadence is unmistakably his. So – 'I do not believe in belief'? *Witchcraft* might seem to be a vindication of E. M. Forster's celebrated assertion of agnosticism: yet Williams, while disliking dogmatic attitudes, believed in the necessity for dogma. At one point he speaks of that 'greatest of virtues – a deliberate belief in God'.[52] This book demonstrates the lengths to which he was prepared to go in the testing of his own.

It is unusual in its blend of historical enquiry with personal concern, and is more like an examination of evidence than the arguing of a case. Williams observed his oaths of silence to the Order of the Golden Dawn: he did not even draw on his knowledge of esoteric rituals, as he does in, for example, *War in Heaven* and *All Hallows' Eve*. A reading of this book should disabuse anyone of the error of supposing that he was a crypto-magician or anything but loyal to those orthodox Catholic formulations he assented to throughout his life, even in the face of a temperamental disinclination to believe in immortality.

This assent to orthodoxy may to some minds appear to limit the significance of what Williams has to say; but only if one refuses orthodoxy a hearing. He was no tub-thumping evangelist. He held his beliefs without apology as an intellectually respectable point of view. And, if he appears to a later generation to be uncritical of his texts, it should be remembered that those accounts of the phenomenon of witchcraft are themselves part of it; indeed, Williams is less interested in the witches themselves than in the effect they had upon their persecutors – say, in the interaction between the two which is the history, as distinct from the practice, of witchcraft. His account of the trial of Gilles de Rais is a case in point. Whether de Rais was self-deluded or not is secondary to the fact that the delusion, if it were one, was shared by his judges. In the trial as Williams describes it, the knowledge of co-inherence reasserted itself. The heightening of the prose in this passage is indicative of where the author's chief concern is to be found.

About the Devil Williams was doubtful. In *He Came Down from Heaven* he remarks that 'the Devil even if he is a fact, has been an indulgence; he has, on occasion, been encouraged to re-introduce into Christian emotions the dualism which the Christian intellect has denied'.[53] It remains a salutary reflection: there is not all that much difference between religion and political ideologies. Certainly there is no lack in *Witchcraft* of the acute and trenchant intellectual dissection of which Williams was a master. Consider, for example, the characteristic footnote on the relation between heresy and inordinate passion. Its fairness is both exemplary and illuminating in its freedom from twentieth-century assumptions.

In the class of grave suspects come those who 'cherish some inordinate love or excessive hatred, even if they do not use it to work harm'. Such persons are thought to have heretical sympathies. The point is well taken. Saint Francis had put it better with his 'Set love in order, thou that lovest me.' But the comment takes us back to the world in which, when all is said, the Inquisitors conceived themselves to be working – the world of motives, desires, spiritual excesses and negations, the powers of the other worlds rather than of this.[54]

Or one may cite the masterly little comment on the ethics of the Salem puritans.

It was a land where everything was immediately translated into terms of God; that is, no doubt, proper, but then they must be His terms and not ours – the terms He deigns to apply, not the terms we force on Him.

And then the surprising, yet obvious, development: 'And this, it seems, is the use of all science – to discover His own terms.'[55] St Thomas says the same thing, as do all Catholic theologians; but the principle is not usually expressed so tersely.

Unlike too many other 'religious' writers, Williams never seeks to bypass intellectual claims with emotional assertions; his peculiarly imaginative way of expressing his ideas frees his readers to think further for themselves. For intellect is a sovereign quality in his scale of values; and in *Witchcraft* he selects it as being the one which, along with sheer exhaustion, rescued Christendom from the lengthy nightmare of taking Satan at his own estimation.

V

Towards the end of *Witchcraft* Williams alludes to William Law as the characteristic voice of true enlightenment in putting forward the idea 'that the darkness of hell is but the Divine Nature falsely invoked by the self and that the only dissipator of it is the Spirit of Love. ... it restored again the light of Redemption, which the bigots of redemption had done so much to obscure'.[56] *The Forgiveness of Sins* completes this quartet of theological studies with a consideration of how the Spirit of Love manifests itself in the context of that hellish darkness. It was written for the same series of short, popular theological books as C. S. Lewis's widely read *The Problem of Pain* (1940), a work about which Williams had his reservations.[57] Certainly the alacrity with which Lewis entered the field of apologetics following his conversion has little in common with the self-distrustful diffidence of Williams's disclaimer at the commencement of *The Forgiveness of Sins* that such a book can properly be written at all unless by the great poets, 'for they understand everything; and saints, for they are united with everything – creatures as well as Creator'.[58] The collocation forms a summary of his own ideals.

This is the most personal of his books, written with a kind of laboured, anguished sincerity.

> All that can really be hoped is that some semi-attentive reader, distrusting or despising what he reads, may turn from it to consider in himself the nature of forgiveness; so, and only so, can this consideration hope to be of any use. . . . Discussion and speculation are amusing enough; there are twenty-four hours in every day and they have to be got through somehow. Any fool can invent theories of the Fall, and when fools were interested in theology they frequently did; nowadays they are more concerned with economics or strategy or 'ideals'. Any fool can discuss how or what God, from his pure self-existence, knows, creates, or sustains. . . . The easy talk of mental distress being worse than physical may occasionally be true; only occasionally. Most men would prefer a month's mental distress to a month's serious neuralgia. It is in our bodies that the secrets exist. Propitiation, expiation, forgiveness, are maintained *there* when the mind has explained them away – the need, and the means, and the fruition.[59]

Nowhere else does Williams write in quite that tone: the debonair scholastic mask has slipped, together with the graceful ironies, the fervours, the pointed wit. This book is full of a sense of travail, a striving after accuracy that results in an over-cryptic style couched in a multiplicity of hints and digressions. Moreover, the lack of a continuous narrative, such as provided the backbone of its two predecessors, deprives it of their colour and imaginative energy.

Williams commences with a consideration of forgiveness as enacted in the plays of Shakespeare, that 'great protagonist of natural life without apparent need – humanly speaking – of the supernatural'.[60] There follows an account of the Fall taken unaltered from *He Came Down from Heaven*, but reinforced with a fuller treatment of the nature and meaning of sin and of God's responsibility for suffering. The latter was a problem that affected Williams urgently, and in his essay 'The Cross', which forms a companion piece to *The Forgiveness of Sins*, he explores it with passion.

> Now the distress of the creation is so vehement and prolonged, so tortuous and torturing, that even naturally it is revolting to our sense of justice, much more supernaturally. We are instructed that [God] contemplates, from His infinite felicity, the agonies of His creation, and deliberately maintains them in it.[61]

There is no avoiding that corollary to the hypothesis of a benevolent Creator: it cannot be explained away. Williams contends that it is the Cross alone which makes the notion of Divine Justice plausible.

> [God] accepted the terms of the creation whom he had limited his omnipotence to create; in that sense he accepted justice. If he meant to sustain his creatures in the pain to which they were reduced, at least he also gave himself up to that pain. The First Cause was responsible for them; he accepted responsibility and endured equality.

The Creation having been determined *for* the Incarnation, the Incarnate Son is compelled to endure the created order and the alienation of his fellow men. More even than that,

> He would not only endure; he would renew; that is, accepting their act he would set up new relations with them on the basis of that act. In their victimization, and therefore in his, he proposed to effect an escape from that victimization. They had refused the co-inherence of the original creation, and had become (literally) incoherent in their suffering. He proposed to make those sufferings themselves co-inherent in him, and therefore to re-introduce them into the principle which was he. The Incarnation was to be a Redemption as well. He became flesh for our sakes as well as his own.[62]

'The Incarnation was to be a Redemption as well.' Williams's mature view of the nature of the life-in-Christ echoes his own words in *Thomas Cranmer,*

> Can life itself be redemption? all grace but grace?
> All this terror the agonising glory of grace?

Nowhere does he write more eloquently of the love of God, that 'intolerable charity', than here:

> Mankind had devoted itself to an egotism which meant des-truction, incoherence, and hell. He would not let it cease to exist. But then the result was that if he was to submit to the choice of man, he was indeed to submit to that choice. He was not merely to put up with it as a Creator, he was to endure it as a Victim. Whatever sin was, it was a thing repugnant to his nature as Man, repugnant to his flesh; that was, in fact, its definition. Whether it was greed or pride or envy, it was still that which the Divine word, in the limits he desired to set upon his earthly existence, would not permit himself to will. He derived, in his flesh, from men and women; but also in that Incarnation he derived from his Father wholly and from his Father's will. Man had chosen an opposite behaviour. Greed or envy or pride, it was opposed to the nature and movement – yes, even the physical movement – of God in flesh. God in flesh was to maintain both incarnation and creation; he must then be the Victim of the choice of man. But why maintain it? there is but one answer – for love. Intolerable charity indeed – but now also intolerable for himself. Indeed, it killed him.[63]

The affinity with the fourth section of Eliot's *Little Gidding* is immediately apparent; but the irony is Williams's own.

The rest of the book concerns itself with the question: what happens to sin when it is forgiven? Is it forgotten? Is it ignored? 'The condition of forgiving ... is to be forgiven; the condition of being forgiven is to forgive.'[64] Under the heading 'The Technique of Pardon' this idea is developed in a witty and searching analysis of how forgiveness does in fact operate in day-to-day experience. 'Where there is love, there is Christ; where there is human reconciliation, there is the Church.'[65] Through quotation Williams acknowledges his debt to his theological masters: Dante, Julian of Norwich, William Law and William Blake. All four proclaim the role of sin in the forgiven life is to be a further and deeper joy. 'He as Man would forgive *thus*, because men also should not merely be forgiven, but also, in every corner of their natures, forgive.'[66] But with characteristic honesty Williams forbore to close his book on this note, and instead proceeded to a sombre discussion of the need to forgive Nazi Germany. His remarks on the impossibility of any real justice in such a case makes ironic reading in the light of the subsequent Nuremburg trials.

VI

Knowledge and justice are of the essence of atonement as Williams interprets it, and one can trace these two elements in his theology, following two interweaving paths. The starting-point of both is the original divine purpose to be incarnate, Fall or no Fall of man. 'The Incarnation is the point of creation, and the divine "reason" for it.'[67] Man loosens the web of creation and the pattern falls apart. 'In Adam' he knows good as evil: but there remains only the good to know. How does he learn to know truly? The question echoes the one raised in *The English Poetic Mind* concerning the nature of free will.

In *He Came Down from Heaven* Atonement is seen as an exchange of the knowledge of good as evil for Christ's knowledge of evil as an occasion of good. It is a transformation in consciousness. This Atonement theology is expressed in terms of its triumphant accomplishment in the redeemed life; but its occasion in individual men and women is the crisis, or condition which Williams calls the Impossibility. The Cross is known in a man's deepest being as an experience of subversion, a division between his nature and his fortune which cannot seemingly be healed. He can seek to change his fortune – but that changes nothing, for he remains himself; he can despair; or he can change his nature. But how does he know what his nature truly is? In true action – or so Williams's commentaries on the English poets would suggest. But truly to act can only be to act in conformity with the will of God, since God alone is pure action; and fallen man can only know that will as potentially, sometimes actually, hostile fortune, a threat to his self-sufficiency. When the threat becomes a trap he knows the Cross. The Cross therefore is the painful evidence of man's sin, and of Christ's freedom from sin. It is, for fallen man, life-in-death; but for redeemed man in Christ it is death-in-life, a death swallowed up in the victory of a new knowledge. There remains the need for fallen man to confront and realise his lack of self-sufficiency, epitomised in the moment of his inability to act. Only when he has chosen that state freely as ordained dependence does he find his true self – which only exists in Christ. Sin separates man's nature from his fortune, but the Cross separates his fortune from his nature. The reversal is complete.

This declaration that the Cross is an integral part of human life relates Williams to such twentieth-century writers as T. F. Powys and Samuel Beckett. It also constitutes his answer to the vexed problem of God's responsibility for suffering. The Atonement is the vindication of his justice. Here Williams's debt to Dante is obvious, but he goes beyond his master. For Dante, God's justice is revealed when Christ in man does what man cannot do for himself; and when man, in the crucifixion of man in Christ, carries out the divine vengeance on sin.

> If, then, the penalty that was wrought by the Cross is measured by the nature assumed, none ever stung so justly; so also none was so great a wrong, having regard to the Person who suffered, in whom that nature was bound up.[68]

Williams carries the idea still further. Burdened as he always was by the difficulty of postulating a just Creator who could yet sustain his creation in an infinity of pain, he sees in the Crucifixion the avowal of divine responsibility.

> Our justice condemned the innocent, but the innocent it condemned was one who was fundamentally responsible for the existence of all injustice – its existence in the mere, but necessary, sense of time, which His will created and prolonged.[69]

And again,

> His will had maintained, or rather His will in His Father's will had maintained, a state of affairs among men of which physical crucifixion was at once a part and a perfect symbol. This state of things He inexorably proposed to Himself to endure; say, rather, that from the beginning He had been Himself at bottom both the endurance and the thing endured.[70]

The work here is the same – the transforming of experience as man knows it into experience as God in Christ knows it; and the point of union and exchange is the Incarnate Life which reaches its culmination on the Cross.

The Cross in Williams's teaching is therefore the inescapable contradiction in human life which has to be accepted as the means of its own resolution. The paradox is borne out by the fact that the Impossibility is both the experience of, and the summons to, the Cross. It may focus on a given situation; but it may also be construed as that pressure of God upon his estranged creatures, that action of the Paraclete against which man's life is set, which is at once the bane of human life and its promise of redemption.

VII

In Williams's writing the cross-fertilisation between literature and theology reaches its fulfilment with *The Figure of Beatrice*. Although properly speaking a work of literary criticism, it takes its place among his more obviously theological works, for in the case of Dante the relationship between poetry and theology is especially close. As early as 1910 Williams had been reading the proofs of a reprint of Cary's translation of the *Commedia*, and Dante, even more than Milton, is his master. Dante's treatment of romantic love in *La Vita Nuova*, his discourses on the City in the *Convivio* and *La Divina Commedia*, his celebrations of order, courtesy and discipline, are all recurring elements in the thought of his disciple; and in *The Figure of Beatrice* that disciple in part repays the debt. The book is Williams's most considered treatment of the nature of imagery, and the absolute relativity of symbols: as such it is also his fullest exposition of the Way of Affirmation as a way of life. A study 'in' rather than 'of' Dante, its character is both theological and expository: theological in the sense that it uses Dante's writings as a text from which to explore the religious significance of romantic experience; and expository in the sense that it is concerned with the content of Dante's verse rather than with a discussion of its construction, background or history. This dual nature is typical of Williams's approach, but, while it accounts for the book's enthusiasm and insight, it renders it at times didactic and oracular. Although he deprecates the fault, the author frequently appears to be rewriting his subject's work, and the result is a feeling of imaginative oppression.

He begins with a cardinal assertion, his belief in the historical existence of Beatrice, since for him her validity as a poetic and religious symbol rests on her actuality as a human being. Only by the realisation of the tangible can transcendence be posited, just as in Williams's novels spiritual reality is destructive unless mediated through the material order. In *Religion and Love in Dante* (1941), a pamphlet which makes a good introduction to the longer book, Williams draws attention to the universal nature of the experience recorded in *La Vita Nuova*; and in *The Figure of Beatrice* he traces the developing meaning of that experience as an element in the poet's spiritual life. Indeed, for Williams, Dante's love for the girl Beatrice is the overriding occasion of all his work, from the early and hesitating attempts at analysis in the *Vita*, through the incomplete attempt to assimilate her image in the *Convivio*, to its triumphant affirmation in the *Commedia*. Such speculations would be irrelevant had there not once been an actual girl in an actual Florence.

Indeed, Florence itself is as significant as Beatrice; Williams treats the two as complementary. The romantic vision takes place within the City where ordinary life is no less important than falling in love. Williams has much to say about both, and in saying it he sticks closely to his text – too closely at times, for the continual quotations in English and Italian, while a concession to accuracy, are an obstacle to attention. An example of his compression is found in the Introduction, where he summarises his themes as being

> (1) the general way of the Affirmation of Images as a method of process towards the in-Godding of man, (2) the way of romantic love as a particular mode of the same progress, (3) the involution of this love with other images, particularly (a) that of the community – that is, of the city, a devotion to which is also a way of the soul, (b) that of poetry and human learning. The general maxim of the whole way in Dante is *attention*; 'look', 'look well'.[71]

Such attention characterises Williams's own approach: he is nothing if not exacting. 'The intention of fidelity is the safeguard of romanticism; the turning of something like the vision of an eternal state into an experiment towards that state.'[72]

In his earlier studies of Wordsworth, Williams examines the contention that imagination, rightly channelled, can wield power; and in the opening chapter of *The Figure of Beatrice* he compares Wordsworth's romantic experience with that of Dante, and finds a pattern common to both – or, rather, common up to a point beyond which Wordsworth does not go. The pattern has four stages, which, as Dorothy L. Sayers points out,[73] can be detected likewise in the work of Traherne and Blake: the first vision or image of glory; the loss of vision, and abandonment of the quest; a second and lesser vision on a more intellectual level; and finally the return of the first image, when the glory is found diffused over all experience. Williams identifies these stages with the salutation of Beatrice; her death and the apostasy of Florence; the consolations of poetry and philosophy; and the process of return set forth in the *Commedia*.

As Williams interprets it, the Way of Affirmation begins with the experience of 'stupor' which the young undergo at their vision of the latent possibilities of the world around them, 'an astonishment of the mind' which focuses on some particular image – a boy, a girl, a landscape, a ship. Whatever arouses this 'romantic' feeling, '(I) it must exist in itself, (II) it must derive from something greater than itself, (III) it must represent in itself that greatness from which it derives.'[74] So, for Dante, 'Beatrice was, in her degree, an image of nobility, of virtue, of the Redeemed Life, and in some sense of Almighty God himself.'[75] Awareness of all these possibilities is conveyed through her to her lover; through her they are to be studied and sought. 'The Way to this knowledge is in the practice of charity and humility and all virtues.'[76]

In the chapter called 'The Death of Beatrice' Williams describes the withdrawal of the sense of glory, again warning against the deduction that it invalidates the vision. Moreover, this withdrawal may itself be the work of that to which the vision points. It is to be a testing time and a means of growth, even though Beatrice is dead.

The recollection of her moves the rational part, even if she no more affects the sensitive. . . . It is by that recollection that the lover is helped towards becoming 'a flame of charity', 'a vesture of humility'. He must, without a miracle, become the perfection he has seen.[77]

The death of Beatrice is necessary for the proper pursuit of the Way. The fact that the glory vanishes is not to mean that the glory was never there, nor even that it is there no longer. But awareness of it has dimmed. In the meantime the lover is to go on loving: – it is the function for which he was created – 'Almighty God did not first create Dante and then find something for him to do.'[78]

The most perplexing feature of the Way, as Williams knew to his cost, is that the vision recurs. Dante saw the Lady of the Window; whether she was a real woman or not, whether she was philosophy or not, is subsidiary to the fact that she was not Beatrice. Outside the way of romantic love in marriage, the re-appearance of the Beatrician quality in a new object is natural and welcome enough: 'such a perfection is implicit in every human being, and (had we eyes to see) would be explicit there'.[79] But, when a second love appears, then an agony of contradiction appears as well. Dante's solution presumably influenced Williams's own.

> Having thriven in one manner, we are offered the opportunity of thriving in another; we are offered the opportunity of being free in the glory. The second image is not to be denied; we are not to pretend it is not there, or indeed to diminish its worth; we are only asked to free ourselves from concupiscence in regard to it.[80]

Intellectually this may be acceptable, but it is hardly easy to practise. Still less so is the succeeding aspiration.

> If it were possible to create in marriage a mutual adoration towards the second image, whenever and however it came, and also a mutual limitation of the method of it, I do not know what new liberties and powers might not be achieved.[81]

'The two great ends of liberty and power'? But this is to tax married love too hard: the idealism borders on absurdity. The weakness in Williams's teaching is that it is deficient in a sense of mutuality and is presented throughout from an intensely devotional point of view. Such co-existence as he points can and does take place, but indifference or moral relativism are as likely to dictate it as are the selfless aspirations envisaged here.

Williams goes on to discuss the Noble Life as defined in the *Convivio* and the *De Monarchia*: his analysis is thorough but tortuous, the chapters twisting and turning upon themselves, their style often parenthetical to excess.

As a proof of this truth – say, of exploration, even of divine exploration, by the grace of divine things; that is, of natural things, for it cannot too often be urged that here there is no dichotomy, or if, it is only of the soul rejecting certain things in order that it may affirm others, but all, though perhaps difficult, is as natural as Beatrice in Florence or Dante writing verse or Casella making music – well, as a proof of this true exploration of the nature of things, Cato speaks.[82]

And high time too, one feels like saying. Williams is happier covering the same ground in his own theological writings, where he could give his imaginative eloquence full rein. His commentary on the *Commedia*, however, is a masterly piece of sympathetic re-creation, in which each part is related to the design of the whole to form a portrait of theology that is comprehensive and inspiring. 'Hell is a funnel; heaven is a rose.'[83] The entire qualitative difference between beatitude and damnation is in that phrase.

The Beatrician moment is itself a moment of judgement.

It is a choice between action and no action, intellect and no intellect, energy and no energy, romanticism and pseudo-romanticism. There is a brief time when the Imagination – the power of grasping images and exploring distances of meaning – remains suspended in a contemplation. ... That Imagination in action becomes faith, the quality by which the truths within the image are actualized within us. But the temptation to turn aside is immediate, swift, subtle and very sweet. It is only to linger in the moment, to desire to be lost passionately and permanently in the moment, to live only for the recurrence of the moment.[84]

The *Inferno* shows the result of such a yielding. The soul 'is incontinent to its function; it treats its function as created for it'.[85] And so it embarks on the perverted Way of Affirmation down the ever-narrowing funnel, through greed and anger and obstinacy, through murk and stench and filth, down to the last cold of self-devouring Hell, where 'the Emperor ... of the sorrowful kingdom', 'that which despairs' is transfixed breast-deep in the everlasting ice.

At the foot of the Mount of Purgation there is another choice: it occasions some of Williams's most concentrated writing, but here the compressions work to good effect, not least as a summing up of much of what he had written in *The Forgiveness of Sins*.

> It was said of God that 'his necessity is in Himself', and this is the only necessity. Hell is the place of those spirits who wish to have their necessity in themselves. But Purgatory is the growing realization that there is no necessity in us, except indeed that of being united with the primal and only Necessity. ... The only illusion is that there is in us a necessity to demand something other than He; the only disillusion is to find it is not so, and that our only necessity is love.

Love, in Williams's teaching, involves the relaxing of a grip. The controlling ego has to learn to let go and enjoy: only so can it enjoy – and enjoy whatever comes. He goes on to face the obstacle to such a disposition:

> there is in us, since the Fall, a kind of necessity of sin, and repentance is by no means so necessary. The unfairness of existence is precisely in this – unless indeed we shared in the Fall and were ourselves personally responsible for the first sin. Even Christ's own mysterious submission to injustice on our behalf does not seem quite to do away with the injustice; we did not ask to be tempted; we do not want, in that sense, to sin. He wishes us to be tempted? very well, but then do not let him blame us. And yet in the first vision of the glory we were, perhaps, reconciled, and not as guiltless but as guilty; then indeed, for a moment, we lived from another root. Romantic Love at once sensitively exposes our guilt, and makes it both tolerable and intolerable. The passage of Purgatory is a passage to justice; in sin the universe is always unfair.[86]

(And 'hell is always inaccurate'. Williams's phrases echo from book to book.) This passage can only be read slowly, ponderingly; even then one may stumble over that 'as guiltless', where the omission of 'being' makes one go back and question what one has read. It is possible, of course, that the trap was deliberately laid. The purgatorial process is the transforming of contradiction, the change from Hell, 'where grace is not known but as a punishment', to Purgatory, 'where grace and punishment are two manners of one fact'.[87] In the paradisal knowledge the image is seen in its fulfilment, at one with the Primal Truth from which all the images derive. It is the state where love is necessity, where 'existence is equal, function hierarchical', where everything may be recalled as a cause of joy. The *Paradiso* is 'an image of the whole act of knowing which is the great Romantic way',[88] in which Dante is the Knower, and God the Known, and Beatrice the Knowing: the image is consistently Trinitarian.

Charles Williams's various themes – the Beatrician vision, the alteration in knowledge, the doctrine of substituted love, the quality of disbelief, are all of them aspects of the Way of Affirmation. That Way may be regarded as a technique of living which springs from an attitude of mind. Indeed, to speak of its being a Way can be misleading, just as it is to talk of the Mystical Way. Phrases such as 'spiritual ascents', 'ladders of prayer', and the like are images which can usurp their own meaning. The Way is no straightforward progress from well-mapped stage to well-mapped stage; rather, it is, to use the image Williams himself valued, an interior movement from the circumference to the centre of a circle, of which the Way of Affirmation and the Way of Negation are complementary aspects. Indeed, the affirmation of images can be related to Gerard Manley Hopkins's concept of inscape and instress – that is to say, to the perception of the essential nature of each created entity as itself evincing in its very quiddity the power and wisdom of the Creator, and in the act of perception relating the perceiver to its source. All Williams's thought works round to the concept of integration as a matter of diverse relationships unified in a mutually related pattern of giving and receiving. It is a process to be found in a fully integrated poem, which itself is 'an image with many relevancies, and not only so, but . . . is itself the expression of the relevancy of its own images each to other'.[89] 'This also is Thou; neither is this Thou.' Once again that definition presents itself as inescapable.

Conclusion

I

The impact of Charles Williams's personality and work seems blunted now. His avoidance of specifically political commitments makes him difficult to place historically, and in a world of terrorism and racial tensions, of the questioning of sexual polarities, and of the secularising of liturgy and doctrine, his views sound reactionary or beside the point. He died before the destruction of Hiroshima and (though he would not have been surprised by them) before the full extent and horror of the European death-camps were made known, so that as a result his portrayal of evil appears at first sight limited and individualistic – even, because of his dealings with the occult, childish. He tends to be regarded as a brilliant oddity, the minor prophet of a dwindling cult. But to study his work with care is to be rewarded by an intellectual vision that is both sane and liberating. If the surest standard for assessing a writer's achievement is, as C. S. Lewis has argued,[1] the quality of reading it elicits, then Williams remains a figure to be reckoned with.

Even in his lifetime he was considered eccentric, not only, as might be expected, by the clergy, but also by the London literary circuit; nearly forty years after his death the slur appears, though from different standpoints. To the present intellectual orthodoxy his unwavering belief in absolute truth is irrelevant enough to dim any awareness of how subtle and sophisticated his assertions of the possibility of truth could be. Similarly, his belief in dogma and spiritual discipline are open to charges of authoritarianism. What is acceptable in Dante's work is less acceptable in that of a twentieth-century disciple.

In the Western Church likewise, Williams's ideas, both in style and content, have become unfashionable. His emphasis on the power of poetic language contradicts the current simplistic preference of intelligible communication to appeals to the imagination and the heart (fundamentalist appeals to the emotions are altogether another thing). It remains a minority belief that the intellect works better when it feels. In Williams's own day his use of language was suspect, even as sympathetic a reviewer as the philosopher E. I. Watkin complaining of 'a terminology distracting and irritating, and a seemingly flippant manner which sometimes jars'. 'Why call Our Lord 'Messias" instead of Jesus or Christ?'[2] The objection remains understandable. When writing discursively Williams could frequently sound evasive or pretentious.

His own enthusiasm also could get in the way. Thus he complains to his wife that

> I sometimes a little despair of the clergy. I have delivered a quite good address – wholly based on you: yes; it is no good denying it, even if you want to, but I hope you do not – and they say, of course it is all on a high and lofty level, and they hint that it is out of touch with the world. I define marriage for them, and they are vaguely uneasy. They were all very nice, but I did tell them what you were like; I talked of the light that you shed, and how I saw the virtues in you (and all), and they say that I am a poet. By which they mean that I am inaccurate. But poets are always accurate and anyone who has known you must try to be accurate. For the glory in you is always accurate. (27 Nov 1940)

This certainly does not sound like the average talk on Christian Marriage Today (nor does it resemble the average domestic communication); but if the language sounds excessively intense it is none the less the language that Williams customarily used. And, whether the projection of a private world or the spontaneous utterance of a visionary, the same kind of thing was said by William Blake.

Verbal mannerisms, and the assumption that what he is talking about is known and accepted, also obtrude discomfortingly in Williams's various essays and reviews. Thus, commenting on Auden's *New Year Letter*, he remarks that 'It is, after its own manner, a pattern of the Way'[3] – but no definition of that 'Way' is offered. Stimulating though most of Williams's occasional writings are, such a self-enclosed vocabulary has the effect of dissociating him from his contemporaries, even from those who share his religious faith.

II

Williams's achievement as a critic goes largely disregarded: it is in any case secondary to his theological concerns. But his perceptions are acute. Thus, commenting on Ford Madox Ford's *Parade's End*, he observes that 'the quietness and the accuracy were so extreme that the voice seemed to come from under one's own skin'[4] – which is not just a picturesque phrase but an actual illumination of Ford's style and fictional technique. Again, he says of Eliot that his landscape is 'his own, but the voice that came out of it was always more like the voice of St John the Baptist in the distance than the croak of the lizard near at hand'.[5] Along with Chesterton, Virginia Woolf and V. S. Pritchett, Williams was a critic who made an analytic tool out of metaphor; it is an achievement which touches the quick of life when more abstract discourse merely talks about doing so. But, where his theological insights are concerned, only G. Wilson Knight among contemporary critics really pursues a line conformable to Williams's own.[6]

In assessing minor writers, taste frequently overrides critical judgement. Major writers are secure from this abuse – too secure, maybe. The virtual canonisation of the greater twentieth-century literary figures makes it possible to discuss them without any indication as to personal appeal, as a glance at any specialist literary journal will confirm. The limitations of individual sensibility can be concealed, though they will be made clear enough should the critic be so rash as to pronounce a verdict on a writer to whom he does not imaginatively respond. The vain quest for total scientific objectivity in the literary realm, which obsesses the late twentieth-century critical mind, betokens disbelief in the power of the imagination. Failing acceptance of transcendence, one falls back on the quest for absolutes, forgetting their inevitable relativity. Criticism becomes a self-justifying art.

Having said this, it is, as Williams himself would say, 'permissible' to discriminate among his writings. With the exception of his verse play *The Witch* and some of the early poems, there is not one that does not reflect the peculiar quality of his mind and voice. Their limitations are self-evident: Williams reveals little interest in his contemporaries, and all his concerns are turned inward to his self-propagating personal myth. To that extent he is a supplementary, not an authoritative, writer. But, where his myth itself dictates the terms of discourse, he reveals his creative power. This happens in the novels, poetry and plays, and, because of the coincidence of myth and subject-matter, the theology.

III

In the novels Williams's art moves towards an ever more perfect fusion of natural with supernatural, so that in *Descent into Hell* and *All Hallows' Eve* he is able to express his vision of co-inherence in a way that overcomes the potential limitation implied in the use of occult symbolism. The magical elements do, certainly, make the novels compare unfavourably as parables of grace with those of William Golding, beside whose psychological penetration and feeling for physical actuality they seem cerebral and rarefied; nor does Williams attempt to integrate theological doctrines with the contemporary world in the way that Golding seeks to do in *Pincher Martin* (1956) and *Free Fall* (1959). Yet the intellectual complexity and denseness of organisation in Williams's novels invite comparison with Golding's work. If one asks why Williams chose to write occult romances, the answer would seem to be that that was the kind of imagination he possessed, just as Golding possesses what might be called an archaeological imagination;[7] and that, while the occult is one way of demonstrating hidden connections and the resolution of dualities within the co-inherence, it also, in its pretensions and yet obvious artificiality, suggests an absolute relativity. There is no confusing the imagery with what it signifies, which remains by definition hidden. The intellectual possibilities of the myths and symbols Williams employs afford his powers of analysis full scope; and, since the symbols are of their nature omnipotent and all-embracing, they can offset the flimsy characterisation by enveloping and subsuming it. Even so, the tension between natural and supernatural remains uneasy. There is an uncomfortable disparity between the grandeur of the novels' themes and the frequently trivial or reductive way in which they are presented.

These faults are least apparent in *The Place of the Lion*, where the characters are little more than cyphers acting out their parts in conformity with the dictates of the celestial invasion. They are personifications in the manner of the medieval mystery plays; indeed, this novel might not unreasonably be designated a mystery in that sense. But, even allowing for this, Anthony Durrant sounds too like a P. G. Wodehouse young man to bear the weight of being the second Adam. Similarly, in *Many Dimensions*, Lord Arglay is often either arch or pompous; his addressing his secretary as 'Child' is tiresome, while his 'O la la!' would be more appropriate in a novel by Ronald Firbank. Where the Stone is concerned, the dialogue turns scriptural and plummy.

> 'Certainly I shall go,' Lord Arglay said, 'for if by chance it was not a thing done to gain the stone then any that he had may still be there. I do not think that I shall find one, but I will take no risks. Besides, as things are, I would not have even Reginald's death quite unnoticed, whatever catastrophe awaits us.'[8]

The worst instances of this kind of thing occur in *The Greater Trumps*, where the emphasis is more interior and psychological. Although Mr Coningsby provides a good example of Williams's ability to mock, love and dissect at the same time, Nancy makes as unbelievable a second Eve as Anthony does a second Adam.

> 'Darling, how gloomy you are. ... Is this what comes of making blizzards and trying to kill your own Nancy's own father? ... It was sweet of you to pick out a nice soothing way of doing what you wanted', she said. 'Some magicians would have put him in a barn and set it on fire, or forced him into a river and let him drown. You've a nice nature, Henry, only a little perverted here and there. All great geniuses are like it, they say. I think you must be a genius, darling; you take your job so solemnly.'[9]

And so on: Williams's own over-anxiety not to be too solemn betrays him into sprightliness and whimsy. It is a temptation frequently succumbed to by the English.

The line between success and failure is more finely drawn in the character of Sybil. She shows a greater self-awareness than her predecessors among Williams's 'saints'. In *Shadows of Ecstasy* Isabel is the perfect wife or partner, wise and disenchanted; while

the Archdeacon in *War in Heaven* is a variant on such semi-play-
ful figures of piety as Giovanni Guareschi's enormously popular
Don Camillo. Both have literary prototypes, and the playing of
their social role helps to mediate their spiritual awareness. In
Many Dimensions Chloe Burnett is described more interestingly;
she is a straightforward, unassuming young woman with a
capacity for seeing things as they are. Her final apotheosis is a
matter of supernatural process, not of conscious virtue rewarded.
But Sybil has no social role to play: she is a leisured lady, though
one 'adult in love'. Williams portrays her interior life with a sure
hand.

> That sovereign estate, the inalienable heritage of man, had
> been in her, as in all, falsely mortgaged to the intruding control
> of her own greedy desires. Even when the true law was dis-
> covered, when she knew that she had the right and the power to
> possess all things, on the one condition that she was herself pos-
> sessed, even then her freedom to yield herself had been won by
> many conflicts. Days of pain and nights of prayer had passed
> while her lonely soul escaped; innocent joys as well as guilty
> hopes had been starved. ... She had tried to enjoy, and she
> remembered vividly when, walking down Kingsway, it had
> struck her that there was no need for her to try or to enjoy: she
> had only to be still, and let that recognized Deity itself enjoy, as
> its omnipotent nature was. She still forgot occasionally; her
> mortality still leapt rarely into action, and confused her and
> clouded the sublime operation of – of It. But rarely and more
> rarely these moments came; more and more securely the
> workings of that Fate which was Love possessed her. For it was
> fatal in its nature; rich and austere at once, giving death and
> life in the same moment, restoring beyond belief all the things
> it took away – except the individual will.[10]

The language here is a good example of the way Williams works
to get the effect he needs, that of an authentic but not
immediately familiar spiritual experience. Sybil lives in
accordance with a mystical quietism familiarised as the practice
of the presence of God; but the obfuscating effect of conventional
terms no longer comes between us and the experience described.
The slight heightening of the language – the mannered inversion
of the adverbs, the balanced stresses and pairings, the faint ring

of incantation coupled with the carefully weighed vocabulary, makes for a piece of religious prose which is persuasive beyond its immediate occasion. Its power is infectious; and nowhere does Williams exercise this particular gift so powerfully as in the chapter describing how Sybil goes out into the storm to save her brother. And yet he falters more than once in his presentation of her, so that her interior assurance takes on a touch of smugness. When, contemplating her toes in the bath, she reflects, 'How sweet of Love to have a toe like that!'[11] all but the most infatuated devotees will flinch.

All of which is to say that Williams was not an instinctive novelist, in the generally accepted sense of that term. His two final novels succeed because in them he ceased trying to be one. For what is most memorable in all of them is the sense of the transcendent as it shines through the world of space and time. In this respect the books are genuinely original and impressive. Especially striking is the way in which the supernatural manifestations are seen as being precisely that – super-natural. They do not engage with the world of appearances, they take it over. There is none of that uneasy intrusion of the paranormal in terms of the normal that we find in the average occult novel, as in Dennis Wheatley's *The Devil Rides Out* (1935) or Aleister Crowley's partly satirical and wholly floundering *Moonchild* (1929).[12] And through his narrative technique Williams, not himself a mystic, is able to present dramatically the conclusion of all visionary experience that spiritual reality co-inheres in material reality. So too he is able to coin, in terms of his various myths, memorable epigrams of redemption, such as 'The Way to the Stone is in the Stone', 'The Knowledge of the Angelicals' and 'The Knowledge of the Dance'. A language for religious experience is being evolved that is specifically symbolic and allusive: no confusion between appearance and reality being raised about or by it, the balance between belief and scepticism can be verbally contained.

The logical outcome of this process is found in *Descent into Hell*. Williams's treatment of occult themes had been moving towards an all-inclusive vision that may be termed multispatial. The debate in *Shadows of Ecstasy* as to the nature and true term of romantic experience concludes with the affirmation of unity set forth initially and dramatically in the four succeeding books, and acted out and set forth definitively in the final one. Parallel to the more selective exploration of division-in-unity leading to unity-in-division carried out in the criticism, biographies and plays, we find Williams using the novel form to enlarge his vision in more general and more widely referential terms.

The novels themselves occupy an ambiguous place in his total output. On the one hand, they are certainly his most well-known and popular writings, and are arguably his most original contribution to the literature of his time. On the other hand, when set alongside novels written out of other traditions than the metaphysical or occult, they dwindle into triviality. Only when read in the context of his total output does their significance become apparent.

The first six reveal an evolving awareness of human power-drives as they are confronted with the inevitable constrictions of human existence. Starting with the consciousness of sublimity, of endless possibility, of romantic yearning, Williams's thought leads inexorably to a consideration of the providence of God. A convinced Christian, he was never a facile one. He did not embrace religious belief because it consoled or even inspired him: rather, he saw it as the necessary accommodation of the self to fact. In his criticism, biographies and plays he concentrates on personal experience; but in the novels the individual dramas are given a wider setting. The metaphysical imagery provides an impersonal set of counters with which to set out the rules of the game.

For a game, in one sense, is what Williams saw life as being – a game for the individual, a dance in reality.[13] The apparent frivolity of the image should not lead one to underrate it: rather it arises from one of Williams's principal beliefs, that the entire creation is necessarily superfluous to God. To this extent his imagination is a dogmatic one: he proceeds from that assertion to reinterpret human experience in its light. He substitutes for the interplay of psychological characteristics found in the main-stream of English fiction, the interplay of spiritual currents and religious understanding; and is thus able to write religious novels that are neither merely tracts nor sociological studies of belief.

The debate, so to call it, in *Shadows of Ecstasy*, sets forth the issues: its conclusion is open-ended. *War in Heaven* has as its central revelation the conduct of the Archdeacon with regard to the Grail: he chooses to defend the Grail by preserving its freedom. This discovery that God is, literally, indefensible, becomes clearer through the pre-Christian imagery of the three succeeding novels. In them the attitude of acceptance (choosing necessity) is vindicated through the imaginative presentation of the workings of that necessity. Williams uses the occult novel in terms of its own premisses, not simply to entertain, but to reveal what lies hidden under the cloak of a logical impossibility. He offers a number of working models for the imagination to accept or reject as it will. *Descent into Hell* is the fulfilment of this method whereby fable and reality are seen as aspects of each other: the metaphysical fantasies of the earlier books are enacted as spiritual reality. The occult has become the visionary.

In their evolution, therefore, the novels work out the perspective from which the theological books and Arthurian poems were written. Less personal in concern and presentation than the plays, they provided imaginative testing grounds for Williams's beliefs about the relation of the individual to the community, of the power-drive to human limitation, and at a deeper level of God's justice to his love.

IV

These beliefs, however, are most subtly presented in Williams's treatment of the Arthuriad. Here the close interconnections, the pursuit of a kind of twentieth-century version of medieval analogies, result in a more wide-ranging, complex and intellectually satisfying model of reality than is to be found in the self-appointed limitations of the novels. Despite this, however, *Taliessin through Logres* and *The Region of the Summer Stars* are little known, and remain an isolated phenomenon in twentieth-century English poetry. The former is unusual among such collections in being a self-integrating book.[14] But, while not lending itself to anthologising, it cannot be read as a long narrative poem. It arises from a world of presuppositions: a full knowledge of the Arthurian literature is assumed at the outset. In some respects this is a source of strength. One weakness of the nineteenth-century poetic versions of the Arthuriad is that, being essentially retellings of the story, they are expressed in part through the naturalistic modes of the day, Tennyson's men and women, for example, being so many Victorians in medieval costume. Similarly, the poems of Swinburne and Morris seem to arise out of the very paintings that so often illustrated them. A kindred difficulty arises in a twentieth-century prose reworking of the legends, T. H. White's *The Once and Future King* (1958).[15] Here the author seeks to bypass the problem by a semi-humorous treatment that effects a delicate reduction of the stereotyped solemnities for the benefit of the human realities that underly them, a method comparable with that used by Robert Graves in *I, Claudius* (1934). The method succeeds, but it is at the cost of diminishing the Grail adventure.

Williams, on the other hand, avoids a specifically humanistic treatment. His world is an abstract world made tangible by a subtle and effective deployment of physical details. Colourful and sensuous passages are interwoven with the narrative and dogmatic elements – often a telling adjective or phrase does the work of whole lines of more formal description. These sudden intensities, flickering amid the hard substance of the poetry like sparkles of quartzite, are furthered by the employment of internal rhyming and the use of the Homeric adjective – 'sea-weighed', 'green-pennon-skirted', 'rain-dark' – with an accompanying compression of phrase that can fuse metaphor and simile with piercing effect, as in 'The Sister of Percivale':

A trumpet's sound from the gate leapt level with the arm,
round with breath as that with flesh, to a plan
blown as that bone-patterned, bound each to a point.

Another characteristic feature is an interfusing of bodily and spiritual perceptions.

Gawaine's thistle, Bedivere's rose, drew near:
flutes infiltrating the light of candles.
Through the magical sound of the fire-strewn air,
spirit, burning to sweetness of body,
exposed in the midst of its bloom the young queen
   Guinevere.[16]

The musical disposition of vowels and consonants in the last line is masterly, as is the effect of the implicit caesura before 'Guinevere'. What Williams is aiming at, and frequently achieves, is a trans-sensuous awareness. The process is imaged in Blanchefleur's sight of the white wolf hurtling through the snow, bearing the infant Galahad:

she saw on the clear horizon an atom, moving,
waxing, white in white, speed in snow,
a silver shape in the moonlight changing to crimson,
a line of launched glory.[17]

In Anne Ridler's words, 'it is at ... a moment of almost
hallucinatory vision held in the senses but on the point of
reaching beyond them, that [Williams's] images must have been
made'.[18]

The use of imagery is similarly effective at the intellectual level.
Williams uses an associative method of notation, which resembles
that of Eliot and Ezra Pound. But, instead of referring to an on-
going historical process, he builds up a metaphysical world, a
pattern or diagram that both reflects and interprets the physical
dimension. The method is a little like that used by David Jones in
In Parenthesis (1937); but Williams lacks Jones's gift for the
integration with the everyday, that power which makes him, in
Jeremy Hooker's phrase, 'a poet of reconciliation'. Indeed, as
Jones himself wrote, reviewing *Taliessin*,

> I wonder whether as a valid spell of permanent efficacy this
> poetry may not be to some degree lacking in one exceptionally
> difficult to express particular? Not in some kind of obscurity,
> not in the form of the writing as such, not in the concepts and
> values in themselves, for these are most permanent and fruit-
> ful, but in something wholly to do with time – with 'now-ness'.
> Somehow, somewhere, between content and form, concept and
> image, sign and what is signified, a sense of the contemporary
> escapes. ... [19]

Taliessin through Logres does indeed remain alien to the
twentieth-century point of view. As Charles Moorman observes,
myth is 'a commentary on the problem of life ... in a language
that we can no longer read'.[20] Most modern verse is essentially
particular, local and personal, but *Taliessin through Logres*
embodies a tale of legendary kings and queens, woods of magic,
lonely seas and rugged peaks, the high region of romantic
tradition. This in itself would not tell against the poems, for the
current popularity of the romances of J. R. R. Tolkien is evidence
of a widespread taste for mythological narrative; but Williams
makes few concessions to the normal romantic temper. The

gorgeousness of imagery is treated with a fine austerity, the story is uncoloured by personal emotion. The poems' style, being at once declamatory and compact, is in marked contrast to most other poetry written at the time or since. Williams's vision is iconographical, static; he seems to be unaware of process. Relativity in time eludes him – hence for many people the curiously unreal nature of his imaginative world. Its beauty is an intellectual beauty, not a vital one; its concern is with a model. Its relativity is not within itself: it posits certainties, pronounces laws. It is everything that is alien to current popular sensibility, and there is none of the fragmenting of experience, that concentration on the moment which, from the poems of Hardy on, have pervaded English verse.

The best indication of Williams's purpose is the use of Byzantium as a focal symbol. Byzantine art was deliberately stylised and created within certain legal conventions, enabling the portraiture of Christ to avoid the misleading naturalistic humanism of later painters, and to concentrate on the essential nature of the God–Man. Williams's poetry is kindred in spirit. Formalised, disciplined by its mythological imagery, and resplendent with colour, it is ideally suited to convey the ordered world of heavenly perfection which Byzantine art proclaims. Its iconographical quality belongs to religious, as distinct from merely pious, poetry. The images are not diminished into an imitative function, and the sense of the Trinity, the Godhead in its fullness of providential operation, is mediated through what is so obviously not a naturalistic mode that there is no danger of the relation between God and man dwindling to a mere matter of degree. It is Williams's achievement to have written a poetry of transcendence which makes transcendence known through the very formalised, materialistic nature of its imagery; as he wrote, reviewing Dorothy Sayers's *The Mind of the Maker* (1941), 'I am too like the Areopagite to be anything but gloomy about analogies with the Uncreated: the damage they do is incalculable.[21] Transcendence means a total *otherness*: nothing but a substantial objectification of images can really make that point, because only so can confusion between what is physically substantive and the transcendent reality be avoided.

The same principle holds good for Williams's treatment of the theme of Britain. His Logres, while embodying the traditional notion of an ideal Britain (ideal through function rather than through attributes) goes far beyond contemporary developments of the theme. Williams grew up in a period which saw Blake's Albion threatened from without as the First World War destroyed the national supremacy which had helped to foster it: the romantic England of Elgar's music and Brooke's poetry was to become matter for nostalgia, to evolve into a kind of inner, quintessential England and a spiritual refuge from the forces of change. In Arthurian terms one can see the concept developing from the rather vapid traditionalism of John Masefield's *Midsummer Eve* (1928) to the more iconoclastic but robust and partially political treatment the story receives in *The Once and Future King*, the first volume of which appeared in the year following *Taliessin through Logres*. But even here the expression is partly nostalgic.

Charles Williams replaces nostalgia with belief: his Arthuriad derives from and is shaped by Christian doctrine. In this he differs from those of his contemporaries who make use of mythological material. For instance, Eliot's portrait of London in *The Waste Land* (1922) is not so much shaped by mythology as illuminated by it: the Grail theme is only fragmentarily realised, and in effect forms part of a far wider, more miscellaneous cultural pattern. In *Ulysses* (1922), Joyce's Dublin is Dublin first and foremost; its Homeric overtones are arbitrary rather than organic, as of necessity they had to be. Myth cannot be geographically transplanted. John Cowper Powys makes use of Arthurian material in *A Glastonbury Romance* (1933) and *Porius* (1951); but in both novels the mythology is secondary to the author's own proclaimed belief in a total, as opposed to an absolute, relativity. In the work of David Jones we find mythology used as an essentially anthropological frame of reference, deposits of belief being depicted as conditioning cultural patterns of the present day. In the work of all four writers the mythological and the everyday are juxtaposed, the former element being employed to further understanding of the latter's essential nature; but in each case it is seen as reflecting rather than as determining the significance of the everyday. The natural is ultimately being assessed on its own terms.

Williams's Logres is very different. It is intended to be a diagram of what truly is, rather than a refuge from what is not. Williams makes no attempt at collocating or conjoining the natural and the supernatural. His world is a deliberate abstraction, a working model of reality, whose laws are intellectually apprehended. Indeed, it is in Williams's studies in history rather than in his poetry that we find him depicting the supernatural in relation to the natural: and the progress of his entire work is towards a fusion of the two. The difference between them is a matter not of kind but of dimension.

Williams's dual awareness of Logres had its origin in the events of his own life. In his version of the myth the Arthurian kingdom both is, and is not. It is, in the sense that its laws and operations are those which reflect the Divine Providence at work in the world; it is not, in the sense that it is an abstract of history, a distillation of the facts of time. It resembles an individual personal mythology objectified. This ambiguity is a positive that arose in Williams's mind from a negative experience, the personal experience of contradiction which he had explored in the early criticism, biographies and plays. The resultant sense of absolute relativity led him to this iconographical portrayal of all that he could see of co-inherence.

Co-inherence is also evident in Williams's method of poetic composition. Acknowledging the gift of a copy of *The Region of the Summer Stars*, W. H. Auden commented that 'You are the only writer since Dante who has found out how to make poetry of theology and history.'[22] The reference to Dante is apposite: Williams's poetic method lends itself to the fourfold level of interpretation which operates in the *Commedia*: literal, allegorical, moral and analogical – say, the ostensible meaning; the meaning signified by the ostensible meaning; the individual application of that meaning; and the meaning of all three in relation to the eternal dimension – what nowadays we may call the eschatological or timeless dimension. The distinctions were laid down by Aquinas before their use by Dante, and their tendency was to exhibit themselves in layers or deposits of meaning. But in Williams's case the exposition operates dialectically, the fourfold interpretation being perceptible through an interior dynamic. To employ Aquinas's distinctions, if the literal meaning is the actual matter of the Arthurian legend itself, the allegorical meaning is the interpretation of those legends as an image of the workings of Christendom. So far this is orthodox enough. But, in the case of the moral interpretation, the one applicable to the individual soul, its apprehension is the *condition* of apprehending the allegorical meaning within the poem itself: 'the lover must become the perfection he has seen'. The relating of all three of these interpretations to each other is what Williams discusses in *The Figure of Beatrice* as the Way of Affirmation of Images; and through this relation of literal, allegorical and moral dimensions the eschatalogical one is apprehended. If Britain, the literal meaning, is to come to Sarras, the eschatological one, it can only be through acceptance of its nature as Logres, and through the dedication in personal action which is summed up in Carbonek, the castle of the Hallows. Thus the poems' methodology itself dramatises the hierarchical medieval mode of poetic interpretation, and re-creates it for the more personal idiom of today.

For the Arthurian poems are not ideograms or versified theological treatises. They call for an intuitive reading, not mere passive receptivity. They also demand a response in keeping with their premises, a blend of perceptive wit and imaginative reason; for wit, in Austin Farrer's words, 'divines its object and begets a representation of it: reason disciplines the product of wit and works out its inspirations to a systematic construction'.[23] Farrer is here referring to a study of the Scriptures, but his words are relevant to literary criticism, and especially to the revived medievalism of Williams's verse. For Williams's technique of interlinked associative symbolism calls not only for an imaginative use of intelligence (common enough in contemporary practice) but also for an intelligent reliance on imagination. If his poems are anachronistic it is because they are ahead of, rather than behind, their time.

V

Charles Williams is not one of the primary artists who creates experience, but one of the secondary ones who defines it. He does, however, offer more than is implied by that distinction. His unique achievement lies in his approach to theology, both as being influenced by literary form and as affected by it. Lewis's description of Williams as a romantic theologian holds good, together with his assertion that this means one who is theological about romance, not one who is romantic about theology.[24] Williams was indeed a romantic of a distinctive kind. The Romantic Revival has been described as a 'prodigious attempt to discover the world of spirit through the unaided efforts of the solitary soul'.[25] Williams's romanticism, however, was a prodigious exploration of the world of incarnate spirit in the conscious fellowship of redeemed and interdependent souls. He saw in literature, theology and history symbols of an existence to which romantic experience points, and it is his linking of that experience to the formulations of Christian theology which is his distinctive achievement as an apologist.

The expression of faith in a faithless age presents a distinct but common literary problem. A number of twentieth-century English imaginative writers have been Christians of various persuasions: the names of Eliot, Auden, David Jones and Edwin Muir come immediately to mind among poets, Graham Greene, Evelyn Waugh and Rose Macaulay among novelists. Williams's influence, such as it is, would seem to have been greater among the poets, and that more on a personal than on a literary level. Certainly his novels do not compare methodologically with those of his contemporaries. He does not, as does Greene in *The End of the Affair* (1949) or Waugh in *Brideshead Revisited* (1945), stress the scandal of particularity *within* the novel, or dramatise the Christian singularity in terms of moral paradox, as a gauntlet thrown down to the unbeliever; nor does he, like Rose Macaulay, present the faith as a rejected but haunting offer of reality. He deals in neither challenge nor nostalgia. His method is parabolic.

It is more appropriate, therefore, to compare his work with that of C. S. Lewis and J. R. R. Tolkien. However, his approach to myth is essentially different from theirs. Whereas Lewis was primarily a teacher and Tolkien a storyteller, Williams was a poet. In Lewis's romances the didactic element predominates, however fresh and vivid the writing, it is subordinate to a design on the reader's beliefs. Tolkien is innocent of such intent; for all the Christian symbolism detectable within it, *The Lord of the Rings* is pure drama, the shape of the story being the burden of its message. In Williams's work, however, the Christian myth is undisguisedly the theme: all his writing springs from his assent to it. And this assent, being imaginative as much as intellectual, both energises the work (so that with a deeper theological understanding there comes a greater command of literary form) and also prevents it from being directed *at* the reader.

At times, however, Williams lays himself open to charges of wilful obfuscation. E. I. Watkin, for example, objected to his discussion of co-inherence as misleading, on the grounds that it 'is usually called the Communion of Saints'.[26] But by 'co-inherence' Williams refers to the whole created order. His sense of the total mutual dependence of every aspect of reality makes it possible for him to recognise both the validity of scientific method (he is notably sympathetic to Bacon's aims) and to the findings of poetic intuition: he will have no schism between the two, for both are methods of discriminating among connections which make reasoning life possible. This incorporation of the spiritual within the natural leaves him free to postulate a transcendence that is convincingly and totally other. His anthology *The New Christian Year* (1941) contains many quotations from Kierkegaard and Karl Barth, in addition to such teachers of the Negative Way as Pascal, St John of the Cross and the author of *The Cloud of Unknowing*, testifying to his realisation that God remains a hypothesis who by his very nature can never be talked about. 'Neither is this Thou': only in that knowledge is he present. But the anthology also contains many readings from Williams's masters in the Affirmative Way, most notably William Law – the Law who wrote *The Spirit of Love*, rather than the author of *A Serious Call to a Devout and Holy Life*. Williams's sense of co-inherence makes for comprehensiveness and catholicity: it also permits, not to say insists on, the knowledge that nothing that is affirmed can escape the possibility that it may for truth's sake have to be denied (a point that forms the climax of *Thomas Cranmer*). This side of Paradise all absolutes are relative.

It is this particular poise which is the distinguishing mark of Williams's mature work, and which makes it so rewarding. He is no mere dualist obsessed with the question of evil: such a concept arises from a misunderstanding of his use of occult symbolism. The nature of evil is of less interest to him than the process by which evil can be overcome.

The theological vision which underlies and unifies Williams's work is expressed with a subtlety and intentness which make that work more satisfactory as a whole than in its parts. In this respect his total output can best be regarded as itself an image, a vision of the incommunicable in terms of a creative meditation on formulae which are, at the most, algebraic symbols for reality. What is impressive about his vision is its consistency and comprehensiveness; it is a total view of life emerging from a variety of occasional writings, and it rings true not so much from intellectual plausibility as from emotional conviction. His religious writing is persuasive because its source is identical with the source of his secular concerns. It has the authenticity of art.

VI

The development of Williams's powers as an artist parallels and indeed mediates his ability as a theologian. This can be seen most clearly in his treatment of the crisis of contradictory knowledge. In the early poetry the crisis is described rather than enacted (the result of using the wrong form and the wrong kind of language), so that the poems proclaim a theology of romanticism in a manner inconsistent with their premises. In the two books on the poetic mind the crisis is objectified and the romantic ideal tested as they describe Milton's way of 'living it out' in the person of Satan, and Shakespeare's manner of 'living it through'. The latter way clearly influences Williams's understanding of the Atonement as the reconciliation of warring opposites in a single action. In the biographies the crisis is examined through actual historical figures; and as a result Williams develops a sense of history as myth which allows for his vision of interpenetrating worlds both in his later novels and verse, and in his theology.

The plays objectify the crisis through personifications, *Thomas Cranmer* bridging the gap between myth and history in its domination by the figure of the Skeleton. This particular dramatised embodiment enables Williams to portray the crisis as itself the manifestation of God's redemptive purpose. Successive figures – the Third King, the Accuser, the Flame – take the concept further, into the realisation that all luck is good and the Kingdom here and now. It is the state evoked by the final movement of Mahler's 'Resurrection' symphony, 'We know and are';[27] by Ashvaghosha's declaration that 'All sentient beings, if only they were able to realize it, are already in Nirvana';[28] in the suggestion by John Cowper Powys that the next Dimension is one that we all unconsciously inhabit now.[29]

But so too, as if in counterpoint, one sees that Williams's Logres approximates to the realised presence of a God known only in absence (Beckett's Godot?), not to be described, defined or in any way to be objectified. By definition he is the (indefinable) eternal subject, the knowledge of whom is an impossibility known as a reality. The knowledge of contradiction, of the Impossibility, of the Cross, is the only knowledge of God that man can surely have. Logres both is and is not; alike in the Arthurian kingdom of Williams's imagining and in the Christian Church of his experience and researches, that truth holds good. From its vantage point the poise of his last books was achieved. As a result they do not exhibit the traces of chronological development that one finds in the earlier ones. Williams's preoccupations were established, his mastery of his material assured: what now emerges is an increasing awareness of the contemporary, the ordinary, even to some extent the colloquial; and with this we also find a deepening sense of the eternal. The systematic exploration of the communal objectified symbols of theology led to a reworking of earlier modes of expression in terms of a more clearly realised apprehension of transcendence. The final creative period is thus one of ease and lucidity – lucidity, not simplicity: and the theology and the poetry illuminate each other.

The unique interest, then, of Williams's thought over all this field of speculation and deduction lies in its formation and nourishing through his parallel enquiries into the springs of poetry and human action. His awareness of the relativity of symbolic statement in verse, and his consideration of the relative worth of human integrity in the plays (a relativity that becomes what is virtually the moral of the biographies), issues in a theological poise that avoids both aggressive dogmatism and the tendency of more insinuating apologists to pander to their audience. If anything, Williams's tendency is too far the other way; as he himself noted, 'only the greatest theologians avoid the disadvantages of their kind, and one disadvantage is that their whole science tends to sound rather remote and unnatural'. (He then proceeds to observe, 'Something of the same surprising result (when we consider the subject-matter) is to be seen in the economists).'[30]

For believer and non-believer alike, Williams's work stands out, both in content and formation, as a testimony to the sovereign power of the imagination. Just as the artist necessarily possesses a kind of disinterested arrogance, so Williams's portrait of Christianity has an assurance that is self-authenticating, free from the need either to impose itself or to truckle to inferior models of reality. In his case *Credo quia impossibile* becomes *Credo ut intelligam*. The values which he puts forward, values native to the artist, of all-inclusiveness (suggested by the term 'co-inherence') and humility before the created order (suggested by 'absolute relativity') issue in theological terms as a sense of inter-relatedness and tolerance. It is this roundedness and balance which makes his theology so satisfying.

His historical studies stress the effects, as much as the intentions, of religious belief. The sense of co-inherence that informs his criticism of poetry by poetry extends to the realm of cause and effect; he never forgets that a creed must be tested by its fruits. Balancing discursive thought by imaginative intuition, he gained an inner assurance resulting in what is essentially a reading of theology, not an arguing for or against any particular sectarian point of view. His work crosses more than disciplinary frontiers, and offers itself as a working model for the apprehension of spiritual realities that transcends the verbal formulations through which they find expression. His assumption that theological statements and symbols are intellectual clothing for, and safe-guards of, the deeper poetic truths of myth, gives his writings an honesty and self-vindicating fervour which makes them accessible to those who, while responsive to his imagination, do not subscribe to his beliefs. If nature and grace are categories of one identity then the experience of their fusion in Williams's work is the measure of his achievement both as apologist and poet.

Appendix

A NOTE ON THE SYMBOLISM OF CHARLES WILLIAMS, WILLIAM BLAKE AND GEORGE MACDONALD

In his monograph on Charles Williams, published by the British Council in 1955, John Heath-Stubbs points out the affinity between certain of Williams's images and those in the later poetry of Blake: thus Logres and Albion correspond, P'o-l'u and Ulro, Broceliande and Beulah, Sarras and Eden. The comparisons may be pushed further. The conflict between the four Zoas, Blake's symbols of the attributes of thought, feeling, imagination and sensation, are recalled in the later poet's vision of 'the Acts in Contention'. The 'geographical' element likewise reflects a kindred working in the two poets' minds. Tharmas, for example, the Zoa of sensation, arises in the west, the west of Williams's 'sea-rooted wood'; and water is the element corresponding to Tharmas in Blake's mythology. Urthona, or Los, Blake's figure of the poetic insight, summed up by Williams in the phrase 'Taliessin through Logres', remains at the north. Urizen, the Zoa of thought, is south, with Gaul's 'trigonometrical milk of doctrine'. As a result of the revolt of Luvah, feeling, against the Self, Albion, the Zoas usurp one another's functions, thought in the place of sensation, feeling in the place of thought; and the reintegration of the Self can only come about when the Zoas are returned to their proper region and functions, 'going to the altar Pelles, and Arthur moving down'.[1] One can also detect affinities between Blake's spiritual geography in *Jerusalem*, with its assignment of the four Zoas of London, Verulam, York and Edinburgh, and Williams's use of Camelot, Caerleon and Carbonek.

The relation of the Spectre image in Blake to Williams's figure of the Skeleton and its fellows is significant. Blake's Spectre can be identified with the 'Shadow' in Jungian psychology. George Macdonald makes interesting use of this image in *Phantastes* (1858), and it appears in another form in the *Doppelgänger* experience which Williams describes in *Descent into Hell*. Blake's *Vala* portrays it as the Spectre who lays down the condition of restoring ordered peace;

> Unbar the gates of Memory: look upon me
> Not as another, but as thy real Self.[2]

In Williams's writings the Shadow comes to be identified with the figure of Christ as it is felt by those who flee from it, their true identity. Blake contrasts Vala, the false *anima* or soul with the true *anima*, Jerusalem (cf. Lilith and Lona in Macdonald's *Lilith* (1880)), but Williams, with his acute sense of the supernatural co-inherence of mankind in Christ, sees true identity as being found in participation in the mystical body of Christ: another example of the development of poetic symbolism into a doctrinal affirmation.

Notes

Except where stated otherwise the place of publication is London.

NOTES TO THE PREFACE

1 Mary McDermott Shideler, *The Theology of Romantic Love* (New York, 1962) p. 47.
2 Dr Brian Horne points out to me the possibility that Williams combined phrases from the Upanishads to make his own definition. 'Believe me, my son, an invisible and subtle essence is the Spirit of the whole universe. That is Reality. That is Atman. THOU Art That.' (From the Chandogya.) On the other hand, the dialogue between Gargya and Ajahsatru in the Brihad-Aranyaka culminates in the assertion of the total transcendence of Brahman above every living thing. See *The Upanishads*, trs. Juan Mascaró (Harmondsworth, Middx., 1965) pp. 117, 127–9.

NOTES TO CHAPTER ONE: THE LIFE

1 'Notes on the Way', *Time and Tide*, vol. 23, no. 10 (7 Mar 1942) pp. 194–5.
2 'Nature and the Poets', *Time and Tide*, vol. 22, no. 27 (5 July 1941) pp. 564–5.
3 Michal Williams, 'As I Remember', *Episcopal Church News*, vol. 119, no. 14 (12 Apr 1953).
4 A. M. Hadfield, *An Introduction to Charles Williams* (1959) p. 70.
5 Gerard Hopkins, 'Charles Williams', *Bookseller*, no. 2059 (24 May 1945) p. 525.
6 C. S. Lewis, Preface to *Essays Presented to Charles Williams* (Oxford, 1947) p. ix.
7 T. S. Eliot, 'The Significance of Charles Williams', *Listener*, vol. 36, no.936 (19 Dec 1946).
8 W. H. Auden, in *Modern Canterbury Pilgrims*, ed. James Pike (New York, 1956); quoted in Monroe K. Spears, *The Poetry of W. H. Auden* (New York, 1963) p. 176.
9 Lois Lang-Sims, *A Time to be Born* (1971) pp. 196–7.
10 'I found him disturbing, physically, psychologically and (I may as well add) spiritually' – Richard Heron Ward, *Names and Natures* (1968) p. 173. It is interesting to compare this with his similarly unfavourable account of T. F. Powys in *The Powys Brothers* (1935).
11 *The Masque of the Manuscript* (1927) and *The Masque of Perusal* (1929). For an account of these see Hadfield, *Introduction to Charles Williams*, pp. 67–75.

NOTES TO CHAPTER TWO: THE EARLY POETRY

1 *The Silver Stair* (1912) p.67.
2 Ibid., p. 39.
3 Ibid., p. 67.
4 *Religion and Love in Dante* (1941) p. 3.
5 *Poems of Conformity* (1917) p. 47.
6 Ibid., p. 55.
7 Ibid., p. 61.
8 Ibid., p. 78.
9 This poem was reprinted by Sir Arthur Quiller-Couch in the 1939 edition of *The Oxford Book of English Verse*, as 'Night Song for a Child'. Most curiously, an exclamation mark was added, and is still to be seen in the paperback edition of 1980.
10 'Renovations of Intelligence', *Time and Tide*, vol. 22, no. 33 (16 Aug 1941) pp. 689–90.
11 *Three Plays* (1931) p. vi.

NOTES TO CHAPTER THREE: CRITICISM, BIOGRAPHIES AND PLAYS

1 F. R. Leavis, *The Common Pursuit* (1952) p. 253
2 T. S. Eliot, *On Poetry and Poets* (1957) p. 147.
3 'Sensuality and Substance', *The Image of the City*, ed. Anne Ridler (1958) pp. 68–75.
4 One of them, Thelma Shuttleworth, writes that 'they were a kind of Mutual Benefit Society, for with Charles the lecturer and the lectured were always on an equal footing.' (From a letter to the author, 15 Sep 1980.)
5 Bernard Blackstone, *The Consecrated Urn* (1959) p. 62.
6 *Poetry at Present* (1930) pp. 60–1.
7 Ibid., p. 62.
8 Ibid., p. 94.
9 Ibid., p. 116.
10 Ibid., p. 120.
11 Walter de la Mare, *Pleasures and Speculations* (1940) p. 179.
12 *Three Plays*, p. 113.
13 Ibid., p. 133.
14 *The Letters of Evelyn Underhill* (1943) p. 15.
15 *Bacon* (1933) p. 106.
16 *The English Poetic Mind* (1932) p. 59.
17 Williams was to commend the phrase used by John Layard in *Stone Men of Malekula*, 'Irresponsible and in all things defiant': 'The whole conception of evil was hardly ever put better and more briefly' – 'Boars of Vau', *Time and Tide*, vol. 24, no. 3 (16 Jan 1943) p. 50.
18 *Reason and Beauty in the Poetic Mind* (1933) p. 79.
19 This progress had already been charted by Williams in his verse play *A Myth of Shakespeare* (1928).
20 *The English Poetic Mind*, pp. 83–4.
21 Introduction to *The New Book of English Verse* (1935) p. 12.
22 See C. G. Jung, *Modern Man in Search of a Soul* (1933) ch. 8.
23 *Reason and Beauty in the Poetic Mind*, p. 10.
24 *The New Book of English Verse*, p. 11.

25 G. Wilson Knight, *Principles of Shakespearian Production* (1949) pp. 31–2.
26 *The New Book of English Verse*, p. 17. The statement needs qualification in view of the continuing and powerful use of myth by such later poets as Edwin Muir and Geoffrey Hill.
27 The six other names are Alexander, Julius Caesar, Charlemagne, Shakespeare, Voltaire and Wesley, with Asoka and Akbar substituted for the last two in the Indian edition. Williams's range was wide: he also wrote short lives of Lord Macaulay (1933) and Queen Victoria (1938).
28 'When a poet's mind is perfectly equipped for its work, it is constantly amalgamating disparate experience – *Selected Essays* (1952) p. 287. It is worth quoting Eliot's essay on the Metaphysical poets in order to point out a similarity to, if not an influence upon, Williams's discussion of the poetic resolution of the Impossibility.
29 *Rochester* (1935) p. 82.
30 'Lord Macaulay', *The Image of the City*, p. 11.
31 *Bacon*, p. 258.
32 *Henry VII* (1937) p. v.
33 *Bacon*, p. 277.
34 *Henry VII*, p. 104.
35 *James I* (1934) p. 136.
36 Ibid., pp. 142–3.
37 Other contributors included W. J. Turner (Wagner) and Francis Birrell (Gladstone). Williams was here associated with members both of 'the Squirearchy' and of 'Bloomsbury'. He was a true literary independent.
38 *Bacon*, p. 308.
39 *Henry VII*, p. 30.
40 Lytton Strachey, *Elizabeth and Essex*, Phoenix Library ed (1928) p. 88.
41 *James I*, p. 205.
42 *Queen Elizabeth* (1936) p. 115.
43 *Bacon*, p. 78
44 *James I*, p. 244.
45 *Henry VII*, p. 255.
46 Williams also wrote *A Myth of Bacon* for performance at Downe House School in 1932. It has been printed for the first time in the *Charles Williams Society Newsletter*, nos 11, 12 and 14.
47 *Bacon*, p. 255.
48 William V. Spanos, *Christian Tradition in Modern Verse Drama* (New Brunswick, N. J., 1967) p. 94.
49 *Three Plays* (1931) p. 190.
50 *Collected Plays* (1963) p. 53.
51 Ibid., p. 6.
52 Ibid., p. 22.
53 Ibid., p. 12.
54 Ibid., p. 14.
55 Ibid., p. 34.
56 Ibid., p. 35.
57 Ibid., p. 47. Note that the metre determines the sense of the line. The stress comes on 'you', not 'were'.

58 Ibid., p. 52.
59 Ibid., p. 54.
60 Ibid., p. 174.
61 Ibid., p. 165.
62 Ibid., p. 153.
63 Ibid., pp. 157–8.
64 Ibid., p. 157.
65 The objector was the Revd V. T. Macy, of St Nicholas, Harbledown. Even
     in secular affairs Williams's sense of irony at times backfired, as when,
     during the Second World War, he speculated that perhaps Hitler had
     'thought the Russian experiment abominable; he signed the Pact against
     his will; as soon as possible he struck at the thing he believed unutterably
     evil. It would be in accord with what we know of the universe (and of the
     Omnipotence) that he should be caught so, that he should be thwarted
     immediately he tried to be honest. The good cheats us, humanly, as well as
     the evil. The experience is common; why exclude Hitler? No, if he loses the
     war, it is proper that he should have begun to lose it in the fatal hour when
     he began again to be truthful. He began to save his soul and (all but
     literally) to lose the world' – 'Notes on the Way', *Time and Tide*, vol. 22,
     no. 37 (13 Sep 1941) p. 769. The following week a reader rebuked him for
     'venturing to offer an impudent and intolerable travesty of the facts as
     sober truth'.
66 *The Descent of the Dove*, 2nd ed (1950) p. 13.
67 John Heath-Stubbs, *Charles Williams* (1955) p. 34.
68 *Collected Plays*, p. 74.
69 Ibid., p. 72.
70 Ibid., p. 90.
71 Ibid., p. 192.
72 Shideler, *Theology of Romantic Love*, p. 86.
73 *Collected Plays*, pp. 226–7.
74 Ibid., p. 330.
75 Ibid., pp. 369–70.
76 Ibid., p. 401.
77 Julia de Beausobre in *Time and Tide*, vol. 26, no. 34 (25 Aug 1945) p. 712.
78 *The Descent of the Dove*, p. 219.
79 *Collected Plays*, p. 299.
80 Ibid., pp. 276–7.
81 'Throughout the play the critic remains unobtrusively present: analysis,
     grown habitual, must be responsible in part for the convincing simplicity of
     the plot' – de Beausobre, in *Time and Tide*, vol. 26, no. 34, (25 Aug 1945)
     p. 712.
82 *Collected Plays*, p. 300.

NOTES TO CHAPTER FOUR: THE NOVELS
1   Evelyn Underhill, *The Grey World* (1904) p. 63; *The Lost Word* (1907)
     p. 314.
2   Ibid., p. 190.
3   Evelyn Underhill, *The Column of Dust* (1909) p. 277.
4   Ibid., p. 3.

5 Ibid., pp. 78, 110.
6 For Machen, see 'The Secret of the Sangraal' in *The Shining Pyramid* (1925). For Waite, see *The Hidden Church of the Holy Ghost* (1909).
7 *The Column of Dust*, pp. 157–8.
8 See p. 144. This phrase might serve as the unifying motto for the whole of Williams's work.
9 *The Column of Dust*, p. 181.
10 Patricia Meyer Spacks, 'Charles Williams: the Fusions of Fiction', in *Shadows of Imagination*, ed. M. R. Hillegas (Carbondale, Ill., 1969).
11 Delivered in Oct 1940.
12 *Shadows of Ecstasy*, 2nd edn (1948) p. 33.
13 Ibid., p. 178.
14 *The Descent of the Dove*, pp. 12–14.
15 *Shadows of Ecstasy*, p. 196.
16 Ibid., pp. 36–7.
17 *Collected Plays*, p. 287.
18 *Shadows of Ecstasy*, pp. 162–3.
19 Ibid., p. 161.
20 Ibid., pp. 16–17.
21 Ibid., p. 114.
22 John Cowper Powys's novel *A Glastonbury Romance* (1933) is another reflection of the contemporary interest in the Grail cult. Unlike *War in Heaven* it is all-inclusive and fundamentally sceptical.
23 *War in Heaven*, 2nd edn (1947) p. 179.
24 Ibid., p. 113.
25 Ibid., p. 203.
26 Ibid., p. 118.
27 Ibid., p. 180.
28 Ibid., p. 173.
29 *Many Dimensions*, 2nd ed (1947) p. 63.
30 Sir Giles is the only character to appear in more than one of Williams's novels. His creator would seem to have taken a wry pleasure in his foul-mouthed malignity.
31 *Many Dimensions*, pp. 217–18.
32 *Poetry at Present*, p. 34. Significantly the phrase occurs in the essay on A. E. Housman.
33 *The Place of the Lion*, 2nd edn (1952) p. 168.
34 Ibid., p. 129.
35 Ibid., pp. 135–6.
36 *The Greater Trumps*, 2nd edn (1954) p. 154.
37 'The Founding of the Company', from *The Region of the Summer Stars*.
38 *The Greater Trumps*, p. 69.
39 *London Mercury*, vol. 33, no. 194 (Dec 1935) pp. 151–8.
40 Shideler, *Theology of Romantic Love*, p. 96.
41 Phyllis Paul is as yet sufficiently little known to warrant a footnote. Between 1949 and 1967 she published nine novels dealing with the psychic and occult borderland. Intricately plotted and precisely evocative, they combine an implacably sombre vision, with a multi-dimensional awareness of reality. *The Lion of Cooling Bay* (1952) and *Rox Hall Illuminated* (1956)

may show signs of Williams's influence; her masterpiece, *Twice Lost* (1961), invites comparison with *The Turn of the Screw*.

42 *Descent into Hell*, 2nd edn (1949) pp. 25–6.
43 Robert Hugh Benson, *Initiation* (1914) p. 61.
44 Ibid., pp. 63–4.
45 Ibid., p. 232.
46 *Descent into Hell*, p. 99.
47 Ibid., p. 53.
48 Ibid., p. 189.
49 Ibid., p. 171.
50 Ibid., p. 174.
51 Ibid., p. 39.
52 Ibid., p. 72.
53 Ibid., p. 124.
54 Ibid., pp. 124–5.
55 Lilith had already been the subject of a poem with Christian connotations in *Heroes and Kings* (1930), a limited edition of some of Williams's Arthurian and domestic verse.
56 *Descent into Hell*, p. 70.
57 *All Hallows Eve* (1945) pp. 72–3.
58 *The Demon Lover* (1945). Kôr is the fabulous city of Rider Haggard's *She* (1886): Haggard's influence on Williams's novels is evident stylistically if not thematically.
59 Both essays are reprinted by Anne Ridler in *The Image of the City*.
60 *All Hallows' Eve*, p. 109.
61 Shideler, *Theology of Romantic Love* p. 138.
62 *All Hallows' Eve*, p. 13.
63 Ibid., p. 190.
64 'Sax Rohmer' was the pen-name of Arthur Sarsfield Ward (1883–1959), another member of the Golden Dawn.
65 *All Hallows' Eve*, p. 76.
66 Ibid., pp. 196–7.

NOTES TO CHAPTER FIVE: THE ARTHURIAN POEMS

1 'Lancelot and Elaine'.
2 'Homage to Mr Belloc', *Time and Tide*, vol. 23, no. 48 (28 Nov 1942) pp. 952 and 954.
3 Four of them are to be found in *Three Plays*, others in *Heroes and Kings* and in *New English Poems*, ed. by Lascelles Abercrombie (1931).
4 'A Commentary on the Arthurian Poems of Charles Williams', *Arthurian Torso* (1948).
5 'Sub Specie Aeternitatis', *Windows of Night*, p. 98.
6 Charles Moorman, *Arthurian Triptych* (Berkeley, Calif., 1960) p. 99.
7 'The imagination is, despite itself, preoccupied, and even love-poetry is not the same as love. To be an object of love and a subject of poetry is not always the same thing; a cruel experience lies in the division' – *Bacon*, p. 197.
8 *The Descent of the Dove*, p. 116.

9 The definition is in Williams's notes on *Taliessin through Logres* (1938) written for C. S. Lewis.
10 'Primary chief bard am I to Elphin, / And my original country is the region of the summer stars' − 'Taliesin', *The Mabinogion*, trs. Lady Charlotte Guest (1906) p. 273.
11 'The Prayers of the Pope', *The Region of the Summer Stars*.
12 *Arthurian Torso*, p. 178.
13 *The Image of the City*, pp. 186−94.
14 *Arthurian Torso*, p. 23.
15 Ibid., pp. 66−7.

NOTES TO CHAPTER SIX: THEOLOGY
1 'The Productions of Time', *Time and Tide*, vol. 22, no. 4 (25 Jan 1941) pp. 72−3.
2 The book formed part of a series called *I Believe*. Other contributors included Gerald Bullett and J. D. Beresford, both agnostics.
3 Thelma Shuttleworth, *Charles Williams Society Newsletter*, Supplement no. 1.
4 *He Came Down from Heaven*, 2nd ed (1950) pp. 10−12.
5 Ibid., p. 33.
6 Ibid., p. 14.
7 Ibid., p. 36.
8 Ibid., pp. 21−2.
9 'John Milton', *The Image of the City*, p. 30.
10 *He Came Down from Heaven*, p. 25.
11 William Blake, *The Marriage of Heaven and Hell*.
12 *He Came Down from Heaven*, p. 24.
13 Ibid., p. 25.
14 Ibid., p. 30.
15 Ibid., p. 42.
16 *Poetry at Present*, pp. 38−9.
17 *He Came Down from Heaven*, p. 35.
18 Ibid., pp. 59−60.
19 Ibid., p. 58.
20 Ibid., p. 81.
21 For Williams's discussion of de Rougemont's thesis, see 'One Way of Love', *The Image of the City*, pp. 159−61.
22 *He Came Down from Heaven*, p. 65.
23 Ibid., p. 71.
24 *Arthurian Torso*, p. 116.
25 *He Came Down from Heaven*, p. 78.
26 Ibid., p. 80.
27 *The Image of the City*, p. 148.
28 Mark 15:31.
29 *He Came Down from Heaven*, p. 85.
30 Ibid., p. 86.
31 Ibid., p. 89.
32 Ibid., p. 98.
33 *The Descent of the Dove*, p. 1.

34   Ibid., p. 59.
35   Ibid., p. 10.
36   Ibid., pp. 38–9.
37   Ibid., p. 31.
38   Ibid., p. 32.
39   Ibid., p. 181.
40   Ibid., p. 57.
41   Ibid., p. 59.
42   'Sensuality and Substance', *The Image of the City*, p. 68.
43   *The Descent of the Dove*, p. 1.
44   Ibid., p. 212.
45   Ibid., pp. 192–3.
46   Ibid., pp. 189–90.
47   'I Saw Eternity', *Time and Tide*, vol. 24, no. 33 (14 Aug 1943) p. 668.
48   'St Anselm's Rabbit', ibid., no. 41 (9 Oct 1943) p. 828.
49   *Witchcraft*, 2nd edn (Wellingborough, 1980) p. 37.
50   Ibid., pp. 154–5.
51   *James I*, p. 92.
52   *Witchcraft*, p. 309.
53   *He Came Down from Heaven*, pp. 18–19.
54   *Witchcraft*, p. 150.
55   Ibid., p. 278.
56   Ibid., p. 302.
57   'All my own emotions rebel against the pattern of this book. I do not want to be shown that pain is, or may be, a good; that (given our present state) its inevitability is a good' – *Theology*, vol. 42, no. 247 (Jan 1941) p. 63.
58   *The Forgiveness of Sins*, 2nd edn (with *He Came Down from Heaven*) (1950) p. 107.
59   Ibid., pp. 108–9.
60   Ibid., pp. 175–6.
61   'The Cross', *The Image of the City*, p. 132.
62   *The Forgiveness of Sins*, pp. 131–2.
63   Ibid., pp. 130–1.
64   Ibid., p. 157.
65   Ibid., p. 164.
66   Ibid., p. 186.
67   'Natural Goodness', *The Image of the City*, p. 76.
68   *Paradiso*, Canto VII (trs. John D. Sinclair).
69   *The Image of the City*, pp. 133–4.
70   Ibid., p. 136.
71   *The Figure of Beatrice* (1943) p. 16.
72   Ibid., p. 51.
73   Dorothy L. Sayers, *The Poetry of Search and the Poetry of Statement* (1963) pp. 45–68.
74   *The Figure of Beatrice*, p. 7.
75   Ibid., pp. 7–8.
76   Ibid., p. 29.
77   Ibid., p. 38.
78   Ibid., p. 40.

79   Ibid., p. 47.
80   Ibid., p. 49.
81   Ibid., p. 50.
82   Ibid., p. 150.
83   Ibid., p. 228.
84   Ibid., p. 123.
85   Ibid., p. 124.
86   Ibid., pp. 147–8.
87   Ibid., p. 162.
88   Ibid., p. 231.
89   Ibid., p. 45.

NOTES TO THE CONCLUSION

1   *An Experiment in Criticism* (Cambridge, 1961).
2   Review of *The Descent of the Dove, Dublin Review*, vol. 206, no. 412 (Jan 1940) p. 199.
3   Ibid., vol. 209, no. 418 (July 1941) pp. 99–101.
4   'Mightier than Most Pens', *Time and Tide*, vol. 19, no. 11 (12 Mar 1938) p. 361.
5   'The Romantic Need', *Time and Tide*, vol. 21, no. 5 (3 Feb 1940) pp. 113–14.
6   Knight's method of spatial analysis, his reading of image clusters and insistence on the spiritual implications of poetic statement are inherent in Williams's more casual methods; while his writings on the spiritual significance of the human body, most notably in *Symbol of Man* (1980), constitute a forceful development of similar ideas put forward by Williams in the Taliessin poems and elsewhere in throwaway remarks and gnomic hints.
7   See, for example, the essay 'Digging for Pictures' in *The Hot Gates* (1965).
8   *Many Dimensions*, p. 233.
9   *The Greater Trumps*, p. 146.
10   Ibid., pp. 124–5.
11   Ibid., p. 135.
12   It is possible that Williams may have had Crowley in mind for his portrait of Gregory Persimmons in *War in Heaven*.
13   It should be stressed here that this statement is an extreme instance of symbolic abstraction. Williams was well aware of what life was like for most people at the everyday level of reality.
14   This is most evident in the first edition, whose end-papers carried a design by Lynton Lamb of the figure of a naked woman superimposed upon the map of Europe. Its subsequent omission is regrettable.
15   Similar oblique approaches to the myth can be found in Martyn Skinner's *The Return of Arthur* (1966) and John Heath-Stubbs's *Artorius* (1974).
16   'The Crowning of Arthur', *Taliessin through Logres*.
17   'The Son of Lancelot', ibid.
18   Introduction to *The Image of the City*, p. lxxi.
19   David Jones, *Epoch and Artist* (1959) p. 209.
20   Moorman, *Arthurian Triptych*, p. 12.
21   'Renovations of Intelligence', *Time and Tide*, vol. 22 no. 33 (16 Aug 1941) pp. 689–90.

22 Quoted in a letter from Charles to Michal Williams, dated 2 Feb 1944. (This and the letter quoted above are in the Wade Collection, Wheaton College, Wheaton, Ill.)
23 Austin Farrer, *The Glass of Vision* (1948) p. 147.
24 C. S. Lewis, Preface to *Essays Presented to Charles Williams*, p. vi.
25 Maurice Bowra, *The Romantic Imagination* (1950) p. 23.
26 Watkin, in *Dublin Review*, vol. 206, no. 412.
27 Gustav Mahler, programme notes on Symphony No. 2, 'Resurrection'.
28 Quoted in Aldous Huxley, *The Perennial Philosophy* (1946) p. 333.
29 John Cowper Powys, *Mortal Strife* (1942) p. 114. This was the only one of Powys's books to be reviewed by Williams, whose conciliatory approach results in an illuminating collocation of vocabularies as he likens Powys's phrase 'a fusion of cold, dry, bare metaphysic with delicious *sensation*' to 'what an unknown modern writer called "geography breathing geometry, the double-fledged Logos" '. The poise of his tolerant understanding is also well (if ungrammatically) illustrated in his remark that 'the idea of the Multiverse is the engine of Mr Powys's freedom as Epicureanism was that of Lucretius and monism (roughly speaking) Hardy's' – *New English Weekly and New Age*, vol. 21, no. 21 (10 Sep 1942) pp. 169–70.
30 'The Virgin Birth', *Time and Tide*, vol. 24, no. 14 (3 Apr 1943) p. 276.

NOTES TO THE APPENDIX
1 'Taliessin at Lancelot's Mass', *Taliessin through Logres*.
2 *Poetry and Prose of William Blake*, ed. Geoffrey Keynes (1927) p. 318.

Bibliography

Except where stated otherwise the place of publication is London.

I. PRINCIPAL WORKS BY CHARLES WILLIAMS

1912 *The Silver Stair* (verse).
1917 *Poems of Conformity* (verse).
1920 *Divorce* (verse).
1924 *Windows of Night* (verse).
1928 *A Myth of Shakespeare* (verse drama).
1930 *Heroes and Kings* (verse).
    Poetry at Present (criticism).
    War in Heaven (novel).
1931 *Many Dimensions* (novel).
    The Place of the Lion (novel).
    Three Plays (verse drama).
1932 *The English Poetic Mind* (criticism).
    The Greater Trumps (novel).
1933 *Bacon* (biography).
    Reason and Beauty in the Poetic Mind (criticism).
    Shadows of Ecstasy (novel).
1934 *James I* (biography).
1935 *The New Book of English Verse* (anthology).
    Rochester (biography).
1936 *Queen Elizabeth* (biography).
    Thomas Cranmer of Canterbury (verse drama).
1937 *Descent into Hell* (novel).
    Henry VII (biography).
    Stories of Great Names (biography).
1938 *He Came Down from Heaven* (theology).
    Taliessin through Logres (verse).
1939 *Judgement at Chelmsford* (verse drama).
    The Descent of the Dove (theology).
1941 *Witchcraft* (theology).
1942 *The Forgiveness of Sins* (theology).
1943 *The Figure of Beatrice* (criticism).
1944 *The Region of the Summer Stars* (verse).
1945 *All Hallows' Eve* (novel).
    The House of the Octopus (verse drama).
1946 *Flecker of Dean Close* (biography).
1948 'The Figure of Arthur', in *Arthurian Torso* (criticism).

190

1958 *The Image of the City* (critical and theological essays).
1963 *Collected Plays*, Introduction by John Heath-Stubbs (*Thomas Cranmer of Canterbury, Judgement at Chelmsford, Seed of Adam, The Death of Good Fortune, The House by the Stable, Grab and Grace, The House of the Octopus, Terror of Light, The Three Temptations*).

For details of Williams's reviews and articles, see the Bibliography in Mary McDermott Shideler's *The Theology of Romantic Love* (1962) and Lois Glenn's *Charles W. S. Williams: A Checklist* (1975).

II. A SELECTION OF CRITICAL AND BIOGRAPHICAL SOURCES

1928 A. C. Ward, *Twentieth-Century Literature*.
1938 David Jones, 'The Arthurian Legend', *Tablet*, 25 Dec 1938; repr. in *Epoch and Artist* (1959).
1939 Hoxie Neale Fairchild, *Religious Trends in English Poetry*, vols v and vi.
1945 Gerard Hopkins, 'Charles Williams', *Bookseller*, no. 2059 (24 May 1945) p. 525.
1946 T. S. Eliot, 'The Significance of Charles Williams', *Listener*, vol. 36, no. 936 (19 Dec 1946).
1947 C. S. Lewis, Preface to *Essays Presented to Charles Williams*.
1948 C. S. Lewis, 'Williams and the Arthuriad', in *Arthurian Torso*.
Anne Ridler, Introduction to *Seed of Adam and Other Plays*.
Bro. George Every, 'Charles Williams – I: the Accuser', *Theology*, vol. 51, no. 333 (Mar 1948) pp. 95–100; 'Charles Williams–II: the City and the Substitutions', ibid., no. 334 (Apr 1948) pp. 145–50.
1949 Bro. George Every, *Poetry and Personal Responsibility*.
F. R. Leavis, 'The Logic of Christian Discrimination', *Scrutiny*, vol. 16. no. 4 (Winter 1949) pp. 339–44; repr. in *The Common Pursuit* (1952).
1951 R. A. Scott-James, *Fifty Years of English Literature 1900–50*.
1953 Michal Williams, 'As I Remember', *Episcopal Church News*, vol. 119, no. 14 (12 Apr 1953).
1954 Dorothy L. Sayers, *Introductory Papers on Dante*.
1955 John Heath-Stubbs, *Charles Williams*.
1956 Glen Cavaliero, 'The Way of Affirmation', *Church Quarterly Review*, vol. 157, no. 322 (Jan–Mar 1956) pp. 19–28.
W. H. Auden, 'Charles Williams: a Review Article', *Christian Century*, vol. 73, no. 18 (2 May 1956) pp. 552–4.
1957 Robert Conquest, 'The Art of the Enemy', *Essays in Criticism*, vol. 7, no. 1 (Jan 1957) pp. 42–55; repr. in *The Abomination of Moab* (1979).
Dorothy L. Sayers, *Further Papers on Dante*.
1958 Anne Ridler, Introduction to *The Image of the City*.
John Press, *The Chequer'd Shade*.
William P. Wylie, *The Pattern of Love*.
1959 A. M. Hadfield, *An Introduction to Charles Williams*.
1960 Charles Moorman, *Arthurian Triptych* (Berkeley, Calif.).
1961 Gerald Weales, *Religion in Modern English Drama*.
1962 Mary McDermott Shideler, *The Theology of Romantic Love* (New York).
1963 Monroe K. Spears, *The Poetry of W. H. Auden* (New York).
Dorothy L. Sayers, *The Poetry of Search and the Poetry of Statement*.

John Wain, *Sprightly Running: Part of an Autobiography.*
1965 Glen Cavaliero, 'Charles Williams on *Taliessin through Logres*', *Gnomon* (New York) no. 1, pp. 37–45.
1966 Charles Moorman, *The Precincts of Felicity* (Gainesville, Fla).
Mary McDermott Shideler, *Charles Williams: A Critical Essay* (New York).
1967 William V. Spanos, *Christian Tradition in Modern Verse Drama* (New York).
1968 W. H. Auden, *Secondary Worlds.*
Richard Heron Ward, *Names and Natures.*
1969 M. R. Hillegas (ed.), *Shadows of Imagination* (Carbondale, Ill.).
1971 Lois Lang-Sims, *A Time to be Born.*
Charles Huttar (ed.), *Imagination and the Spirit* (Grand Rapids, Mich.).
R. J. Reilly, *Romantic Religion* (Athens, Ga.).
Gunnar Urang, *Shadows of Heaven.*
1974 John Warwich Montgomery (ed.), *Myth, Allegory and Gospel* (Minneapolis, Minn.).
1978 Humphrey Carpenter, *The Inklings.*
Peter Sutcliffe, *The Oxford University Press: An Informal History.*
Glen St John Barclay, *Anatomy of Horror.*
1980 Alice Mary Hadfield, 'Charles Williams and his Arthurian Poetry', *VII* (Wheaton College. Illinois), vol. I, pp. 62–80.
1981 Joe McClatchey, 'The Diagrammatised Glory of Charles Williams's *Taliessin through Logres*', *VII* (Wheaton College, Illinois), vol. II, pp. 100–25.
1982 Brian Horne, 'Known in Another Kind: a Comment on the Literary Criticism of Charles Williams', *VII* (Wheaton College, Illinois), vol. III, pp. 83–92.

Index

1. WORKS BY CHARLES WILLIAMS

'Advent of Galahad, The', 98
All Hallows' Eve, 7, 8, 56, 59, *90–6*, 143, 161
'Ascent of the Spear, The', 100, 109–10

Bacon, 27, 32–8
'Ballade of Travellers', 17
'Bors to Elayne: The Fish of Broceliande', 100, 105–6
'Bors to Elayne: On the King's Coins', 100, 108–9

'Calling of Arthur, The', 101, 104, 114, 115
'Calling of Taliessin, The', 118–19
Chaste Wanton, The, *25–6*, 77
'Coming of Galahad, The', 107, 113–14
'Coming of Palomides, The', 100, 107–8
'Cross, The', 127, 146–7
'Crowning of Arthur, The', 101, 105, 114

Death of Good Fortune, The, 48–9
'Death of Palomides, The', 101, 114
'Departure of Dindrane, The', 117, 120–1
'Departure of Merlin, The', 101, 114
Descent into Hell, 35, 47, 56, 57, 59, 61, 78–90, 95, 112, 130, 135, 142, 161, 164, 166, 179
Descent of the Dove, The, 6, 38, 64, 127, *137–42*
'Domesticity', 9
Divorce, 11, 16–18, 20

English Poetic Mind, The, 5, 27, 28, 63, 101, 149
'Et in Sempiternum Pereant', 78–9

Figure of Arthur, The, 124–5
Figure of Beatrice, The, 6, 7, 151–7
Flecker of Dean Close, 7
Forgiveness of Sins, The, 6, 127, *145–9*, 156
'Founding of the Company, The', 117, 121

'Ghosts', 17–18
Grab and Grace, 49
Greater Trumps, The, 57, 58, 59, 60, 62, *76–8*, 91, 134, 162–4

He Came Down from Heaven, 6, 127, *128–37*, 141, 144, 146, 149
Henry VII, 32–8
Heroes and Kings, 185n
House of the Octopus, The, 7, *51–3*, 65
House by the Stable, The, 49

Image of the City, The, 127
'Image of the City in English Verse, The', 92

James I, 32–8
'Joan of Arc', 32
Judgement at Chelmsford, *47–8*
'Jupiter over Carbonek', 124

'Lamorak and the Queen Morgause of Orkney', 100, 108
'Last Voyage, The', 101, 115–16
Letters of Evelyn Underhill, The, 26
'Lord Macaulay', 182n

Many Dimensions, 57, 59, 60, 62, 70–3, 74, 85, 102, 162, 163

Masque of the Manuscript, The, 5, 39

'Meditation of Mordred, The', 116, 122

'Mount Badon', 101, 104–5, 111

'Myth of Bacon, A', 182n

Myth of Shakespeare, A, 181n

New Book of English Verse, The, 29, 30–1

New Christian Year, The, 174

'Night Song for a Child', 18, 181n

'Palomides before his Christening', 101, 112–13

'Percivale at Carbonek', 101, 114–15

Place of the Lion, The, 59, 60, 61, 73–6, 123, 161–2

Poems of Conformity, 11, *15–16*, 17, 19

Poetry at Present, 23–5

Prayers of the Pope, The', 117, 122–4

'Prelude' to *Taliessin through Logres*, 101

Queen Elizabeth, 32–8

'Queen Victoria', 182n

'Queen's Servant, The', 117, 121–2

Reason and Beauty in the Poetic Mind, 5, 27, 28, 29, 140

'Redeemed City, The', 92

Region of the Summer Stars, The, 8, *116–24*, 166, 171

Religion and Love in Dante, 152

Rite of the Passion, The, 40, 41

Rochester, 32–8

Seed of Adam, 44–7, 104

Shadows of Ecstasy, 14, 31, 60, *62–6*, 91, 92, 162, 164, 165

Silver Stair, The, 2, *13–14*, 72

'Sister of Percivale, The', 101, 110–11, 167

'Son of Lancelot, The', 101, 111–12

'Star of Percivale, The' 100, 109

Stories of Great Names, 32, 182n

'Taliessin at Lancelot's Mass', 101, 116

'Taliessin in the Rose-Garden', 117, 119–20

'Taliessin in the School of the Poets', 100, 106, 108

'Taliessin on the Death of Virgil', 100, 106–7

'Taliessin's Return to Logres', 101–2

'Taliessin's Song of the Unicorn', 100, 105

Taliessin through Logres, 7–8, 98, 99, *100–16*, 120, *166–72*

Terror of Light, 50

Thomas Cranmer of Canterbury, 5, 34, *38–44*, 45, 47, 48, 49, 147–8, 175

Three Plays, 25, 39, 40

Three Temptations, The, 50

'To Michal: On Bringing her Breakfast in Bed', 19

'To the Protector, or Angel, of Intellectual Doubt', 19–20

'Two Domes, The', 19

'Vision of the Empire, The', 102–3

War in Heaven, 19, 57, 58, 59, 60, 61, *66–9*, 75, 142, 143, 163, 165, 184n

Way of Exchange, The, 135–6

'Window, The', 19

Windows of Night, 5, *18–20*, 25, 79, 86

Witch, The, 39, 160

Witchcraft, 6, 127, *142–5*

2. GENERAL INDEX

Abercrombie, Lascelles, 25

Amen House, 5, 39

Arnold, Matthew, 97

Auden, W. H., 4, 159, 171, 173

Barth, Karl, 174

Beckett, Samuel, 150, 175

Belloc, Hilaire, viii, 9, 33
Benson, R. H., 56, 59, 82
  Initiation, 82–3
  The Necromancers, 56
Beresford, J. D., 186n
Birrell, Francis, 186n
Blackwood, Algernon, 55
Blake, William, 16, 23, 99, 131, 148, 153, 159, 170, 178–9
  Jerusalem, 176
  Songs of Innocence and Experience, 16
Blunden, Edmund, 9
Book of Common Prayer, The, 20
Bowen, Elizabeth, 92
Bowra, Sir Maurice, 7
Brecht, Bertolt, 41, 44
Bridges, Robert, 20, 31
Brooke, Rupert, 25, 170
Brooks, Cleanth, 29
Bruce, J. D., 124
Buchan, John, 59
Bullett, Gerald, 186n

Canterbury, 38, 47
Cary, H. F., 152
Cecil, Lord David, 7
'Celia' (Phyllis Jones), 5, 25, 29
Chambers, E. K., 124
Chesterton, G. K., viii, 3, 9, 55, 58, 59, 67, 124, 141, 160
  The Everlasting Man, 124
Christendom Group, 6
City Literary Institute, 3, 5
Cloud of Unknowing, The, 139, 174
Colchester, 44
Companions of the Co-inherence, 5
Conrad, Joseph, 90
Criterion, The, 22
Crowley, Aleister, 164, 188n
  Moonchild, 164

Dante Alighieri, 2, 6, 48, 61, 91, 101, 133, 134, 148, 150, 151–7, 158, 171
  Convivio, 151, 152, 155
  De Monarchia, 155
  La Divina Commedia, 151, 152, 155

La Vita Nuova, 151, 152
  Inferno, 91, 155
  Paradiso, 157
De la Mare, Walter, 24, 25, 55, 59
Dickens, Charles, 7, 54
Dublin Review, The, 6, 124
Dunne, J. W., 59
Duns Scotus, 12, 132

Elgar, Sir Edward, 170
Eliot, George, 90, 94
Eliot, T. S., 4, 10, 15, 17, 22, 32, 40, 42, 44, 52, 53, 78, 80, 124, 142, 160, 168, 170, 173, 182n
  Ash Wednesday, 44
  East Coker, 17
  The Family Reunion, 52
  Little Gidding, 18, 148
  Murder in the Cathedral, 38, 39, 52
  Prufrock and Other Observations, 15
  Sweeney Agonistes, 42
  The Waste Land, 170
Empson, Sir William, 29

Farrer, Austin, 172
Firbank, Ronald, 162
First World War, 3
Ford, Ford Madox, 160
Forster, E. M., 2, 143
Fry, Christopher, 38
Fulford, Roger, 33

Genet, Jean, 103
Geoffrey of Monmouth, 124
Gershwin, Ira, 50
Gibson, Wilfrid, 9
Glastonbury, 67
Golden Dawn, Order of the, 4–5, 143
Golding, William, 161
Graves, Robert, 167
Greene, Graham, 173
Guareschi, Giovanni, 163
Guest, Lady Charlotte, 116

Hadfield, Alice Mary, 3
Haggard, H. Rider, 185n
Hardy, Thomas, 169
Hawker, Robert Stephen, 10–11, 12

Heath-Stubbs, John, 47, 178, 188n
Herbert, George, 15
Hill, Geoffrey, 182n
Hooker, Jeremy, 168
Hopkins, Gerard Manley, 7, 12, 98, 102, 116, 132, 157
Hopkins, Gerard, 3
Housman, A. E., 26, 132
    A Shropshire Lad, 26

Ibsen, Henrik, 82
Inklings, the, 6

James, Henry, 54, 81, 87
    'The Jolly Corner', 81
    'The Turn of the Screw', 185n
James, M. R., 54
John of the Cross, St, 139, 174
Johnson, Samuel, 2
Jones, David, 10, 124, 168, 170, 173
    In Parenthesis, 168
Joyce, James, 170
Julian of Norwich, 83, 148

Keats, John, 23, 28, 101
    'Ode to a Nightingale', 28
Keble, John, 15
Kierkegaard, Søren, 41, 138, 140, 174
Kipling, Rudyard, 82
Knight, G. Wilson, 31, 160, 188n

Lamb, Lynton, 188n
Lang-Sims, Lois, 4
Law, William, 145, 148, 174
    The Spirit of Love, 174
Lawrence, D. H., 22, 31, 90, 93
    Women in Love 93
Layard, John, 181n
Lean, David, 26
Leavis, F. R., 22
Le Fanu, J. S., 54
Lewis, C. S., viii, 4, 6, 99, 122, 124, 133, 135, 145, 158, 172, 173
    The Allegory of Love, 133
    The Problem of Pain, 145
Lytton, Edward Bulwer, 56

Macaulay, Rose, 173
Macdonald, George, 178-9

Machen, Arthur, 4, 55, 57, 58, 59, 60, 79
    Hieroglyphics, 55
    The Hill of Dreams, 55
    The House of Souls, 55-6
Macy, V. T., 183n
Mahler, Gustav, 175
Mann, Thomas, 93
Marvell, Andrew, 29
Masefield, John, 25, 38, 170
    The Coming of Christ, 38
    Midsummer Eve, 170
Mercury Theatre, 38
Meynell, Alice and Wilfrid, 2
Milton, John, 22, 27-8, 31, 130, 151, 175
    Comus, 101
    Paradise Lost, 130
Montaigne, Michel de, 140
Montanus, 138
Moorman, Charles, 168
Morgan, Charles, 26
Morrell, Lady Ottoline, 4
Morris, William, 97, 166
    The Defence of Guinevere, 98
Muir, Edwin, 173, 182n

Nietzsche, Friedrich, 63

Ouspensky, P. D., 59
Oxford, 6-7, 48
Oxford University Press, 2, 3, 5, 6

Pascal, Blaise, 174
Pater, Walter, 63
Patmore, Coventry, 9, 10, 11, 12, 15, 133
    The Angel in the House, 10
    The Rod, the Root, and the Flower, 133
    The Unknown Eros, 15
Paul, Phyllis, 80, 184-5n
Pilgrim Players, 48
Pius X, 26
Poe, Edgar Allan, 81
Pound, Ezra, 168
Powys, John Cowper, 63-4, 80-1, 170, 175, 189n
    A Glastonbury Romance, 80-1, 170, 184n

Maiden Castle, 63–4
Porius, 170
Powys, T. F., 59, 150, 180n
   Mr Weston's Good Wine, 59
Pritchett, V. S., 160

Quiller-Couch, Sir Arthur, 181n

Radcliffe, Ann, 54
Rais, Gilles de, 144
Rhondda, Viscountess, 6
Ridler, Anne, 127, 165
'Rohmer, Sax' (A. S. Ward), 59, 95, 185n
   The Brood of the Witch Queen, 95
Rossetti, Dante Gabriel, 2
Rougemont, Denis de, 133–4

St Albans, 1
Sayers, Dorothy L., 7, 50, 153, 169
   The Man Born to be King, 50
   The Mind of the Maker, 169
Shakespeare, William, 27–8, 122, 146, 175
   Antony and Cleopatra, 28
Shideler, Mary McDermott, 79
Shuttleworth, Thelma, 181n
Sinclair, Margaret, 5
Skinner, Martyn, 188n
Strachey, Lytton, 33, 36, 37
   Eminent Victorians, 33
Swinburne, A. C., 97, 98, 116, 166
   Tristram of Lyonesse, 98

Tambimuttu, M. J., 8
Tennyson, Alfred, 25, 97, 111, 125, 166
   Idylls of the King, 97
Thackeray, W. M., 2
Thompson, Francis, 3, 9, 11, 12
   Time and Tide, 6, 126
Tolkien, J. R. R., 6, 168, 173
Traherne, Thomas, 153
Turner, W. J., 182n

Underhill, Evelyn, 4, 26, 55, 56–8, 59, 60, 79
   The Column of Dust, 56, 57–8 , 60
   The Grey World, 56

The Lost Word, 56

Voltaire, F. M. A. de, 92, 141

Wagner, Richard, 133–4
Waite, A. E., 4, 57, 124
Waldman, Milton, 33
Watkin, E. I., 159, 173
Waugh, Evelyn, 173
Wells, H. G., 58
Wheatley, Dennis, 164
White, T. H., 167
   The Once and Future King, 167, 170
Williams, Florence ('Michal'), 2, 3, 5, 6, 128, 159
Williams, Walter, 16–17
Wodehouse. P. G., 69, 162
Woolf, Virginia, 81, 160
Wordsworth, William, 7, 23, 113, 153
   The Prelude, 23, 116
Working Men's Club, 2
Wuthering Heights, 54

Yeats, W. B., 3, 4, 24, 25, 66, 72, 102, 114
   'The Phases of the Moon', 114
   The Shadowy Waters, 72

3. SPECIAL SUBJECT INDEX

Affirmation of Images, Way of, ix, 116, 118, 139–40, 151, 157, 172, 174
Allegory, 31–2
Atonement, 34, 127, 132, 149–50, 175

Beatitude, 79, 91, 127, 141
Beatrician Vision, 153–4, 155, 157
Byzantium, 100, 102, 169

Cabbala, the, 4, 73, 76
Celian Moment, the, 29, 30–1
Ceremony, 2, 31
Chastity, 14
City, the, 1, 13, 17, 85, 91–6, 128, 133, 152
Co-inherence, viii, 19, 32, 50, 70, 79,

98, 111, 113, 120, 123, 127, 131, 133, 139, 161, 164, 171, 173–4, 176–7
Contradiction, 5, 27–8, 40, 117, 129, 154, 171, 175
Creation, 74, 117, 118, 130, 132, 147
Cross, the, 89, 146, 149–51, 176

Damnation, 79, 80, 91
Death, 93–4
Derivation, 79, 82, 92, 130
Devil, 143, 144
Dharma, 139
Disbelief, 20, 30, 65, 140–1, 142, 157
Doctrine, 9, 14, 24, 30, 98, 127, 141, 170
Doppelgänger, 81–2, 89

Eschatology, 40, 116, 129, 171–2
Evil, 60, 69, 93, 94, 114, 130, 149, 158
Exchange, viii, 26, 71, 74, 77, 80, 84–5, 89, 92, 94, 95, 100, 109, 111, 114, 115, 116, 119, 129, 132, 133, 136–7

Fall, the, 77, 103, 117, 129, 132, 146, 149
Forgiveness, 146–9
Fortune, 33–5, 41, 48–9, 76, 149

Glory, 128, 129, 137, 153–4
Gnosticism, 4–5, 59, 130
God, 62, 70, 77, 137–8, 139, 141, 146, 149, 166, 169, 175
Gomorrah, 85–6, 89, 93, 108, 130, 133
Grace, 101, 110, 112, 114, 117, 177

Heaven, 78, 86, 128
Hell, 79, 80, 86, 91, 93, 123, 130, 156
Holy Grail, 57, 67–9, 76, 98, 100, 115, 117–18, 124, 165, 167, 170

Imagery, 3, 12, 14, 30, 31, 78, 79–80, 168, 169
Imagination, 63, 65, 70, 78, 143, 153, 155, 165, 176
Impossibility, the, 26–7, 29, 32, 33–5, 36, 38, 42, 60, 74–5, 77, 86, 94, 97, 140, 149, 151

Infamy, the, 92–3
Intellect, 28, 31, 45, 159
Irony, 2, 8, 19, 29, 42, 64, 84, 106, 110, 112, 121, 141, 142
Islam, 46, 62, 70, 107

Joy, 19, 31, 60, 61, 85, 131, 141
Judgement, 79–80, 93, 118
Justice, 19, 149, 150, 166

Law, 14, 66, 85, 95, 171
Lilith, 89–90
Literary criticism, 23, 24, 27, 129, 160, 172
Logres, 99, 104, 110, 116, 117, 169–71, 172, 175
Love, 13, 15–16, 17, 26, 60, 61, 62, 74, 76–7, 93, 95, 127, 128, 134–5, 138, 142, 143, 148, 156, 157, 166

Magic, 4, 5, 60, 61, 69, 95, 143
Marriage, 15, 16, 18, 154, 159
Mathematics, 107
Metaphysics, 9, 30, 39, 59, 60, 168
Modernism, 25, 125
Money, 1, 109
Myth, mythology, 12, 24, 30, 31, 32, 77, 99, 114, 117, 129, 132, 160–1, 164, 170, 171, 173

Nature, 1, 114, 120, 123, 161, 170, 177
Necessity, 37, 61, 83, 93, 120, 141, 157, 166
Negation, Way of, 157, 174
see also Rejection, Way of
Neo-Platonism, 55, 58, 59–60, 73

Obedience, 113, 121, 130
Occultism, 4, 54, 59, 60, 61, 90, 91, 93, 95, 158, 161, 164, 166

Parousia, see Second Coming
Perversion of Images, Way of, 130, 142
Pessimism, 15, 19, 69
Poetry, 9, 22–3, 24, 25, 29–30, 31–2, 75, 102, 106, 113, 119, 127, 169, 177

Power, 60, 67, 92, 143, 165

Redemption, 45, 50, 52, 62, 72, 74,
    117, 130, 133
Rejection of Images, Way of, 118,
    120, 139–40
    see also Negation, Way of
Relativity, ix, 19, 30–1, 64, 69, 113,
    121, 160, 161, 169, 170, 171,
    174, 176, 177
Religion, 14, 113
Renunciation, 13
Romanticism, 5, 25, 26, 172–3, 175
Romantic love, 77, 102, 105–6, 113,
    128, 133–5
Royalty, 33–5, 36

Sacrament, 3, 9, 15, 53
Salvation, 42, 48, 59, 61, 74
Sanctity, 4, 77, 79, 93
Second Coming, 117, 118, 123

Sex, 15–16, 26, 63–4
Sin, 130, 148
Spiritual dimension, 3, 12, 175
Style, 37, 39, 41, 49–50, 53, 75–6, 98,
    108–9, 126–7, 146, 151–2, 159,
    163–4, 167–8
Substitution, 82–5, 89, 132, 133,
    135–6, 157
Superfluity, 119, 121, 141
Supernatural, the, 5, 7, 60, 67, 78,
    161, 164, 171
Symbolism, 21, 161, 164, 171–2, 173

Theology, 6, 9, 12, 17, 23, 28, 29, 30,
    49, 68–9, 125, 127, 151, 161,
    172–3, 176
Timelessness, 40, 46
Transcendence, 164, 169, 174, 176

Witchcraft, 142–4